From Cadet to Commodore

The End of a Sea-going Era

by

Robert Royan

Librario

Published by

Librario Publishing Ltd.

ISBN: 978-1-909238-42-8

Copies can be ordered via the Internet
www.librario.com

or from:

Brough House, Milton Brodie, Kinloss
Moray IV36 2UA
Tel/Fax No 00 44 (0)1343 850 178

Printed and bound in the UK

Cover Design: Monika Gromek

Back cover: Covesea Lighthouse.
Photograph by Lumley Photography

Typeset by 3btype.com

Cadet Royan, aged 19.

Contents

Acknowledgements

After some persuasion from my daughter Nicola I started writing of incidents, occasions and people that come to mind during my time at sea. Starting with going to the training ship HMS *Conway* in September 1944 and retiring from the sea on 2nd January 2000. I found that, once I started, one incident led to another and I am fortunate in having quite a good memory. I was helped by the fact that I have retained my Seaman's Discharge Books which records every vessel I have sailed on.

I was fortunate to have parents who did not deter me from going to sea being the eldest in the family and doing something very different to the family tradition. I had this drive to see the world and was very fortunate that when I went to sea the war had just ended.

I must also say I could not have continued with my seagoing career had I not married the ideal seafarers wife. My wife Carol made a home with a warm welcome to all, bore and brought up our son and daughter of whom I am immensely proud. In the twenty-seven years I was at sea as a married man, I was a total of sixteen years away and eleven years at home. I was at home for nine Christmas Days and away for sixteen.

In conclusion I must convey my sincere thanks to VONEF, Cupar, without whose expertise, help and encouragement this epistle would never have been published and in particular to Ann Muir who translated my writing into typing.

Introduction

I left the training ship HMS *Conway* in July 1946 at the age of sixteen and joined my first ship of the Clan Line on 12th August at the beginning of her maiden voyage. I soon realized how fortunate I was to have missed the war at sea. Just listening to the stories of fellow shipmates torpedoing; bombings, sinking, convoy duties and POW camps both German and Japanese was reason enough. I sailed with FW Thornton and JP Smythe, OCs whose names appear in the Honours Board

On my first voyage we carried food relief from the US to India which was suffering from famine and I saw real poverty for the first time. On arriving at the Sandhead Pilot we picked up our Hoogly Pilot who was an OC. called Colquhoun accompanied by his bearer and a wooden trunk of his personal effects. This was style. I believe that up until the war the Hoogly Pilot service used to recruit from HMS *Conway*. In Calcutta we were witness to the 1946 Hindu Moslem riots which were particularly bad round the dock area with a curfew enforced at night. The following voyage was to South Africa and Australia which was something of a contrast. We carried part of the Royal Train to Cape Town for the Royal Tour of South Africa. Arriving at Sydney Heads early in the morning we witnessed the sight of the sailing vessel *Pamir* making sail, not something to be seen much in the future. My next port of call at Calcutta was in August 1947 on a Liberty or Samboat bought by the Clan Line. We were at the river moorings and there for Indian Independence Day. There was no work for forty-eight hours and all the crews were confined to their ships. We cadets however, were able to see some of the celebrations in the Chowringee centre of the city by climbing the masts and sitting on the cross trees. One of our engineers was ashore during all the celebrations and survived but that is another story.

The following voyage found me on one of the old vessels berthed in Bombay when Mahatma Ghandi was assassinated. There was an immediate curfew and no cargo work. The following day when I walked to the Red Gate of Bombay Docks, there were only two people in sight a Policeman and a Customs officer. It was, normally a seething mass of people day and night as any seafarer who has called at Bombay would remember. When next in Durban, on another new vessel, there was serious rioting between African and Indians and many deaths. Our Indian crew had been threatened. As now a Senior Cadet I was given the job of gangway night watchman armed with the instructions to cut the gangway ropes if I saw Africans trying to board. Life as a cadet was not without interest. When in Hamburg on my last voyage as a cadet it was pointed out to me that the white haired gangway watchman employed by our company agent had been Master of one of the German transatlantic liners pre-war.

My required sea time was completed in 1949 but I had to wait until I was twenty to sit for Second Mate FG. On gaining my certificate I was immediately appointed to a ship as Third Officer. I later discovered the Clan Line Glasgow office had a hot line to the Board of Trade offices and usually knew before the examinees if they had passed and one had barely time to celebrate before one had a ship. Later as Third Officer of one of the refrigerated ships we went to the assistance of one of our old vessels with a cargo of tea which had lost its rudder in bad weather off Cape Finisterre. We managed with difficulty to get her under tow and out of immediate danger, handed over to a salvage tug which had been contacted by the company, so that we could resume our voyage to Liverpool. Other than the experience gained from the incident, the highlight was that all the crew received a month's wages as a salvage payment. Riches untold.

Once I had completed the necessary sea time I sat for First Mate FG between Christmas and New Year 1951 as one did in those days. I was immediately promoted Second Mate but had to forego any leave hoped for at that time until later. It was on this vessel awaiting to dock at Birkenhead, that I was part of an occasion I will never forget. When the Liver Building clock struck 14.00 hrs. there was a two minute silence for the funeral of King George VI at Westminster Abbey. We had just made fast our stern tug and all vessels stopped engines and the whole of Merseyside fell silent and shore cranes dipped their jibs. At the end a gun fired and activities resumed on what was a very busy river at that time. In 1953 the sister ship that I was now on was at the Spithead Review while we were in Glasgow hosting the company's coronation parties there, after cargo-work had finished, of course. The Master of this ship was a Manxman and seemed to know his opposite number on the IOM ferries which involved much whistle blowing when entering and leaving the Mersey.

With another period of sea-time completed I passed for Master FG in March 1955 and appointed Second Mate of a vessel three days later. At the end of that voyage I was promoted Chief Officer, somewhat earlier than I expected, but the company was experiencing a shortage of mates and engineers as a result of conscription coming to an end. On this vessel, outbound for India, we had a Greek Master as Suez Canal Pilot as the regular pilots all left on nationalisation. This was the first vessel he had taken through but we made it. Homeward bound on that voyage, we had just cleared Port Said after the canal transit, when the bombers flew overhead to bomb Port Said at the start of the attempted takeover. We were fortunate to be clear.

In 1958 I was flown out to Bombay to take over from a chief officer who had been landed sick. This was a first flight for me and the company had to rustle up a passport for me. Up until then a UK seaman's identity card and discharge book was normally sufficient for travel. During my time on this vessel we were in Dar es Salaam for Independence Day, for what is now Tanzania. We were in port with three other UK vessels and all ships were to dress overall on the day. HMS *Belfast* arrived the day before the big event and we received instructions to take our cue from her. On the day, at 08.00 hrs, when her answering pennant was raised, we all did our bit. However, with all our flags flying we looked over to *Belfast* to see her dressing flags had been caught up in her main radar antennae! I wonder what happened to that operator. It was an eventful stay altogether but that is another story. We had no further contact with *Belfast*. I remained on this vessel, which carried twelve passengers, for three and a half years. On my last voyage from CT we carried two young ladies among the other passengers, one of whom became my wife. That was the last voyage the ship carried passengers. Coincidence or not I don't know.

In 1964 the company decided that all the sea staff of the various companies in the group should be merged. I was then transferred as chief officer to the Union Castle passenger vessels. This was the commencement of a steep learning curve, having to sail with UK crews for the first time and adapting to a different life on passenger vessels. In all I sailed on six different ships in six years.

In 1966 I was chief officer of *Cape Town Castle* which was the last of our passenger vessels to resume service after the seamen's strike. By the time we were manning, all the regular men had been taken on the earlier vessels and many had left the sea. As a result we sailed with a very inexperienced catering crew and full passenger complement. To say the least it was an unusual passage to CT In 1967 I was chief officer of *Rhodesia Castle* on the final voyage of the East African service, via Suez, which was quite a sad time for many. Having transmitted the canal and steamed quietly in the Med we heard that the canal had been closed for a second time due to conflict. Did our management have forewarning I often wonder? I then returned to the mail service as staff commander until I was appointed master in 1970.

My first command in 1970 was a Bowater newsprint/timber carrier trading mainly from Newfoundland and Nova Scotia to US east coast ports as far as Florida and occasionally to Europe. Navigating in ice in the Gulf of St Lawrence for the first time was another interesting experience. In 1971 we traded from Newfoundland to the US ports in the Great Lakes with newsprint. One of the first deep sea vessels into the seaway that year and encountered more ice in Lake Erie. I obtained my Great Lakes licence after examination at the Department of Transport offices at midnight while the vessel was bunkering. It was very interesting berthing in unfamiliar ports without pilots or tugs with a very handy little vessel. My next command was an ageing products tanker on charter to BP I had no previous tanker experience but attended the usual tanker courses. I had a very experienced chief officer who had been with Shell Tankers who quickly brought me up to standard. I was very fortunate to sail with him.

During my two years on that vessel, and as is usual on a hard working one, a close bond was created with the men who sailed on her and shared the varied situations in which we found ourselves. On one occasion when discharging at the oil terminal in Lourenço Marques, now known as Maputo the then revolutionary government in Lisbon announced that the colony was now free. This resulted in all work stopping, except us, and certainly the Portuguese population disappearing to their homes not knowing what would happen. The oil company managed to persuade one Portuguese pilot to assist us out of the oil terminal, on payment in US dollars. As we sailed past the main port and city it was quite weird. No sound of life and few people to be seen except for the crews of the vessels in port. At our next port of call, Durban, South Africa, my problem was persuading officials that having no clearance papers from the previous port was not illegal given the circumstances. At the beginning of my time on this vessel in 1972, the new revised Merchant Shipping Act was implemented which changed many of the procedures in operating UK flagged ships.

My next appointment was a return to the passenger mail service to South Africa. This came as a surprise to me as these ships had a limited time to operate with the competition from flying. I joined the *SA Orange* sailing under the South African flag and previously called the *Pretoria Castle*. I had sailed on her before and so was familiar with the vessel and many of her crew. Sadly, on my second voyage I had to break the news to the ship's company that the vessel was to be withdrawn from service after three further voyages. It was not really unexpected but still not a pleasant task to carry out. The final voyage went well due to loyal support from the ship's company and we had a very fine send-off from each South African port. At Durban the last passengers disembarked and the majority of the crew were flown back to the UK that same day. Those of us remaining unloaded cargo and de-stored the vessel before departing toTaiwan for scrapping. The passage was like sailing on a ghost ship and at the end, to leave a fine old vessel at a scrap yard on the beach was not very pleasant. The end of the passenger service was in 1977 and prior to that I was relief master on other passenger vessels.

My next appointment was to standby the completion of a VLCC at Swan Hunter's Wallsend yard on the Tyne. This was to be the last very large vessel built on the Tyne. The ship was being built for an American oil company and our company had the contract to supervise the building and the management and manning of the vessel. The ship was handed over after twelve days of trials in the North Sea on the 7th July 1977, two years late on the projected delivery date. The original agreement was for the vessel to operate under the British flag but two weeks before the trials the owners decided that the ship would now be registered in Panama but with our company still managing and manning it. This meant, among other things, that all the officers and ratings had to be supplied with Panamanian certificates to sail under the Panama flag which incurred fees.

Prior to the trials I visited the Panamanian Consulate in London to obtain the ship's register and other papers and of course the crew's individual certificates. I had a company cheque to use for the various payments but to my surprise this was not acceptable. The bill had to be paid in cash. It certainly caused some surprise at head office as they gathered the cash, as I sat enjoying a malt whisky with the Consul, toasting the well-being of the then to be largest vessel under the Panamanian flag at that time. I found out later that all dealings with the Panamanian authorities world wide had to be paid for in cash and US dollars.

I served two and a half years with this vessel, trading from the Persian Gulf to Curacao, carrying 255,000 tons of crude oil, each voyage to the USA. The cargo was off-loaded at Curacao into smaller tankers as the ship was too large to berth at a US port. We stored off-shore each time we passed Cape Town. Of the many different experiences on this vessel, one comes to mind in an international way. We were completing loading at Kharg Island off the coast of Iran when the agent rushed on board and urged us to sail at once. The reason for this was that the Revolutionary Guards had just over-run the US Embassy in Tehran and a detachment had just arrived on Kharg Island and expected to stop all ship departures. Fortunately we were able to slip our moorings and get underway, otherwise a lengthy stay would have been our fate especially carrying a cargo for the USA.

Following my time on the large tanker I was transferred to our reefer vessels on worldwide trading and another contrast in size and speed. By this time the shipping side of our company had drastically reduced in size; in part due to containerisation, increased competition with flags of convenience, and becoming too expensive. I completed two voyages on the reefer ships one of which took us round the world. En route from Seattle to Jeddah, off the north of the Philippines, we picked up the crew of a vessel that had recently sunk in the bad weather we were encountering and in the middle of the night. We had diverted on receiving information from the Japanese Marine Safety Agency. We picked up all twenty-two crew and, as is common these days the ship was Panama flag, the crew Korean and the owners Japanese. Fortunately we were able to contact the owners and to disembark the crew as we passed Singapore saving us any possible immigration problems. Incidentally, three other vessels had ignored the distress messages from the now sunken ship and at the time were much nearer to the distress position than we were. When I eventually returned to the UK I was interviewed by the smaller vessel's insurers as to the possibility of the vessel having been scuttled. I thought not. Later we arrived at Hodeida in North Yemen on the wedding day of the Prince of Wales. We were preceded into port by a Royal Naval Frigate which anchored and we berthed to unload our cargo. Our agent advised us that an Official Reception was to be held aboard the RN vessel that evening to celebrate the wedding and the VIP guests would be taken by the ship's purser from our berth. We became useful in allowing our VHF to communicate between the RN ship and her shore party. Later in the evening after cargo operations had ceased I was confronted in my cabin by a very drunk armed Yemeni policeman and a very agitated ship's chief steward. The policeman was demanding that we supply him with drink even though our bond was sealed. An interesting situation in a country with a total ban on alcohol. Eventually we managed to get him on the jetty and then lifted our gangway. I thought of calling up the navy for protection but then thought it might ruin a good party!!

On leaving the reefer ship I was very fortunate in being appointed to our containership *Table Bay* and taken on by the OCL. management in 1981. Interestingly I was on the vessel on three consecutive Christmas's with three different names, showing the diversity of loading patterns even in container shipping. In 1986 OCL was wholly taken over by the P&O Group and became POCL. In due course the chairman of P&O decided there should be a Commodore of the container fleet and I was appointed to the position. On my penultimate voyage prior to my retirement I had a reminder, if needed, of the power of the sea. We had departed Southampton bound for the Far East with a forecast of severe weather expected in the Biscay area. The Solent pilot was disembarked at Cowes Roads because of current weather conditions.

As we entered Biscay that evening the conditions were poor in a severe westerly gale and our speed reduced. Already several Mayday messages had been received and acknowledged but none near to us. At 23.00 hrs we received and SOS from a small German owned, Singapore flagged cargo vessel, indicating that it was sinking and they were abandoning ship. We acknowledged the message and hoped to be in the position given in about an hour, then all contact was lost with the vessel. On arrival at the position – and with crew on stations floating debris was observed and so we stopped to search the immediate area. This resulted in our coming beam on to wind and sea. With being a high sided vessel plus containers on deck the vessel now had a permanent nearly ten degree list due to the wind. Otherwise the movement of the vessel was reasonable considering the current weather conditions. An empty lifeboat was identified and lights from floating lifejackets were checked but no sign of survivors. Meanwhile a French coastguard aircraft had appeared on the scene and dropped two life rafts and released parachute flares which of course initially destroyed our night vision. In spite of this we could see no sign of survivors. Meantime two of our crew were washed overboard by a rogue wave. Unbelievably one was washed back on board by the next sea and the other retrieved by the rope attached to his safety harness.

Remarkably both men had only mild bruising but were somewhat shaken. The French coastguard instructed us to remain in the area and continue our search. To do so we had to get underway again to try and hold our position. In doing so until we gained steerage way, conditions on board were difficult and we sustained some structural damage as well. Once daylight arrived the French coastguard and our owners were informed that we were having difficulty maintaining our position in the prevailing conditions and so were permitted to proceed. Later we heard that eighteen crew including two wives were on board the vessel. I was informed later that about 120 people had been lost at sea during that storm, more than half being fishermen. These situations continue to occur at sea but seldom if ever appear in the press. The incident reminded many of our crew that even large ships are not necessarily foolproof to the force of the wind and weather. It should always be treated with great respect.

I retired nine months later having spent two years on the training ship HMS *Conway* followed by forty-four years at sea and consider myself fortunate in doing the job I enjoyed and was able to do so until my retirement in a rapidly disappearing industry.

School Days 1938

A t the age of eight my father received permission to take me away from school in 1938; because of my early interest in ships he took me to Glasgow to see the launch of the *Queen Elizabeth* from John Brown's shipyard. We stayed with my mother's two sisters at Bridge of Weir which was very convenient. On the big day we had seats in one of the grandstands on the opposite bank of the river near to the mouth of the river Cart where the stern of the ship launched would enter for a short distance, the river Clyde itself not being wide enough. A very big crowd had gathered and an announcement was made by loud speaker for everyone to move back from the immediate river bank but many ignored the warning. The scene was very impressive with the tug boats standing by to hold the vessel once launched.

Then Queen Elizabeth, mother of our present Queen, swung the bottle and named the ship. It slowly started to move and increased speed, an impressive sight. Unfortunately, with it being high water spring tides when the ship entered the river it created its own tidal wave which came over the opposite bank into the field and those who had ignored the warning, were suddenly nearly waist deep in water. The new ship was safely secured by the tugs and towed to the fitting out basin for completion. A day to remember. When we left the scene of the launch I was taken to the Empire Exhibition at Bellahouston Park which was also very interesting even for a small boy as each country had its own pavilion. The day was rounded off with a fish and chip tea. The only down side to the great occasion for me was having to write an essay of the event for my teacher at school.

Sometime later when I was a cadet on HMS *Conway* I had the opportunity of attending another ship launching. My father had a friend in Elgin who also had a good friend who was manager of the Greenock Dockyard Shipbuilding Company which was owned by the Clan Line This gentleman on hearing of my intentions of a seagoing career invited me, aged fifteen to the launch of a ship at his yard. It was fortunate that it was to take place at the beginning my Christmas leave from the training ship. Again I was able to make use of my aunts living at Bridge of Weir.

I duly presented myself at the Greenock yard at the time and date given in December 1945. With the country still at war, there was no real ceremony but a shipyard wife would break the bottle and the workers would down tools to watch. I was then introduced to the Clyde pilot who would be in charge on board and I was to accompany him which was quite unexpected. For the times it was quite a large vessel to be used for transporting heavy items of cargo, railway engines, tanks and such like. When we reached the bridge we were about level of the tops of the shipyard cranes and the ground seemed a very long way below. The vessel was really a skeleton with no fittings as yet and instructions given by hand whistle to the tug boats and hand megaphone to the mooring men on deck. I had moments of thinking the ship might fall over before reaching the Clyde. The pilot however had a voice like a fog horn and I was told to follow him around. The moment came, the ship named *Empire Canute* and it slowly started to move with cheers from the workers on shore. It truly was an amazing experience for me. Once we were fully afloat in the Clyde and the tugs now made fast we proceeded through the lock into James Watt Dock to our fitting out berth. By now it was a dark, cold December evening. As it would be some time before a gangway could be rigged we were to be lifted off individually by crane. A crane swung over the ship and I was told to put one foot on the hook and hang on to the crane wire. This I did knowing the quayside was a long way down. I was aware of being whisked up with my eyes tightly shut, swung over the side and lowered very quickly with me hanging on. I then was aware of laughter and encouraged to put my other foot down and there was the solid ground – I not really aware I was there. It certainly gave big light entertainment to the onlookers. I was then off to catch the bus to Bridge of Weir and relate the amazing experience to my aunts who were always an appreciative audience.

HMS *Conway* 1944–1946

When I was a boy I always had a desire to go to sea and see the world. My father, through help from his brother, applied for me to go to HMS *Conway* a well known sea training school ship. I sat and passed the 'Conway' entrance exam. I had to have special tuition in trigonometry, as in Scotland you did not have trig until your third year. The fees for 'Conway' at that time were £150.00 a year and the course was for two years. At the time I was not aware of it but this was a considerable outlay for my parents plus the extras of uniform and transport to and from the ship.

My father and a friend, Tom Watson, took me by train to join the ship at Bangor in North Wales. This would be the first time my father had crossed the border, though he had been to Ireland as I recall to buy cattle. I did not want my family to see me off wearing my uniform for the first time. However, to my mortification one of my aunts, the gym teacher at Elgin Academy wearing her gym slip insisted in seeing me off, cycling along the platform as the train drew away. I remember we stayed the night at Llandudno before going to Bangor the following day.

At Bangor pier we were taken by launch to *Conway* which was anchored off in the Menai Straits. I can remember well being met at the top of the gangway by the ship's Warrant Officer, known to all as bossy Phelps. He introduced himself to my father saying "right now Mr Royan, just leave him with us, we will take care of him, we make or break them in a fortnight". My father left and I believe it was a year before he told my mother what was said and I was grateful for that.

The *Conway* had been one of Nelson's ships and originally called HMS *Nile* a typical wooden wall as better known. There were 250 cadets living on board in what was called the orlop deck. We each were given a black painted wooden trunk with our name on it which housed all our possessions for the next two years. You learned quickly how to arrange your chest neatly with all your clothes. At the same time we were given a hammock for the two years. The hammocks were slung from the deck head prior to turning in and lashed up each morning and stowed away.

We new boys, 'New Chums' we were called had a senior and a junior cadet captain in charge of us. They were to instruct and lead us in the ship's routine. A fortnight was the time given to become familiar with the routine. We were shown how to sling our hammock and at first we had trouble staying in them which was soon overcome. Reveille was at 06.30 hrs and lights out at 21.30 hrs and by that time we were too tired to fall out. Each morning we lashed our hammocks as shown and the cadet captain would then bend them double and if any bedding showed you were obliged to do it again. If this happened after a fortnight you received one across your rear with the ropes end, known as the teaser.

The washing facilities were a bit of a shock. There were four rows of wash basins, each with a tap and they were up in the bow of the ship where the anchor chains ran out and the wind whistled in which was not pleasant in winter. The water supply was poor and as juniors you were at the end of the line and frequently had to suck the tap to get the water to flow. Everything was done by seniority so term by term these conditions improved.

All orders and instructions were given by bugle call; another thing you had to learn in the first fortnight or pay the price. All these orders had to be carried out at the double, one soon learned that you did not take your time.

The food was terrible on board even allowing for food rationing in the country as a whole. Each term sat at its own table under the supervision of their respective cadet captains. When (seldom) there was some extra food cooked it went to the senior hands. Rumour had it that our catering officer owned a café in Bangor which did rather well. We ate our meals on the main deck which during school became our class rooms. Partitions were put in place to make individual classrooms which had to be removed for each meal by the cadets. You always knew when a cadet had received a food parcel from home. He was always surrounded by so called friends.

The basic routine on board was reveille at 06.30 hrs by bugle followed by lashing up and stowing hammocks followed by washing. We then had gym on the upper deck irrespective of the weather followed by breakfast. Then on week days, school morning and afternoon followed by the evening meal and other duties until lights out at 21.30 hrs. Virtually no spare time as cleaning routines of various kinds followed. There was one bath night a week which went by term so Sunday night no baths. Saturday mornings were heave-ho where we scrubbed decks in bare feet and polished all brass and silver. In winter we were allowed to wear sea boots. In the afternoon it was games where we had to walk to the playing fields at Bangor or Beaumaris or partake of a cross country run. Any spare time left was usually spent gathering something to eat. Our parents were limited to 2/6d per week for pocket money which was paid out weekly. Sundays featured inspection by the captain of all cadets in full uniform with the heels of your shoes of special interest. This was followed by a general inspection of the ship where cadets mustered at the places for which they were responsible. Then at 11 o'clock we had church service on the main deck, a watered down Anglican service conducted by the full time ship's padre. Exceptions were made for Roman Catholics to go ashore for mass and the odd non conformist who put their name forward. I was not smart enough to think about it. Sunday afternoon was time set aside to write letters home. In summer if the weather was good you were allowed ashore to walk. You were landed on the Anglesey side and had to walk to the Menai Bridge and on to Bangor where you were picked up. Little time for other diversions.

One morning in my third term I felt quite unwell and reported to sickbay where a formidable lady called Sister Perry held sway. She looked at me and said I was just trying to miss gym on the upper deck so I left. My first class that morning was Seamanship taken by a seagoing officer on secondment. He called me out in front of the class and remarked that I did not look well and I told him of my Sister Parry interview. He then told me to pull up my shirt to find I was covered in spots and taken swiftly to sick bay and presented to Sister Parry. German measles was diagnosed and before I knew it I was ashore at our sanitorium on Anglesey and the ship put in quarantine. I enjoyed my time there as I listened to the bugle calls and enjoyed much better food, As I remember no one else caught the disease but the annual dance on board was cancelled which disappointed our more mature boys and some of the girls from Normal College who would have been invited. Fortunately for me I was sent straight home from sick bay!

On our fourth term we were in turn sent for a fortnight at the original Outward Bound Sea School at Aberdovey in West Wales. This really was a fitness course for boys going to sea and also boys from the London area who had appeared in court and were sent to Aberdovey instead of borstal for their offence and possibly to go to sea. As you can imagine we were quite a mixed bag. During the day it was physical exercises and athletics and very competitive with standards you were expected to reach. In the evenings there were classes in map reading, route planning and the like and each in turn to give details of our backgrounds and ambitions – all very interesting.

Our spell was the four weeks before Christmas and so pretty cold. We were accommodated in an old country house with about eight beds to a room. First thing at 06.30 hrs you dressed in a vest and shorts and as a group ran down the avenue to the main road and then back again overseen by merchant navy officers fully clothed. You then returned to the stables, having worked up a good sweat, where each of the stalls had a shower in position. The water for these showers came directly from a hillside stream to a tank in the loft. On one morning they had to break the ice on the tank. Each in turn had to shower monitored by these officers wearing duffel coats and a stop watch. How we hated them. However in that four weeks no one fell sick and we were lined up before each breakfast and given a spoonful of cod liver oil. The best bit was that the food was good and plentiful and compared to the Conway was perfect.

Each in turn were crew on a sailing schooner for three days in the Irish Sea. On our turn we experienced a gale and had to spend a night in Fishguard having all been seasick and scared at times. Our final exercise was a mountain trek. We were divided into teams of six and I was the leader of our team. The evening before, each team were issued with the route they had to follow along with an ordnance map and a compass, all of which we had been taught to use. After breakfast the following morning, when still dark, we boarded an old country bus, driven into the hills and each team dropped off at their own starting point, each person having also been provided with a packet of food. We had check-in points to make where we had to pick up proof that we had been there but saw no one. At one point a hill mist formed and at about the same time we saw a farm cottage. I thought I could confirm our position there but no one answered the door though we could see people peering from behind the curtains. I am glad to say we all completed our routes and by that time dark it was again. We had all covered twenty-two miles and were exhausted but well pleased with ourselves and ready for the food placed before us. When I mentioned the cottage incident we were told there was a borstal school in the area and the occupants probably thought we were escapees and in fairness we probably looked like that. On our last day we all received a certificate with our best performances listed and I have still held on to mine to produce to family now and again. From Aberdovey we all headed home for our Christmas leave.

On return to the ship for my fifth term at the beginning of 1946 I found I had been made a junior cadet captain under a senior cadet captain. We were now in charge of a number of boys on their first term. I had to remember what it was like for me eighteen months before. When I returned to the ship for my final term, to my delight I had been made a senior cadet captain in charge of the ship's largest motor boat with a crew of four. It was not the best rating as such but in many ways very desirable. Handling the boat every day gave me considerable experience which stood me in good stead in my career. Looking back now I had more authority then at sixteen until I was promoted to chief officer. There was much poor weather that summer and often we were the only boat operating, kitted out in oilskins like lifeboat men!

Each summer term there was a King's Gold Medal awarded. The officers and scholastic staff between them selected five cadets in their last term. The ship's company was then mustered, except for the first termers, and each had to vote for one of the five names. On the day it came as a shock to me that I was one of the five names on the board. We were then all called, one by one, to indicate our choice. I really could not believe it when it was announced that I had the most votes. It took some time for it to sink in.

Towards the end of that term the King and Queen accompanied by the two Princesses visited Bangor. They were engaged in a grand tour of the UK at the time. The *Conway* provided a guard of honour that day in recognition of the role the Merchant Service had played during the war. Eighty of us paraded on the big day outside Bangor Cathedral. Being North Wales it was raining but that did not prevent us putting on a very good show. I was presented to the King as the winner of the Gold Medal and had been well briefed beforehand. When we were dismissed and news reporters asked me what the King had to say I could not remember but fortunately a friend who had been on parade next to me was able to answer for me. I did not receive the medal until three years later because of wartime restrictions. The following day a photograph of the event appeared on the front pages of the Liverpool daily paper. However, life carried on as usual on board till the end of term.

At the end of my two years I was a different person. Now able to look after myself and had grown up. The discipline and teamwork on board were to stand me in good stead in the years to come at sea.

We were fortunate that, at the summer prize giving on the two years I was on the ship, we had two distinguished guests. In 1945 we had Admiral Max Horton who was Commander in Chief North Atlantic during the war and in 1946 we had Admiral Bruce Somerville of H Force looking after the Western Mediterranean during the hostilities. They both gave very impressive speeches to the boys who were enthralled.

During my time on *Conway* Commander T.M. Goddard was the captain. There were three chief officers, Digby, Jones and Pilcher; Blue Funnel Line chief officers on secondment and in my last term C. Douglas Lane, Commander RNR, who returned after having left the ship at the start of the war as the second officer. I kept in touch with him until he died having last visited him at his care home. He was remarkably unchanged. For some considerable time he was coach in charge of the ball boys for tennis tournaments. After he retired, girls were introduced and he confided in me that it would not be the same especially since all were to be addressed by their Christian names instead of their surnames. How would you tell them apart? He was an excellent officer and should have been the last captain of the *Conway*.

Cadets with an overnight journey to get home at the end of term could leave the ship the afternoon before . For me, this involved taking the train to Llandudno Junction where I had to change to the Crewe train. Crewe station in December 1944 was a heaving mass of humanity, mainly members of the armed forces, and an amazing sight for a fourteen-year-old boy. The London-Inverness train arrived at 2.00 am and was already full. Each carriage I approached, I was told in no uncertain terms there was no room. However, when I heard the guard's whistle, I had to board, so opened the nearest carriage door, causing three soldiers of the HLI, who had been leaning out of the window, to end up on the platform. I climbed aboard, closely followed by the three soldiers, who subjected me to verbal abuse of the highest standard – a swift learning curve! – as we sat on our baggage in the corridor, all the way to Stirling, between snatches of sleep. At Stirling, my three tormentors left with further parting shots and I had relative peace for the rest of the journey. I reached home a much more worldly-wise person.

On VE day, a day's leave was granted to those who could get home on the same day. Those of us who came from further away, remained on board. It was a funny feeling, on board a nearly empty, quiet ship. There was no shore leave but we were aware of festivities ashore at Bangor, with music and fireworks

At the end of my last term, my mate Philip Gyton invited me to spend a few days at his home in Nottingham. Again, we had to change at Llandudno Junction to get to Crewe and hence Nottingham. At Llandudno Junction, when the train drew in a little early, we asked a porter if it was the Crewe train, which he said it was. We boarded and as usual, it was full. However, when our tickets were checked, the guard informed us this was a special excursion train to London and did not stop at Crewe. We certainly did not have enough money to travel to London and back to Nottingham. The train couldn't stop at Crewe by signals, as it would be on the through line. We asked the guard, if the train stopped anywhere, could we jump off, his reply was he did not want to know. But luck was on our side as the train was stopped by signal. We opened the door, threw out our cases and jumped down to the embankment, and the guard kindly shut the door behind us. But the engine crew spotted us and were waving us on board; we waved them on as we scrambled up the bank. By now, people were peering out of the windows and shaking their heads. We just hoped no one could identify us as Conway boys. Our luck was still in when we were given a lift into Crewe, twelve miles away, by a kind lorry driver – we were still in time to catch the Nottingham train. By now, we decided that, after our two years on the Old Ship, we were ready to face the challenges of going to sea.

I must mention before I forget that there was a strict rule of no smoking on board *Conway*. As was the case in those days boys were very often tempted to have a sneaky drag and this was true on the ship. A favorite place was the 'heads' in other words the lavatories which were very basic. However if caught by an officer it was 'six of the best' administered by the PT warrant officer which was painful I am sure. On one leave I was discussing this with my parents and thought it hard on those boys who smoked at home. My father was a heavy smoker and with a smoker's cough in the morning. I then suggested that he would have difficulty giving up smoking where upon he handed over his packet of Churchmen No 1 and his lighter to my mother. I then bet half a crown he would not give it up – with my mother holding the stake. Believe it or not he never smoked again. I was suitably impressed.

Conway Days

My term at HMS *Conway* held a fiftieth reunion at a hotel in Carnaervon at which eighteen attended out of a team of about forty. Wives were also invited. We had an enjoyable weekend and I was amazed at how few had changed all that much other than they were now all pensioners. Of course many incidents and events were recalled. The one which stood out was recalled by AR Worthington who had come all the way from Fremantle, West Australia where he had been a labour pilot before retiring. He was still nursing an injustice which he had suffered these many years ago.

This incident occurred at a church parade which a squad of cadets was to attend led by the ship's Drum and Bugle band which was much in demand at that time towards the end of the war. I was not included in this particular parade which was fortunate. On the Sunday of the parade the band and parade squad were mustered at the end of Bangor Pier, but at the last minute the Drum Major, RJ Bostock went sick and so Worthington, the senior bugler, was put in charge to lead the parade. It would appear that he was not properly briefed as to the programme – his story – or he just misunderstood his instructions. He thought they were to attend the church at the top end of Bangor next to the railway station which everyone knew.

However, this church was a Welsh church with the whole service in Welsh and needless to say the cadets were not expected. Space was made for the cadets at the back of the church and a spot found for the instruments and the squad had to sit and stand through a service all in Welsh. At the end of the service the party was mustered and marched off back to Bangor Pier watched by a much bemused congregation. On reaching the pier they were met by the captain who, to say the least, was not amused. Apparently the church parade was to be at Bangor Cathedral which was about half way up the hill to the station and the Captain, Bishop and the Dean of the cathedral were outside to take the salute and welcome the party. They stood there in shock as the church parade continued up the hill to the other church.Poor Worthington had his shore leave stopped for three weeks and was still brooding, fifty years later, of this grave injustice. One wonders what the Welsh minister and congregation made of it at the time. The captain in due course apologised to the minister of the Welsh church.

During the war the Conway band was much in demand with a marching squad of cadets very often for fundraising purposes. There would be a Spitfire Week and other similar schemes and we would be at the head of the parade behind our band followed by Scouts, Guides, Boys Brigade and the like with possibly an army or RAF detachment. If you were selected for the marching squad you missed out from the Saturday scrub and polish morning. One parade of which I was part particularly comes to mind. Our band had a fast march beat which we were trained to follow and on this occasion we were joined by a detachment of a Highland Regiment which was training in Snowdonia. They arrived late and were taking up the rear of the parade. What we did not know before we started marching was that they had brought a solitary piper. Once the march began we were soon in trouble. The piper's beat, as it were, was slightly slower than the bugle band which in time caused chaos as some heard the band from the front end and some the pipes from behind. It was just too easy to unwittingly change step. We were all much relieved when that parade was over.

VE Day was during my third term. All those who lived in England and Wales were granted two day's leave if their parents agreed. Those others with long distance to travel had to remain on board with no shore leave. We were all aware of the celebrations ashore as we could see and hear them. For two senior cadets, both rebels, one from Glasgow and one from Northern Ireland, decided they were going ashore. Our rubbish was collected in tubs – large wooden barrels cut in half. These two secretly launched one into the Menai Straits and using planks as paddles set off after dark from the ship for Bangor Pier. However they were spotted by the duty officer who sent the motor boat after them. Luckily the boat arrived at the same time as the tub filled with water and they were only halfway between ship and the pier. The strong tide could easily have swept them away. They were suitably chastened when back on board and were let off with a warning on this occasion.

On the ship in my time the winter term was when the boxing matches took place. A list of the different fighting weights was posted and cadets who wished to take part were instructed to put their names down at the appropriate weights. When the list was closed the PT instructor would check it over and see how it looked. If any weight was short in numbers he would look around for volunteers as such. Needless to say first term innocents were fair game.

To my horror I found my name down at one of the very light weights which was not surprising as I was only fourteen and a half years at the time. I went along to the PT instructor to say that I had never had boxing gloves on in my life and knew nothing about boxing. Predictably, my views were swept aside with the assurance that it was time I knew how to defend myself if I was to go to sea and that he would give me some training. When the lists were posted of those taking part in the first rounds I was to face a cadet called Macbride who I did not know him as he was senior to me. When I asked around I was told, with much glee by those not boxing, that Macbride was captain of the ship's official boxing team. I was horrified. I eventually managed to meet Macbride, who was so much senior to me, and I explained the situation to him. He was very understanding and promised he would go easy on me and would of course win on points after we had completed the required three rounds. Those of my term, who had not been picked to box, encouraged me by saying I would not know what had hit me in the ring!

The big night came and the ring rigged up in the ships hold. Everyone not boxing were there to enjoy the show and of course hoping for blood. We light weights were on early and soon it was my time. As my opponent circled around I was being encouraged by the PT instructor and my so called seconds. In the first round Macbride danced around me, giving me comparatively light taps and I could not get near him as the crowd shouted for blood. In the second round Macbride stung me once or twice and I took a swing at him, which he was not expecting, right on his nose. That was the last I remembered until I was carried out of the ring and revived by my seconds to the cheers of the crowd. Macbride looked me up the next day to say no hard feelings but that I had really stung him with the blow to the nose. Incidentally I learned later that Macbride had been killed in Burma leading the opposition to the Junta there. In his early days he had been sailing to Rangoon and had met his bride, from a high ranking family who were opposed to the Junta and by this time Macbride had been living there. We Conways go around.

During my last term we heard that Sister Perry was to retire and a replacement was being sought. One Saturday afternoon when I was preparing to take No.1 motor boat to Bangor Pier to pick up the cadets returning from shore, I was informed by the duty officer that there would be a lady to pick up (I cannot recall her name) who was to be the replacement for Sister Perry the next term. She was joining to double up with her for the rest of this term. I was told that once she was on board she would be introduced to the ship's company and not before. This was interesting news.

When I arrived at Bangor Pier there was a youngish lady with a suitcase and of course a crowd of very curious cadets obviously wondering who she was. Following procedures our passenger was the first to board and requested by me to go to the cabin up forward to be followed in order of seniority with some senior cadets very anxious to get into the cabin as well. The remaining cadets followed full of curiosity and excitement at the unknown lady.

On returning to the ship, the usual procedure was followed. Space was made on the motor boat to allow our passenger to leave first with the coxen saluting – that's me. She emerged somewhat flustered from the cabin with one of the senior hands carrying her suitcase having been in close proximity to some very interested youths and followed in orderly fashion by the rest of the cadets, all closely watched by the officer of the watch at the top of the gangway I understand that our new nursing sister only lasted one term after I left. I think she was possibly too young for the post and the ship had the tough Sister Perry back until they found another replacement.

Another *Conway* Memory
– The Captain's Daughter

The Captain's daughter called Rosemary used to live aboard with her parents from time to time and was married to an old Conway at that time, a Lieutenant RN in the submarine service whose name for the moment I cannot remember. When we were more senior we were on a rota for anchor watch from between 22.00 and 06.00 for two hours. The duty included fire patrols around the ship. Any incidents had to be written up in the night logbook when handing over to your relief as keeper.

I was on watch on one occasion from midnight until 02.00 and was patrolling round the poop deck, at the stern of the ship. Below this deck was the Captain's quarters. I was unexpectedly approached by the Captain's daughter in her dressing gown who informed me that the Captain's cat had caught a rat under her bed and could I do something about it. Armed with a brush and shovel I entered the Captain's quarters for the first and only time. Under the bed I found the cat and the now dead rat and managed to retrieve the rat from the reluctant cat and disposed of the body into the Menai Strait and was thanked by the lady. I duly entered the event in the logbook and mentioned it to my relief who was suitably impressed. The following morning the news was round the ship and even senior hands inquiring of the incident and wondering why it had not been them. Many of them at that time were more interested in girls than I was.

In my last term the Captain's daughter lived aboard as she was expecting a baby. The more enterprising of the senior hands were running a sweepstake on when the baby would arrive. I was quite shocked. As the maximum pocket money allowed was two shillings a week it was surprising how many took part. A baby girl was born ashore and the proud grandparents rowed back to the ship late at night in the ships dinghy with just the oarsman as the ship's company were all fast asleep except the duty officer. I never knew who won the sweep and it did not come to the attention of the officers until after the event.

Early Days at Sea as a Cadet

Prior to leaving the *Conway* we were encouraged to apply to a shipping company for a position as deck cadet. I knew very little about shipping companies but heard of the P&O and going to the Far East appealed to me. However, when I received the information about P&O I realised that my parents could not afford the outlay uniforms that this would involve. I applied to join the Clan Line as at least it was Scottish, and was accepted.

Within two weeks of leaving *Conway* I had a letter appointing me to my first ship as a deck cadet. Little time to arrange new uniforms and the like. I joined the *Clan Cumming* at Princes Pier, Greenock on 12 August 1946 and only realised it was the first new ship to join the company since the end of the war. I was one of three cadets on board. The senior cadet was nineteen and the other one had been a year ahead of me on *Conway*. I now found myself the lowest of the low again and to start afresh the climb up. The ship had Indian ratings and UK officers. When I went into the dining saloon and was handed a menu I could hardly believe it after *Conway*. The following day the ship left on sea trials in the Firth of Clyde and when completed to the owner's satisfaction the ship was formally handed over by the shipbuilders, and the ship stored for deep sea. The following day the Cayzer family boarded, about fifteen in all, the owners of the Clan Line. The ship then went on a cruise down to Ailsa Craig and back to Greenock for the benefit of the owners and they had lunch on board. This resulted in we cadets not eating till 3 p.m!

The following day we departed for New York to commence loading for South Africa. Most of the officers had been through the war and the captain had been torpedoed on a Malta convoy and taken prisoner by the submarine that had sunk his ship *Clan Ferguson*. The chief officer had been captain of a frigate, as RNR officer, on convoy duty on the North Atlantic. I was seasick for a day or two but the chief officer told me the only cure was hard work and it seemed to be effective

We arrived at New York on a Friday and steaming past the Statue of Liberty and viewing the city skyscrapers was very exciting. This was what going to sea was about. We anchored off Staten Island to await orders and were boarded by the Port Health doctor who was to check everyone. All the officers mustered in the dining saloon when everyone, except the captain, was told to drop their trousers for an inspection for VD! This was one part of going to sea that I had not known about. After that surprise our orders were to remain at anchor over the weekend but no shore leave so no money was ordered. However, when the ship's agent came on board he had US dollars to give to the senior cadet. This money had been provided by a friend of this cadet's father who lived in New York. Because of this gift we three cadets were allowed ashore on the Saturday to the irritation of the ship's company. We went first to what was known as the Apprentices Club run by two respected and well known ladies for cadets and apprentices to gather to enjoy the amenities, and advise on what to see in the city. We then visited Times Square with all its lights, theatres, cinemas and the like. So different to the UK at that time. It was decided we would go to a cinema and the film was the *Big Sleep*. There was a notice outside which said US Forces half price. We were in uniform as we were obliged to do and I was nominated to go and buy the tickets. I somewhat reluctantly approached the ticket office manned by, to me, a very glamorous blonde who looked like Betty Grable. when I made my request she pointed out that I was not US military but as only a kid, she gave me three half price tickets. In the cinema there was a famous dance band playing between the films. We had been told to buy the Sunday papers to bring back to the ship. No one had told us how large they were and we carried them on board on our shoulders.

The ship then received new orders, and instead of loading for South Africa it had been taken over by UNRA (United Nations Relief Agency), to load a cargo of wheat and flour for India, which had a famine at that time, and we loaded a full cargo at Baltimore. From Baltimore we called at Trinidad to take on fuel and then carried on round the Cape of Good Hope to our first port in India which was Madras.

On our arrival at Madras I came face to face with real poverty for the first time. It was quite a shock. One evening we three cadets walked out to the Seamen's Club which was not far outside the main gate to the docks. On our way back we were walking on the road as the pavement was taken up by the very poor living in makeshift tents. We came to a small crowd gathered round a woman lying on the pavement who it turned out was giving birth to a baby. Something I did not mention in my letter home at the time. We then sailed on to Calcutta to complete our discharge and commence loading for home. At the time the city was under night curfew because of rioting between Hindus and Moslems. My two fellow cadets were given an afternoon off and decided to go up to the city centre by tram. At the time each tram was carrying a policeman to prevent trouble. However, their tram was attacked and they ended up lying on the floor as the driver headed the tram at full speed to safety. They admitted to having been really scared when they returned to the ship.

Our final loading port was Chittagong which was still part of India at that time and is now in Bangladesh. There we completed loading tea and jute. In these days Chittagong was a main trading port for the Clan Line and where we recruited our Indian crews. On leaving Chittagong I was on the bridge keeping the bridge book, when the ship's steering gear jammed and we hit the bank, Fortunately it was composed of soft mud and we bounced off. I was reminded of keeping times and notes rather than enjoying the drama. One of the propellers was damaged and we had to dry dock in Colombo which gave me a chance go and see another place for the first time. It was very much like the East as I had imagined.

Homeward bound, we called at Aden for fuel and then up the Red Sea and through the Suez Canal all very interesting for the first time. Meeting in Port Said, the agents approved a trader or bum boat man, as commercially known. As a good Egyptian and wily trader he had adopted the name of Jock Mackay when dealing with Clan ships. We arrived at Tilbury with the largest cargo of tea since the beginning of the war. However we sailed from Tilbury on Christmas Eve bound for Dundee in dense fog. Ship-owners always tried to have their ships at sea over holidays rather than have the vessel lying idle in port. This happened to me quite often over the years.

When the ship arrived in Glasgow I was given a week's leave and had plenty to tell. On return I found the ship loading for South Africa another new country to see. We had a full cargo of an amazing variety of goods from Scotch whisky and seed potatoes to two railway coaches to form part of the Royal train in South Africa for the King and Queen's tour later in 1947. We also had one of the grandsons of the founder of the company travelling to South Africa with us along with his car and driver.

We arrived at Cape Town early on a beautiful morning and the sight of Table Mountain for the first time was unforgettable. Once alongside, I went to see all the wonderful fruit to buy which was so cheap and in sharp contrast to the rationing and shortages at home. There was an excellent Mission to Seamen in the port which we cadets frequented when ashore. They arranged trips to the beaches and elsewhere.. We then called at Port Elizabeth, East London and Durban to unload. finally completing our discharge at Lorenzo Marques and Beira two ports in the Portuguese Mozambique By this time the ship had received orders to proceed in ballast, otherwise empty, to Australia to load for home which was much appreciated by all on board.

We arrived at a small port in the Spencer Gulf called Port Pirie which had a facility to process zinc ingots which we loaded for bottom weight. It was a typical frontier town at that time where the train ran along the main street but the people were very friendly. We then sailed round to Sydney, arriving again in the early morning, and entering its magnificent harbour and of course passing under the famous bridge. As we arrived, a square rigged sailing ship called *Pamir* had just departed and was making sail. A splendid sight. One of the reasons why trading with Australia was popular with ships' crews was that time in port could be prolonged due to the frequent strikes called by the dock workers union, and our stay in Sydney extended to two weeks which included Easter weekend which was a public holiday. When my family heard that I was heading to Australia I was advised of an uncle of my father who lived near to Sydney and was given his address. He had fought in the

1914–18 war and on being demobbed decided to emigrate to New Zealand then on to Australia where prospects were better. He had married, had no family and was now a widower. He had never been back to the UK and neither had any of his family been to visit him. I had written him from Port Pirie and had a letter awaiting me on arrival at Sydney. As the ship was not working at Easter I was given leave over the weekend to visit him. He was retired in a small town called the Entrance on the Shore of Tuggerah Lake. I travelled by train and then bus to meet him and it was all very exciting. He lived in a small bungalow type house and had a very nice housekeeper also of a good age. Needless to say there was much to talk about and I was taken around to meet his friends. Many of them were Scots and I was amazed at how they seemed to recall their accents when talking to me. Their nostalgia for the 'old country' was strong especially as they had a far better life and working conditions in Australia than they would have had in Scotland. He brought me back to the ship on the Monday calling at the Royal Easter Agricultural Show on the way. To me a quite spectacular event. We departed from Sydney and called at Fremantle to load more wool on deck and water and provisions for the voyage home.

Our first unloading port was Antwerp where I first saw the effect of the war in Europe. In Antwerp docks all the buildings had been flattened and rebuilding had not yet commenced. We unloaded the bales of wool on the quay which were then covered by tarpaulins until such time as it was ferried away by horse and cart. No motor transport and the railway line still not repaired. We finished our unloading in Hull before going round to Glasgow through the Pentland Firth again. I was given leave and told I was to be appointed to another ship. Before leaving, the chief officer told me now was the time to leave the sea before it was too late as it was not much of a life. I was quite taken aback.

My next ship was the *Clan McFadyen* which I joined in Glasgow as the senior of two cadets. My first promotion! This was one of the mass produced American ships built to make up for the losses during the war. Built in 1943 the company had just bought it from the US and had painted it in company colours. These ships were of a different design and in ways more up to date in that we had hot and cold water to each cabin and rotating ventilation fans. Just as well as these ships are very hot in the tropics with all accommodation above the engine room. The second officer of the *Cumming* was promoted chief officer here and so I knew at least one person. We loaded for Ceylon and India carrying four race horses to Colombo which we cadets looked after.

One incident I shall recall was during our passage through the Red Sea. It was very hot and many of the officers were sleeping on the boat deck where it was cooler than the cabins. I was getting up at 4.30 to give the horses a drink and wash down their legs with sea water. On this particular morning on the boat deck among others was our rather fat chief steward flat on his back covered with just sheets. The engineers had just blown the soot out of the boilers and because of a following wind it had landed on the chief steward among others, and had formed a black pile on top of this large fat stomach and with each breath he took it quivered gently. I was transfixed and only wished I had owned a camera. Something not common in these days.

We were in Calcutta for Indian Independence day which I have mentioned elsewhere. The other incident from that vessel I recall was also to do with someone's stomach, this time the captain's. Going round the UK coast on our return from India I was on the eight–twelve watch with the third officer. He had just taken bearings of three light houses and went into the chartroom to put these bearings on the chart and so have the ship's position. The captain was leaning over the chart table waiting to see this position. The third officer found the top drawer partly open which was preventing him plotting the position. He gave the drawer a firm push which resulted in a roar of pain from the captain whose large stomach had overhung the drawer. I could hear the roar from the bridge and the third officer appeared looking somewhat shocked and not knowing if it was the end of his career. Again on returning to Glasgow I was given leave and waited for my next appointment..

The next ship I joined was the *Clan Macnair* one of the oldest ships in the fleet having built in 1921. I was the senior cadet and the other cadet on his first trip, had me as his cadet captain on his first term on *Conway*. Having started on the latest ship in the fleet and now on one of the oldest I was doing the rounds. All the officers' cabins were lined with tongue and groove panelling which was the home to numerous cockroaches before the days of an effective repellent. In the hot weather the ship was alive with them. Our washing facilities was a forty gallon drum which was filled up each day by one of the Indian stewards using a hand pump and we used a bucket to rinse ourselves down. We loaded for India and back and mentioned elsewhere of being in Bombay when Gandhi was killed and carrying mares in foal to Bombay. We had very bad weather both out and homeward in the Bay of Biscay. At that time I did not realize how bad it was, just very exciting if very uncomfortable. Once again when the ship reached Glasgow I was sent on leave and would be told in due course what ship I would be joining.

HMS *Conway*

HMS *Conway* was built in 1839 at Plymouth and was originally named HMS *Nile*, a second rate ship of the British navy. She was renamed *Conway* in 1876 and turned into a training ship anchored off Liverpool.

In 1949, HMS *Conway* was towed from a mooring off Bangor Pier in the Menai Straits to a mooring off Plas Newydd the home of the Marquis of Anglesey. This was a tricky operation due to the very strong currents in the area and the rocky foreshore, the most dangerous area known as the Swellies. It also involved passing under the road suspension bridge and the tubular railway bridge. The operation was successfully carried out on 14th April and a number of cadets were then housed ashore thus improving conditions aboard ship. All the school classrooms were based ashore.

In 1953 it was decided that the ship would have to go to dry dock in the river Mersey. The vessel's underwater part of the hull required cleaning and repaired where necessary to ensure her future afloat. Once again careful planning was required to ensure ideal tidal and wind conditions. On 14th April, with two Mersey tug boats to assist, (though three had been considered necessary by some) the moorings were slipped and the tow commenced. However things did not go to plan. The tidal strength was stronger than expected and one tug's tow wire parted. Sadly the old ship ran aground on a formidable rock formation and was stuck on the falling tide. This resulted in the wooden shjp breaking her back and being declared a total loss. Had the ship survived she would have been to Liverpool what the HMS *Victory* is to Portsmouth.

The School was eventually handed over to Cheshire Education Authority and it was closed in 1974.

So ended the old motto *Quit ye like men be strong*

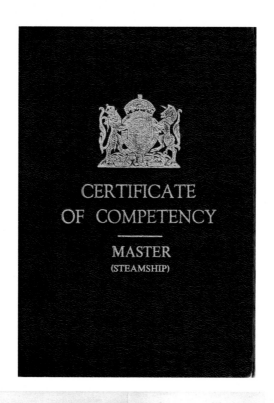

CERTIFICATE OF COMPETENCY
AS
MASTER
OF A FOREIGN-GOING STEAMSHIP No. 74180.

To *Robert Pryce Royan.*

WHEREAS you have been found duly qualified to fulfil the duties of Master of a Foreign-going Steamship in the Merchant Service, the Minister of Transport and Civil Aviation, in exercise of his powers under the Merchant Shipping Acts and of all other powers enabling him in that behalf, hereby grants you this Certificate of Competency.

SIGNED BY AUTHORITY OF THE MINISTER OF TRANSPORT and CIVIL AVIATION and

dated this 1st day of **March**, 19 55.

Countersigned

Registrar General

A Deputy Secretary of the Ministry of Transport and Civil Aviation.

REGISTERED AT THE OFFICE OF THE REGISTRAR GENERAL OF SHIPPING AND SEAMEN.

Cadet Royan being presented to King George VI.

Staff Commander of the Oranje.*(right) Pictured with his wife Carol and children Bruce and Nicola. Chief engineer Bob Gemmel (centre).*

Robert Royan pictured receiving his Commodore's Flag.
Left to Right: *Sir Geoffrey Sterling of P&O Containers, Robert Royan, Kerry St Johnston CEO POCL and R. Gemmell Chief Engineer who also received the honour.*

A WARM WELCOME FOR 'TOLAGA BAY'

After the ceremony, a tour of the bridge for Irene Manuel and other members of the welcoming party.

Maori carver Mark Kopua presents a Maori carving to Captain Robert Royan, Master of 'Tolaga Bay.'

Dwarfed by the cliff-like wall of the giant vessel, the official party watching the ceremony.

Tolaga Bay was the biggest ship to visit New Zealand which generated publicity.

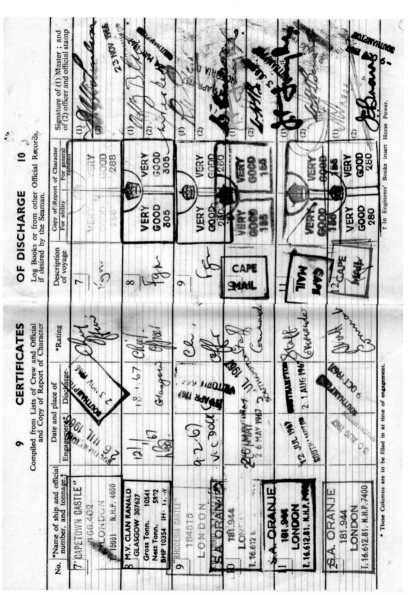

Robert Royan's Discharge Certificate.

Conditions at Sea

When I went to sea immediately after the war, conditions on different ships varied considerably. Certainly in the wartime built vessels it was compactums in cabins with a basin and a small tank above to be filled each day. No plumbing in cabins. These same ships had the steam pipes supplying the cargo winches going round the outside of cabins making the living quarters even hotter in the tropics. Both these vessels, and pre-war vessels especially, were alive with cockroaches which enjoyed living in the tongue and grove panelling used in the accommodation spaces. It was common practice for the sandwiches for the watch keepers at night, to be held in a wire cage suspended from the deckhead in the chartroom as the safest places from the cockroaches. With newer material used in cabin fittings and the introduction of an anti cockroach spray life improved considerably. When taking stores in hot countries one had to be on the lookout for these vermin in the supplies being taken on board.

At the end of the war at least half our fleet still had the magnetic compass but all new vessels were also fitted with gyro compasses which was a great advantage. In due course they led to automatic steering in open waters. Radar too was not common but all the new ships were fitted. Smaller radar was fitted to the older vessels and when the radar was required the engineers had to be informed so that they would start up another generator to provide the power! By the time I retired satellite navigation was fitted in most vessels and of course vastly improved radars and unmanned engine rooms.

In my earlier days at sea, fresh water was also precious as each ship had to carry enough for daily use remembering that good water was in short supply in many parts of the world. The same also applied to the older passenger vessels and it was not uncommon for water to be rationed. Again by the time I retired most modern vessels were able to distil their own water and as a result it was treated more casually. I used to get quite annoyed when I would find a large washing machine in operation to deal with one pair of underpants!

Air conditioning was another great advance on board ship especially in the tropics, and in port in particular. The only downside was that germs in the circulating air could spread easily as is the case in passenger vessels and aircraft in modern times.

When I first went to sea the crew of the average cargo vessel was around fifty men. By the time I retired in 1990 the average crew numbers were around the twenty mark on very much larger vessels and this has reduced even more since then with more sophisticated automation. The British flag fleet had almost disappeared and has only increased of late through it becoming an upmarket flag of convenience where any nationality can be employed provided officer qualifications are of a recognised world standard and no so called UK rates of pay are required. In other words we, as an industry, became too expensive and now very few UK genuine ship owners remain, as is the fact that very few men and women from the UK go to sea as a career.

On reflection, as one does from time to time, if I had the chance I would go to sea again if the industry was the same as I experienced but alas this is no longer the case. As we all know it is all about progress.

Leave was somewhat limited and as officers we had a few days extra in lieu of overtime – this based on a ten hour working day, seven days a week. Leave was given very much depending on whether there were men to relieve you and originally you could be recalled at short notice and could not leave the country when on leave. On two separate occasions as a very young officer my mother had already received a telegram recalling me before I had reached home. As a single man it was irritating but to married men and their families it was not appreciated. As the years progressed the leave improved and the company became obliged to guarantee at least three weeks leave before calling on you. Latterly full leave was guaranteed at the time but again it made us more expensive as an industry as men from Eastern Europe and Asia would be cheaper to employ and so the jobs disappeared.

India celebrate the Day of Independence

On 15th August 1947, India celebrated the Day of Independence from Britain. On that day I was on the *Clan Macfadyen* as a cadet. We were moored at the Calcutta Jetties on the Hooghly river, and close to the main square of the city, called Chouringee. On that day a forty-eight hour curfew was imposed and, as I recall, all work stopped – certainly at the docks. Shore leave was forbidden in case there was any rioting or public disorder. At the time of the big occasion we cadets climbed the mast and had an excellent view of the celebrations of the vast crowd, and could feel the general exhilaration.

Next morning, the ship's fifth engineer who should have been night engineer watch keeper was missing and certainly not on board. This gave cause for concern to senior officers as he may have run into trouble in the curfew with dire results, not only from the ship's and company's point of view but also politically in a very tense atmosphere.

Later in the morning, the curfew lifted and normal working resumed. The fifth engineer was spotted walking towards the ship's gangway with a very attractive Anglo Indian lady on each arm. The Master and Chief Engineer did not share the pleasure and excitement of the cadets. What followed exactly we were never allowed to know but the two young ladies were very disappointed at not being allowed on board, but dispatched about their affairs by an unkind authority.

In due time, when the opportunity presented itself, we had our hero's version of events. First of all he was older than usual for a junior engineer. He had served his time as an engineering apprentice in the Clyde shipyards and was called up into the army, namely the HLI – the Highland Light Infantry. He had been all through the North African and Italian campaigns and so was a war veteran. When he was demobbed in 1946 he decided to go to sea rather than return to the shipyard.

The story he told us was that ashore pre-Independence Day he was having such a good time that he ignored the curfew. He must have been one of the very few British around the Square at the big moment – all police and soldiers had been confined to barracks. He told us he was carried shoulder high and passed at that level from one to another – occasionally let down to refresh himself. We were enthralled and considered him a hero.

To be honest, I don't think he could remember too much of what happened but he was not harmed in any way. He was best pleased at meeting two very attractive ladies. On the voyage home he would regale us with his war time stories. We admired him enormously.

However, when we finally arrived in Glasgow the company found it had no further need of his services which we considered unfair as he was a good engineer.

Assassination of Mahatma Gandhi 1948

On 30th January 1948, Mahatma Ghandi was assassinated. At that time I was in Bombay Docks as a cadet on the *Clan Macnair*.

Prior to the above event I had been invited to lunch in the city by a couple from my home town Elgin. I had managed to get time off for this invitation from the Chief Officer somewhat grudgingly I might add. The husband was the cashier at the Bombay Branch of the National Bank of India.

When news of the assassination was released all work in the port ceased and a day of mourning was announced and I believe the authorities were expecting some civil unrest.

The following day, Saturday, was the day of my lunch invitation. There was no way I could contact my friends, and our agent had not attended the vessel. I knew if I stayed on board I would be given work to do and really did not like the idea of missing out on my day off.

I changed into my best day gear and set off for the main dock entrance called the Red Gate. In normal times the area around the Red Gate was a seething mass of humanity twenty-four hours a day but on this occasion when I arrived there it was deserted. Only two people in sight a policeman and a customs officer. All the shops and trading stalls were shuttered up and closed. There were no taxis, gharries, rickshaws to be seen. The silence was quite uncanny, neither official stopped me and I decided to walk to my friends' flat in the city centre which was quite close to the docks. I walked up the middle of the street with virtually nothing in sight other than the occasional scavenging dog. I reached my friends' flat and when they answered the ringing of the doorbell were quite shocked to see me there. In the circumstances they did not expect me to come as many disturbances were expected. I enjoyed my lunch and afternoon and when it was time to return to the ship some life had returned to the city and they drove me back to the Red Gate.

I can only imagine that the population as a whole were so shocked at the death of Ghandi that they entered into mourning and prepared for the worst. It was only when things returned to near normal that disturbances began to take place. Not many people had ever seen the Red Gate deserted other than for a policeman, customs officer and an eighteen-year-old cadet

Clan Macnair

The third ship I joined as a cadet was the *SS Clan Macnair* which had been built in 1921 and the oldest ship I was to sail on. I was the senior cadet and the other was a lad called Geoff Potter who had been a new chum on *Conway* with me as his cadet captain. We sailed again later when he was third mate and I was second mate and he was a character. He left the sea after obtaining his Master's certificate and died sadly a relatively young man.

We sailed from Birkenhead on Christmas Eve 1947 and spent Christmas Day in very bad weather in the Irish Sea. In fact it was a voyage of bad weather having encountered very bad weather in the Mediterranean Sea with our four horses on board which I have written about elsewhere. The ship being old and having come through the war was showing its age. All the accommodation was lined by tongue and groove panelling which, as usual, was home to thousands of cockroaches. They were everywhere. The sandwiches for the bridge night watch keepers would be hung in a wire cage from the deckhead to try and evade these creatures. In the hot weather with no bed clothes if you put the light out you would awake to find them walking over you. One defence was to put a large jar on the cabin deck with a little drop of honey pinched out of the dining saloon. This attracted the cockroaches and they could not get out of the jar and heaved over the side with relish in the morning. Washing facilities were primitive and the fresh water had to be pumped up by hand and into a forty gallon drum in the wash place. With a bucket this was your bath/shower. Only the captain and chief engineer had a little bathroom. The captain was a very nice man called Jenkins and the chief officer, called Freestone was somewhat different. The chief engineer was called Low and on his last voyage before retiring. He was also the senior chief engineer in the fleet. He could have had a new ship but wanted a trouble free last voyage. I believe he got it as far as the engine was concerned but we had terrible

47

weather in the Bay of Biscay homeward bound and as I was going on watch at 04.00 hrs I saw him bailing out his cabin which had been flooded, using a bucket and wearing his combination underwear! At sixty-four, some way to end your last voyage before retirement.

Early Days

When I was attending the School of Navigation at the then Glasgow Technical College in 1949, our lecturer reminded us that our examiners, whichever ones we had encountered, had all been through the war and some of them through the depression before that and had experienced tough times. Just to remember that as young men, we did not know it all, and were very lucky in that the industry was needing men and so work could easily be obtained. Another item which affected employment to some extent was that serving in the merchant service exempted young men from National Service but if you left the sea before National Service was stopped you were immediately called up.

When the end of National Service was announced there was quite an exodus from the industry especially among engineers who were much in demand ashore. Others had married and found the life unsuitable and those that knew they would not be called up, left. This resulted in much faster promotions than usual in the better companies for a time.

When I obtained my Master's Foreign Going certificate at twenty-five I had anticipated doing about three years more before being promoted to chief officer. However after one voyage of four months I was promoted, and though excited at this, I knew of the increased responsibility that went with the position. I was appointed to a wartime American built ship called the *Clan MacBean* at Tilbury. The officer I relieved had been on the ship for more than two years and was well known in the company as a bit of a character! When we met I was hoping he would give me a good summary of the job but when I asked for the inventory of stores, certificates, etc. he referred me to his settee which was piled high with papers and said it was all there, wished me well and was gone. I quickly realized that nothing had been filed or recorded since he had joined. I set to in trying to bring some order into what I found which included all his letters from his wife and his now redundant clothing coupon book. In the meantime, it was necessary to supervise the ship which was loading for East Africa and to supervise the deck sereng who required my instructions. The dock superintendent called in and wished me well in restoring some order to the records and to say the Master or 'old man', was joining the following day and was also newly promoted. He had no more advice to offer other than he would have the stevedore give me cargo figures so that I could check the stability figures. Needless to say I worked late into the night and realized promotion had its draw-backs.

The new Master joined the following afternoon and I awaited my summons. Time passed and so I went up to the Master's quarters and introduced myself. I told him I was newly promoted a little earlier than expected, but was getting through the paperwork. I would be grateful, however, for any advice he could give as required or necessary. He then informed me that he had waited long years for this moment and it was up to me to get on with it and not expect any advice from him. I was somewhat taken aback and realized I was at the bottom of a very steep learning curve and to get stuck in. We sailed together for three voyages and really felt rather sorry for him; he was not a well man. He took no exercise, consumed sixty cigarettes and a bottle of gin a day and had food as his passion. It stood me in good stead however and to quickly realize that one is always learning and very willing to offer advice or help to those who ask it and to those who think they know. He died sometime before retirement and he had a very nice wife whom I met on two occasions when she visited the ship in the UK

Clan Macleod

M y next and last ship as a cadet was the *IMV Clan Macleod* which
I joined in July 1948. She was a new vessel and the whole ship's
company joined a few days before going on trials. This was the first
diesel engined ship I was to sail on and also had electric instead of the
very noisy steam winches of the previous vessels. We completed trials
in the Firth of Clyde, before the ship proceeded to Glasgow to load her
first cargo. The other cadet was called Barber doing his first voyage to
sea. His mother was Belgian and his father British and he was fluent in
both German and French. I was very impressed.

There was an interesting mix of officers who remained friends till
they died, some comparatively young. The captain was called Gough
and had been torpedoed four times during the war which I am sure had
an effect on him. After his sinking for the fourth time the company had
him in a shore appointment returning to the sea after the war was over.
Not an easy man to sail with. The chief officer was called Mitchell and
also a character and one of the untidiest men I sailed with. I was quite
sure by the end of my time I was one of the hardest worked cadets in
the Clan Line. In fact when I left the ship to study for my Second Mates
Certificate the other cadet refused to carry on sailing on the vessel and
so was transferred to the oldest ship in the fleet built in 1914. When he
finished his apprenticeship he emigrated to Canada and we lost touch.

By this time the Merchant Navy Board was fully operational and all
UK cadets were given correspondence courses to complete and at certain
stages exams were to be taken aboard ship under the supervision of an
officer. With both the captain and chief officer of the old school they
did not believe in time off for study. In fact when I did one exam the
chief officer had me on the four–eight watch with him. I did each paper
under his supervision at the chartroom table, had breakfast and worked
on deck until lunch. Told to study during the afternoon and back on
watch on the bridge at 16.00 hrs. No time wasted. The captain sent for
me on our first Saturday at sea and said that every Saturday afternoon

from then on I had to slice up his slab tobacco called 'Fair Maid' as I remember. This tobacco came in slabs and I was to slice it as thin as possible which took time. When I presented the first delivery he said it was not thin enough and to try harder. I tried and could not improve any. I took it back without comment and he accepted it and this performance continued all the time we sailed together. Saturday afternoon being our time off from other duties. Those were the days. I was on the ship at the time of the Durban riots which I mentioned elsewhere. One other story comes to mind of when we were in Cochin South India. The ship was moored at Buoys in the harbour for loading and to get ashore we had the use of a small rowing boat. This evening I was on cargo duty and had to row the chief officer and a couple of engineers ashore to the jetty of a nice hotel called the Malabar close by where they would spend the evening. I was to return at 22.00 hrs to bring them back to the ship. When I arrived they were waiting and in high good spirits. Once on the rowing boat the chief officer stood up and started to rock the boat ignoring calls to sit down. The inevitable happened and he fell overboard to everyone's amusement. As he thrashed around calling for help as he could not swim the second officer told him to put his feet down and he found the water only waist deep. This caused great amusement to all except the victim. On returning on board, he took it out on me as I had to dry out his rupee notes on the galley stove without burning them.

Incidentally, this chief officer eventually became one of our marine superintendents at our London office where I used to meet him from time to time. Sadly he died just as he was about to retire and had left in his will a request for me to scatter his ashes at sea – somewhere warm. This I did off the Comoro Islands as we headed up the Persian Gulf to load. I think it would have amused him that at the time the ship was flying the Panamanian flag.

My sea time required to sit for my Second Mates (Foreign going) certificate was reached at the end of my second voyage on the *Clan Macleod*. I was not allowed to sit the exam until I was twenty which meant I had to do another voyage as a cadet. I asked if I could sail as a fourth officer giving me a little more money, but the request was turned down.

Shoregoing

In my early days at sea, when we younger ones would go ashore to the dancing or whatever, I often found myself in charge of the kitty, principally because I did not drink in those days. You would also have the duty of informing the lads when the last train or bus was leaving for the docks. This latter duty pulled a bit when some would reject my advice as they were having too good a time and they would then blame me the next morning because they had to walk back to the ship. They felt I should have insisted they came.

One particular occasion is still very clear in my mind. We had docked in Hamburg homeward bound from India with little opportunity of going ashore. This was around the early '50s when Germany was slowly recovering from the war. We headed for the Rieperbahn which was the famous entertainment area of the city which we had heard much about from other shipmates who had been there. One thing which gave us some pleasure were the big notices stating the area 'Out of Bounds to Allied Forces' and Military Police checking identities. A merchant navy identity card, which we were obliged to carry allowed us in! It was a swinging place with lights and music and girls everywhere. We elected for this particular dance hall night club because it had a floor show and in we went and had a table for the five of us. As holder of the kitty I reminded everyone that beer or soft drinks and no buying of drinks for attractive young ladies as our funds were limited I must also add that each table had a number on a little flagpole and a telephone.

The floor show was an eye stopper for us lads. There was an excellent brass band, the cast spoke in English and German and the chorus line on a raised section of the stage were topless and very attractive young ladies. This was life. At the end of the show the band played for dancing and then the chorus appeared fully dressed and sat around the floor. This of course was the reason for the phones. You could phone the ladies or if you made a move they phoned you. We had been well warned about this and the cost of buying drinks for the girls, which was allegedly champagne, at vast expense, when in reality it was coloured sparkling water. Again I had to remind the group that we did not have the finances to buy phoney drinks and I also had the taxi fare to the ship to safeguard. Anyway I had cause to make myself comfortable and warned my shipmates of the rules regarding drinks. On my return I found young ladies from the chorus with drinks at our table and the waiter waiting to be paid! I was not amused and had to delve into reserves including the taxi fare to pay the bill. At this moment the band struck up and I decided if nothing else I would have a dance with one of the girls at the table. We stepped on to the dance floor but I was unaware that I was being guided to the back of the floor and only realized this when floor rose and we were now on the elevated stage. Any others inclined to dance stood back and my partner really gave me the once over. I tried to disengage which was impossible and so rose to the occasion with roars of approval and the band played on. It was with difficulty I managed to retain my clothes and it was certainly embarrassing being cold sober. Eventually the stage was lowered and I made my escape to a series of cheers and jeers. At last we departed and had to face the walk back to the ship after quite a night out. When we left Hamburg at 06.00 hrs, all on board had a somewhat embellished account of the evening.

This reminds me also of one of the first occasions I attended a dance at the Marine Club in Madras. I invited this young lady to dance and had been aware she was wearing a sari. When we began I was a little taken aback that my hand to her back was on bare flesh. Whether up or down it was bare. Once I realised that this did not bother her I was able to carry on dancing.

Making Friends

I joined my first ship as third mate having passed my Second Mate Foreign Going Certificate. I joined the *Clan Macilwraith,* one of the older ships having been built in 1924, in Glasgow on 10th March 1950. That same afternoon the second mate joined as well and this was his first voyage in the Company. He had arrived along with his young wife and, not knowing that wives were not allowed aboard Clan vessels without a pass from the Chief Superintendent, was not allowed to stay overnight. However, as it was too late to find accommodation she stayed overnight without the shore staff knowing. The following morning the ship was advised that the Dock Superintendent was coming on board to meet the new second mate and welcome him to the Company. This caused a certain amount of alarm to those concerned and I suddenly found the second mate's wife shown into my cabin and instructions to put her in the 'wardrobe', an upright locker really, until the Superintendent left the ship. I was then to sit at my desk on a camp chair and to be writing up the daily rough log book.

As I sat there I was very much aware of the voices next door which was the second mate's cabin. At the same time I was also aware of a very pleasant perfume coming from my wardrobe where my lady guest was standing. This all in contrast to the smell of an old ship and food being prepared in the galley. All I could think of was how I was to explain to my mother that I had been sacked from the Company for having a woman in my cabin and a married one at that!

The visitors departed from next door and luckily did not call on me. After a few moments the second mate came to retrieve his rather hot and flustered wife. He was a great support to me on the ensuing voyage and Ivan, Shelagh and I have been good friends ever since.

TSS *Clan Macrae* 1950

I was appointed to the *Clan Macrae* as third mate in August 1950. It was built at the Greenoch Dockyard in 1942 and was one of the refrigerated ships in the fleet. I was very pleased to find myself on one of the larger vessels in the fleet after only one voyage as third mate. The master at the time was called Coulthart who had interviewed me prior to joining the company, when he had been the Liverpool marine superintendent and to his disgust had been sent back to sea. The chief officer was very senior called Taffy Lewis and was promoted at the end of the voyage. He was a real martinet and I never stepped over his cabin door in the eight month voyage. The second mate was Tommy Aitchison with whom I sailed on the *Clan Macleod* and became firm friends from then on.

The second engineer was called Angus Meek also ex *Clan Macleod* who came ashore as an engineer superintendent, much respected but died prior to his retirement. He was on one of the company ships when it was torpedoed at night. There was time to do a head count in the lifeboats and Angus was missing. The second mate re-boarded the ship and found him still asleep in his bunk having slept through all the crisis. Since then Angus had trouble sleeping at sea and woe betide anyone who banged a cabin door near his when he was turned in. The radio officer 'Sparks' as known on board, had been a Japanese prisoner of war and his stories horrified me. He had malaria twice during the voyage.

We discharged our general cargo in South Africa and proceeded to Mombasa in Kenya to load soda ash and sisal for Australia. We spent three months on the Australian coast mainly due to l disputes with the dock labour who were known as 'Whorfies'. When we unloaded, a big cleanup was necessary before loading our refrigerated cargo for Europe, mainly beef and mutton, also wool and tinned products. In Sydney I was able to visit my great uncle Alec again who was dying of throat cancer. Since first meeting him in 1947 he had married his housekeeper who was a lovely little lady. We were in Sydney for Christmas and New Year about which we had no complaint. While docked, the agent informed me that a large package, addressed to me from the UK, was being held by the harbour Customs for me to collect. On opening the parcel in front of the Customs official I found a beautifully iced cake for my 21st birthday on the 2nd January. Recorded in the enclosed letter were the ingredients, as food was still rationed, and my mother had Austins the bakers bake the cake. The effect and thought put into the cake and for it to arrive between Christmas and New Year after a six week sea voyage on the PO mail service was quite remarkable. Half the cake gave all twenty officers a decent pierce on the day and the rest was appreciated by special friends.

We completed loading at Freemantle, West Australia, with a deck cargo of bales of wool – which brings me to another incident of note. Australian regulations at that time required that any pet, being cat dog or bird had to have a deposit made to Customs at the first Aussie port. In these days £50 (before the Aussie dollar), for each animal on board, which would be refunded at the final port, subject to the animal still being on board, or the deposit was not returned. This was quite a sum in 1951. By the time we reached Freemantle the ship's cat had disappeared. Not really surprising after three months. The night before sailing I was summoned by those on high to take the two cadets with me after dark and find a cat. As you can imagine no easy task though badly lit streets were to our advantage. After some time and many near misses we obtained our cat which was put in the spare cabin next to the Captain's quarters, fed and watered in grand style and produced to Customs before sailing and the old man had his £50. The cat settled well, with no lack of goodies plus the bonus of flying fish on deck on occasions. It decided to emigrate at Liverpool. Any time I have been in Freemantle since then I have been aware of the long arm of the law!

On our way back to the UK we discharged frozen meat for the armed services at Aden, Port Said, Malta and Gibraltar. After leaving Gibraltar and approaching the Bay of Biscay we went to the assistance of an old company vessel called the *Clan Maciver*. She had damaged her rudder in bad weather and was in danger of being blown ashore. She was carrying a full cargo of tea from India to London. When we made contact there were clearly two salvage tugs anxious for the prize. We managed to get a line to her and towed her away from the shore. In the meantime the company in London had contacted a large UK tug called *Turmoil* to take over the tow and allow us to continue our voyage to Liverpool. It was a very interesting event to be involved in and I learnt a great deal from it. In due course we all received a month's salary from the company, in lieu of a salvage award, had it not been one of our own vessels. On my second voyage on this vessel we loaded direct for Australia and now had a very pleasant man in the chief officer. As we left the Gulf of Aden round Cape Guardoafui we ran into the south west monsoon and encountered very rough seas. Crates of machinery we were carrying above deck shifted and we had to 'heave to' to allow us to rescue our cargo. Another event to broaden my experience. On our way to Freemantle I was relieved on the bridge as usual by the second mate, Tommy Aitchison at midnight. The radio officer was also there to hand Tommy a telegram. He opened it to discover he was now the father of a baby girl to be called Joan and mother and baby were well. We then toasted the baby's health with tea and the radio officer left. Two hours later, and endless cups of tea, before I managed to get to bed and leave the new father to his thoughts. Many years later Carol and I were able to toast daughter Joan's health at her wedding with something stronger than tea! A very happy occasion. When in Sydney I managed a day off to visit my great uncle's widow which was good as by the next time I had visited Australia she also had died. We then returned to the UK with another cargo of frozen meat and wool. On reaching Glasgow the second mate left the ship to become an assistant dock superintendent for the company and I left to study for my First Mate's Certificate at the Glasgow Technical College.

I decided to begin my studies at the college as soon as I left the ship in October and hopefully take some home leave after I had passed. At that time we were given two month's pay from the company for both Second Mate's and First Mate's Certificate. Beyond that time you were off pay. The courses ran continually and you could join and leave as suited you when you thought you were ready to sit the examination. When I enrolled I was advised that the examination format was to change at the end of the year and two additional subjects added which would not be taught at college until then. The lecturer in charge at the time suggested I applied to sit for the last exam of the current syllabus though I did not think I would be ready. He thought it worth the risk since, if I failed I would have to do extra time to learn up the new subjects. In the end I put in for the last exam which was held in the three days between Christmas and New Year. No nonsense about Christmas holidays in these days. I was being very well looked after by my two aunts at Bridge of Weir and travelled each day to college by train. The week after New Year I found that I had passed, to my great relief, thanked my lecturer for his advice and headed home to Elgin for some relaxing time. A usual, I was barely home before I received a letter from the company informing me I was to be promoted to second mate and to join my next ship the following week in Tilbury. So much for my relaxed spell, I was off to buy my new braid from the naval tailors!

Animals as Pets

Up until 1965 British ships were allowed to carry animals as pets. They were principally cats and many ships cats became well known. I have to say that most ship's cats just appeared on board, only someone very senior would bring their own pet cat. In earlier days cats were encouraged as a way of keeping rats in check.

One cat we had on the *Clan Macinnes* was quite a character and I cannot remember for sure when she decided to take up residence but I think it was somewhere in the UK. On that voyage we were bound for South and East Africa and our lady established a routine, watched with interest by us all. In each of our ports of call she would be seen going down the gangway all spic and span or bright and bushy tailed. At first we assumed she would find pastures new. However, back she would arrive before sailing time looking a bit ragged and in need of food and rest. At the next port rested and ready she was away ashore again. It became a source of interest to be the one seeing her return before sailing. In due course the Indian steward came up with my early tea to the bridge and said I should look at my cabin. I left the senior cadet in charge for a few moments and went to my cabin. Lying comfortably on my pillow was our cat and three kittens who had to be found a more appropriate spot. In due course we found a stevedore foreman to give the kittens a good home. Our cat continued her lifestyle but on return to the UK at one of our ports she did not return. Her real party however occurred in Lorenzo Marques, now called Maputo. The company agents had arranged an evening drinks party for cargo shippers and port agent. It was held on our boat deck as the weather was good and under the canvas sun awnings with the coloured lights it was very festive. The guests were all there in their party dresses and everything going well. Suddenly there was a shriek from a Portuguese lady and she fainted. What had happened was that she had looked upwards just as the ship's cat had stuck her head through an opening in the canvas to see what was going on, as one does! The cat withdrew and a stiff brandy restored the patient.

Another party we held on board the *Clan Macinnes* also brings back memories. The ship was anchored off shore at a port called Mangalore on the Malabar Coast of India. At that time the port was not big enough to accommodate our size of vessel alongside.

The party was for tea planters and shippers of other commodities and port officials. At that time this area had prohibition problems but as we were anchored off shore we could open our bar. Hence the party. The guests were brought out to the ship in the large agent's launch and all in their finery. It was a lovely clear evening with a full moon and it was my duty as the chief officer to get the guests safely on to our accommodation ladder. There was however, a slight ocean swell running and the ship and launch moving slightly. The right moment had to be chosen and folk move quickly, not all that easy in high heels and tight dresses. All boarded safely and proceeded to have an enjoyable time. My main thought though was how we would get them safely back on board the launch at the end of the gathering. This did not bother our guests whose free and easy approach was a trifle disconcerting. The ladies removed their shoes and were all for jumping into the launch provided we were there to catch them! They had to be cooled down a bit and all departed without any obvious damage and in good fettle. I do hope it obtained for the Clan Line many more cases of tea.

Horse Riding, Pony Riding

My father's family had a farm and from a very young age I had a pony. Starting off with a Shetland pony upwards. I learned to ride bare backed initially and Shetland ponies are spirited creatures at the best of times. My father had been a territorial soldier with the Scottish Horse until he married my mother and so he was very keen on us children being able to ride.

Prior to my going to *HMS Conway* in 1944 I had progressed to a very good dapple greyed Welsh pony called Tony. On Saturday mornings I would cycle out to the farm, two and a half miles from town, and yoke the pony into a small flat cart and drive into Elgin to my father's butchers shop. I would then load up the cart with the weekend deliveries for his customers. The cart could take four bike baskets at one time and so was quicker with the help of the message boy. On completion the pony and I returned to the farm where I watered, fed and groomed him before returning for my dinner and pocket money.

On one occasion I ended up with a passenger that I still remember so well. Near to our farm was an old tumble down cottage lived in by an elderly lady known to people round and about as the Batchy Wifey. She was well known as a fortune teller, reading palms and known to have the second sight in those days. Not known, as I recall, as someone who bothered about a tidy house nor personal hygiene. Driving home one Saturday, minding my own business, I suddenly noticed someone in the middle of the road waving me down. As I came closer I saw it was the Batchy Wifey with two bags of supplies and wanting a lift home. For a minute I wanted to drive on but thought I might knock her down and I like to think my better side prevailed. I had to lift her on to the cart at the tail end along with her shopping and made the detour to her cottage which I had only seen from a distance. I disembarked my passenger and her shopping and to be fair she invited me in for a cuppa tea. I declined with thanks with the excuse that the pony had to be fed.

On returning home I related my story to my mother and she ordered me upstairs to have a bath as she took my clothes for washing!

But, I digress, it had always been my hope that I could have a pony again as long as the farm was available and my father was well aware of this. I was home on leave in 1951, by this time third mate, when my father announced that Gordonstoun School was closing down its riding stables and that there were one or two good ponies for sale. We went down to the school stable and met the farm manager. One animal immediately caught my eye, a gelding called Paddy, a big Irish hunter. At the time my father was surprised it had not been sold and I had a ride and was impressed. The deal was done and I took delivery of the hunter and as I recall he cost me one month's salary £30.00 and I rode him out to the farm. I returned to sea and heard afterwards that the German riding instructor had been hoping to acquire the horse for himself and was not at all happy when he found him sold.

In the meantime my mother's brother, a dairy farmer near Bridge of Weir had heard of my purchase. He was a keen heavy horse person, Clydesdales especially, but did not ride. His farm was adjacent to the kennels of the then Lanarkshire and Renfrewshire hunt and he was a keen follower of the hunt on foot on a Saturday afternoon. One of the rules of the hunt was that any farmer, over whose land the hunt could ride over could join them without being a member. When I informed my aunts, who lived near my uncle's farm, that I hoped to be living with them again to study for my First Mate's certificate, my uncle insisted I brought my pony and I could ride with the hunt on a Saturday. Looking back I get the feeling all this had been taken out of my control. The horse was taken by rail from Elgin to Bridge of Weir with the horse wagon attached to a passenger train and the animal watered and fed. I could have travelled with the horse all for £10.00.

The first Saturday I was at the farm my uncle had me mounted to see how good a jumper Paddy was. He indicated one of the farm's dry stone dykes and hit the horse with his bonnet. Away we went and the animal sailed over the wall with ease and to my amazement I was still on board. He then indicated I should be on my way to the hunt meet about five miles distance. Fortunately in 1951 not many vehicles were on the roads. I was very fortunate to have a horse who was a born hunter and discovered that the moment Paddy heard the huntsman's horn – he was away. All I had to do was to stay on board. As I was, shall we say, informally dressed I would try to keep a low profile but once there was a chase I would find myself close to the lead whether I liked it or not. I also discovered that not all jumped every fence as well. A considerable number headed for the nearest gate held open by a foot follower like my uncle.

Two occasions come to mind of this period. At one meeting I found myself in the company of a girl possibly younger than me as we waited for something to happen. When the call came we were confronted with a high stone wall and those around us proceeded to the nearest gate. Not this girl, she turned her horse and made to jump. The horse swerved at the last moment and she ended up on the wall. I trotted up to give help but she indicated she was fine and remounted. I was faced with a problem, head for the nearest gate and be sensible I thought, or remember my male pride and jump. I knew the horse was up to it but was I? Paddy sailed over but when we landed we parted company. Fortunately I still held my reins and the look of contempt on Paddy's face was quite wounding! Not helped by the arrival of the young lady who had just safely jumped and bent from the saddle to enquire of my well being. I was on my feet and remounted albeit with the odd twinge.

The next occasion was after the end of another hunt day and I was heading back to the farm a few miles away. Ahead of me was another rider, a redcoat, one of the full members, going the same way. I could not hold Paddy back as he obviously wanted the company. The other rider asked me to join him as that was what my horse wanted. He then made conversation and admitted to knowing my uncle. When I told him I was studying for my ticket and employed by the Clan Line he said he knew the Cayzer family. We then reached the gateway to a large mansion and he indicated that he would leave us there saying that he was Donaldson of the Donaldson Shipping Line. Fortunately I had said nothing uncomplimentary of my employers or ship owners in general.

It also turned out that the girl who had been at the jumping episode was his daughter

Having passed my exam, Paddy returned to the farm at Elgin but my father was getting too old to exercise the him while I was at sea. He sold him to the wife of a local landowner and the horse sadly died of grass sickness.

When I came ashore to study for my Master's my uncle and father went to the Kelso Horse show and bought a little mare on my behalf! She was called Donetta and was very fast but not as good a jumper as Paddy I was at the Navigation school at the Tech for three months at the end of 1954 beginning of 1955 and was able to attend a number of the hunt meets. During my times at a hunt I never saw a fox killed nor wished to but very much enjoyed being able to gallop across the countryside legally and without needing to worry about traffic. On participating with the hunt on this second occasion I was obliged to wear a hat for safety reasons otherwise my ordinary riding gear was acceptable. Possibly because of the shape of my head, when we jumped my hat would come off and end up trailing behind on its cord. On my last hunt before sitting my exam I came off my pony when we hit very soft ground at speed. She stopped and I continued! I was able to remount but had sprained an ankle and had considerable trouble getting my boot off on return to the farm. With a strapped ankle and the aid of a walking stick I made the college on the Monday. Needless to say my excuse of falling off a horse was treated with derision and jumping out a window was considered more likely. On passing my exams the days of having a pony were over and my Donetta was sold. It was all fun while it lasted.

Animals Carried

In my earlier days at sea we regularly carried animals to various destinations. As the war was now ended much pedigree stock was on the move and it was the cadet's role to look after them. The only time I had people travel to look after the animals was when carrying wild animals which was not a pleasant experience.

Having come from a farming background I enjoyed looking after the animals and when no longer a cadet was willing to help out when we had young cadets from an urban background who had no experience of them. One particular voyage comes to mind when I was a cadet. We had on board four beautiful pedigree fillies, They were race horses bound for the stables of the Maharajah of Baroda, to be off-loaded at Bombay. They were all in foal.

We sailed from the Mersey on Christmas Eve and encountered bad weather nearly all the way to the Suez Canal. Horses cannot be sick as such but are miserable with their heads hanging between their forelegs. They normally don't lie down because of the difficulty of getting up in the confines of the horse box. On the night of New Years Eve we were in particularly bad weather in the Mediterranean and the vessel was moving violently. When I checked up on our horses I found that one had fallen and could not move and I was not sure if she had broken her leg. I told the Chief Officer, not a very pleasant man that I would stay with the mare till daybreak. At daybreak we managed to get her to her feet and, thank goodness, no broken bones. For the rest of the passage to Bombay I was the only person that she would allow into her horse box.

The ship was about three days from Bombay when the Captain was notified that the we would have to anchor for a few days until a cargo berth was available. I was quite concerned about the news as our four mares were showing signs of giving birth. In fact the horse that had fallen was beginning to leak milk which is a sure sign, and after her fall could be early. I told the chief officer who in turn told the captain who contacted the ship's agent. In due course the ship was informed that it would be allowed to berth to land our livestock and then go and join the queue of ships at anchor. The evening before arrival the junior cadet and I spent some time grooming the horses so that they looked their best for their new owners. When it came the turn of my special lady she unexpectedly turned on me and I had to make a very fast exit. When she settled a little I tried again with no success and was quite disappointed.

We berthed the next morning at the passenger ship quay where the Maharajah's British racing manager was waiting together with a very small grizzled Indian groom. When we met at the horse boxes I mentioned the episode of the previous night so that he could warn his groom. He told me not to be concerned or hurt about the animal turning on me as most likely it had smelled the land in the air. Not desert as it had been previously but verdant growth. He then told me to watch the groom who now had bundles of lush green grass in his hands which he was feeding in turn to the horses who were now totally amenable. I enquired what would happen to the horses now and was told they would be taken to local stables and then, each led by a groom, would be walked round a paddock for a day to relax muscles and get rid of any poisons in their system having been standing in their boxes for more than four weeks. The following day the agent informed us that the first mare had dropped her foal and all was well.

In the days when animals were carried it was usual for those receiving them to give a tip, gratuity, to whoever had tended them. In this case I remember the second officer asking us how much we had received from the chief officer and we told him ten rupees each. He left us saying that he would see about that and shortly afterwards the chief officer arrived and handed us each a 100 rupee note. He did not look a happy man. We learned afterwards that the second officer,(from Dundee I remember him well) told the chief officer he was going to the Captain unless we cadets received our just due.

We carried many animals in these days after the war. Pedigree cattle, horses, domestic animals and even pigs which I have mentioned separately.

One memory when chief officer, of carrying a really splendid White Shorthorn Bull to Cape Town. The evening before arrival the two cadets and I set about scrubbing him down with soap and he seemed to enjoy the attention. When finished we gave him a fresh bed. On arrival at daybreak when we went to the box with the new owner our pride and joy had done his business and then lay down. Instead of the pristine creature we had a white bull and brown patches. Rather like modern art.

Pigs carried

In 1963 it was decided at a lofty level to improve the breeding stock of the bacon industry in South Africa

I set sail on *TSS Clan Mactavish* with a full cargo for Durban, Mozambique, LM and Beira. On the deck were heavy drums of hazardous chemicals and on the after deck four horse boxes on each side, each of which contained six young pigs, forty-eight in all, bound for Durban.

Travelling with them was a Mr Carruthers from the pig industry to oversee their well-being. We met prior to sailing when the care of the animals was discussed. Usually in our line the cadets looked after any animals carried but on this occasion they could expect no help as the crew were mainly Muslim. They would need hands-on assistance from Mr C. He was not too pleased about this – I rather think he had envisaged a restful voyage of sunshine and relaxation to South Africa.

We sailed on the night tide and proceeded down the Irish Sea to the Bay of Biscay. There we encountered a full summer South West gale. Because of the hazardous deck cargo the Master decided to reduce speed and heave to until the weather moderated. I came to the bridge at 04.00 hrs, and the Master retired to the settee in his cabin. Within minutes the secunny (standby quartermaster) arrived on the bridge to say all was not well on the after deck. I called the Master and went to see what was up.

You must try to imagine the scene. It was pitch black at 04.30 hrs; the ship moving quite considerably and the sea rolling on board at a whim. I discovered with a torch that a rogue wave had come aboard and struck three of the four horse boxes on the starboard side, and the contents of eighteen pigs were loose on deck! The roar of the storm and screaming squealing of the pigs was a noise difficult to forget.

I called the cadets and carpenter and organised lighting. A serious concern was not allowing the animals to escape into the crew quarters. The deck serang felt that catching pigs did not fall into his remit, or any other of the Muslim crew – so the cadets and I armed ourselves with brooms and set about catching our cargo while chippie made the boxes secure once more. Anyone who has ever tried to catch mercury will know what it is like to catch pigs made ever more excited by the rolling of the deck, the water, and the blackness of the night. I sent messages to the man in authority but he was too sick to care what happened to his precious cargo. We heard no more from him about the care of pigs.

The valiant chippie made one of the horse boxes secure and one by one we managed to catch the eighteen pigs who were quite wound up by their adventures. Dawn was breaking when we had nine pigs in each of the two boxes, but there was unexpected worry when we found we had the sexes all mixed up – so much for careful breeding plan! I did my best by leaving a cadet in each box armed with a broom and instructions to hit any head that got lifted in the crowd. With belated assistance the chippie made the other two boxes secure and we managed to restore order. It was quite remarkable that we did not loose a single pig.

In due course the vessel arrived in Durban and we docked at a particular quay to disembark our passengers. The government vet wanted them at the quarantine station at the other end of the docks on Point Road. I expected cattle trucks to be ready and waiting for the onward journey and was very surprised to see open lorries especially knowing what a lively crowd of pigs we had. I was over-ruled and the lorries drove off with each pig held down by a very large Zulu. They didn't like it and the screams and squeals could be heard for a long time as they drove down the esplanade. If you visit South Africa please think of us as you enjoy your bacon.

A Brush with Celebrity as it is now known – 1953

In 1953 I was second Officer of the *Clan Sinclair* loading cargo for the UK and North Europe when we learned of a Saturday evening dance to be held at the Nyali Beach Hotel a few miles to the North of Mombasa. The function was open to non residents provided they were considered respectable and able to pay. Four or five of us decided to attend as the Purser Catering Officer could arrange transport for us, to and from the hotel, courtesy of the laundry man servicing the ship during our time in port.

On Saturday evening, we set off in the back of the laundry van having pooled our financial resources which we considered adequate but no more and I was the bagman. We were deposited at the hotel well away from the main entrance and car park to avoid publicising our entrance.

We were shown to a table out on the hotel veranda where the dance was being held. We looked out at a calm sea on a lovely evening. We then ordered up a quart bottle of local Whitecap beer each which would last us through a good part of the evening. At the table adjacent to us were a family party who were up-country Kenyans staying at the hotel. One of the men approached us and asked if we would like the two daughters one from each couple, to join us, he was sure they would enjoy themselves more with us. Needless to say we agreed and were duly introduced and they were very pleasant, aged about nineteen. They also only had soft drinks which our budget could accommodate! It was an enjoyable little gathering and we all had a dance in turn. Further round the dance floor was a larger gathering of folk who were quite noisy to say the least. Our two ladies were able to tell us they were part of a film crew who were staying at the hotel while filming *West of Zanzibar.* Before long one of that party, attracted by the ladies with us decided to join us and who turned out to be Anthony Steele, one of the actors. He had already consumed enough to drink and was quite coarse and rude in his conversation. He insisted in ordering a round of drinks, despite our refusals and invited one of the girls to dance. That triggered off something in me and I approached the tables where the film crew sat and invited Sylvia Syms, it turned out be, to dance which she accepted. She was very pleasant and advised me not to pay any attention to Anthony Steele. At the end of the dance I returned to our table to find that the girl whom Steele had invited to dance had left him on the floor over something he had said. He did not return to the table to everyone's relief.

When it came to settle our bill I pointed out to the duty manager that one round of drinks had been ordered by Steele despite our protestations. He told me not to worry as he was known to do this and this cost would be transferred to Steele's account. That was a relief as we were running close to the bottom of our funds.

Some time later I caught a glimpse of the Indian laundryman waving to me from the vestibule and it was time to go. We made our farewells to the girls and parents for a very pleasant evening. As we passed the cocktail bar on our way out we had the pleasure of seeing Anthony Steele being punched by the husband of a lady who had been accosted by him. What a finale. We departed discreetly in our laundry van with a kindly view of the world. I have followed Miss Syms' career with interest every since.

Clan MacQueen, Tilbury 1953

I joined the *Clan Macqueen* in Tilbury. She was another wartime built ship in the USA to UK specifications, in other words with minimum executive comforts. The ship was to proceed to Antwerp and Hamburg on leaving Tilbury and my first duty was to bring the North Sea charts up to date from the Notices to Mariners, issued by the Admiralty, which were put on board at Tilbury. Ever since the end of the war the North Sea had special routes marked by buoys to avoid the mine fields which took many years to clear. The last time I saw a magnetic mine was in 1960 which we duly reported as all vessels were instructed to do.

We loaded for East Africa in the west coast of the UK. The master was Marr who I had sailed with on the *Clan MacIlwrath,* the chief officer was Mike Ure and the third officer Colin Gowens, both good to sail with. The chief steward/purser was Gibson whom later became the company's catering manager in South Africa. His claim to fame on the vessel was having a set of tropical kit made from old settee covers of a delicate pastel pink! There was port congestion at Mombasa when we arrived, something quite common around the world at that time. We were anchored at Mombasa for fifty-six days until we obtained a berth. During that time we all painted out our cabins, caught up with the ship maintenance and played deck tennis every evening when it cooled down. Once a week we had an agent's boat give us a trip ashore for those of the crew who wished to take advantage. The ship's lifeboats were also made use of for swimming but this was not encouraged because of sharks being present. On completion of discharge we proceeded to India to head for home.

On my second voyage on the *Clan MacQueen* we loaded for India and then back to the UK. We now had a newly appointed Captain called Paie Thorpe May who was a real gentleman and a new chief officer called Vaughan who later became a Trinity House sea pilot. During that period a sister-ship called the *Clan Macquarrie* was blown ashore at the North of the Isle of Lewis during a wild storm. Amazingly the ship was driven ashore on the only beach for miles on either side. The entire ship's company was rescued the next day by breaches buoy after the wind had subsided. The local people rendered assistance to the crew until they could be transported to Stornaway which included forty Indian seamen. It was the same storm that caused the sinking of the ferry *Princess Victoria* on its way to Larne with considerable loss of life. On return to the UK, I was told that after some leave I was to be appointed to another company vessel.

Indian Wedding 1956

When I was a young chief officer we were in Chittagong in what is now Bangladesh. I was on one of three clan vessels in port loading tea and jute. In our limited leisure time we used to ship visit and exchange news and other stories. On one of the other vessels was a chief engineer who was known as quite a character and when he heard I came from Elgin he asked me to come and see him. When I had the time I called on him and then realized why. He was a bachelor living in Ayr, and used to regularly visit a maiden aunt who lived in Elgin, and who was of comfortable means. I was given to understand however, she was a lady of strident views with regard to strong drink and thought her favourite nephew was of the same persuasion. He was when visiting her, but not otherwise. She was also a well known customer of my father's butcher shop so on no account was I to reveal to anyone at home in Elgin that the man enjoyed a dram. Otherwise his hoped for inheritance would be put at risk! I told him that my lips were sealed. He was good company and very erudite. I discovered he also had a great knowledge of Burn's poetry and prose..

Just before our ship, the first one, was due to finish loading an invitation was received by all three vessels for the captains, chief engineers and chief officers to attend a luncheon arranged by the local ship's chandler in celebration of his eldest son's wedding. They were a Muslim family. On the day we all mustered in our white dress uniforms and I was informed that, as the junior one there and alleged friend of the chief engineer mentioned above, I was instructed to sit with him and keep a weatherly eye on him. This was an honour I could do without but my companion had had a couple of drinks beforehand knowing it would be soft drinks only at the reception. We were at a long table and, to my relief, we two were towards the bottom end. We had a very enjoyable Indian meal of generous proportions but it was also quite warm. This long before air conditioning. At the end some speeches were made and the senior captain made one for us. However, this was too much for my companion, carried away by emotion shall we say, decided to recite some of his favourite Burns. I realised I could not stop him without making a scene but what I was now to find out was that he had loosened his trouser belt for comfort after the big meal and there he was in full flow and his trousers were slowly slipping down! I had no option but to go under the table and pull his feet from under him. He sat down with a thump, but the true artist that he was, he never missed a word as he finished sitting down. There was a round of applause but I managed to persuade him that a follow up was not required. I don't remember getting much credit from my superiors for avoiding a potential disaster. Sadly some time later when visiting up North he was killed in a car accident when he was a passenger.

Sudanese Doctor 1958

In 1958 I was chief officer of the *Clan MacLennan*. During the loading of tea on the homeward voyage one of my legs slipped between two chests of tea and was grazed. These things happen and I thought no more about it. On the voyage back to the UK we called at Port Sudan to load cotton. As the vessel was berthing at Port Sudan I collapsed without warning and had to be carried to my cabin. The agent on board was instructed to call a doctor. I was a little taken aback when the agent, the captain and the doctor all arrived at my cabin. He was Sudanese, wearing a leopard skin coat and his hair was in long ringlets. He was a graduate of Edinburgh University medical school and spoke excellent English.

On examination he announced that I had a poisoned leg and this was running into my groin where he found a lump which would need to be lanced immediately. I remember he produced a cigarette case and suggested I had one indicating that one side of the case had ordinary cigarettes and the other side others! I declined both so he gave me as I recall one of the early biros to bite on. He was right as when he lanced my lump I bit through the biro which he said was better than my tongue. He suggested that I be taken to hospital which did not appeal to me and the captain agreed to carry me on with a course of penicillin injections to be given four times a day. The ship sailed the following day after a final visit from the doctor. As our purser chief steward at the time had a very shaky hand the second and third mates were given the duties of injecting me in the bottom. Needless to say it gave them a certain perverse pleasure, especially as each time they arrived with a file to allegedly sharpen the needle. The drug worked, helped by the fact if it didn't I would be landed in hospital at the Suez Canal. By the time we transited the canal I was fit for duty. At sea there was no time for convalescence! I had been very fortunate in getting medical attention quickly.

I returned to Port Sudan about seven years later and when the same agent boarded I enquired of the doctor. He told me he had died unexpectedly about four months previously. When word reached his tribe they all converged on Port Sudan from the surrounding desert for his funeral. The city Governor had put the police on alert expecting trouble but it was all very peaceful with the people just wishing to pay their respects before returning to the desert.

Apparently nothing like this had happened before and this man had been revered by his people. He was the first of the tribe to qualify as a doctor and on his return home had set up a free clinic in Port Sudan for his people. I was among very many to be grateful for his skill and professionalism.

I regret to say that forty-odd years later there was a Clan Line Reunion in Liverpool, and as I arrived at the bar I found the two mates still laughing at their joy wielding the needle.

Tuticorin – Attempted Rescue
1958

I was Chief Officer in 1958 of the *Clan MacLennan* at anchor off the
port of Tuticorin at the southern end of India. We were there to load
bales of cotton brought out to the ship by sailing barges. At that time
the port was not deep enough to allow deep sea ships to berth alongside.
Our main communication with the shore was by signal flags or morse
code on aldis signalling lamps.

This particular evening the sun had just set and a fresh wind was
blowing an indication of the approach of the SW Monsoon when the
port would be closed. We received a message from the port authorities
that a local fishing vessel had been seen in distress and possibly had
sunk. Could we search for survivors in our vicinity. It would have taken
some time to get the ship underway and as it was also empty very high
in the water and not very suitable in the prevailing circumstances. The
Captain decided to launch the ship's motorboat with yours truly in
charge. I had the third engineer, one cadet and three Indian seamen as
crew when we were lowered into the sea which was quite choppy when
in a lifeboat. We managed to clear the ship with difficulty and headed
in the direction of the distress. Before long the only person not feeling
the effects of sea sickness was the grey bearded Indian quartermaster
who was greatly enjoying the search. After some time the captain
signalled us back and when reasonably close to the ship our engine
failed, not an unusual thing with lifeboat engines which have improved
greatly since then. Now it was all hands on the oars as we headed for
the ship. It began to look as if we would be swept past the stern but
those on board managed to float a line to us which we were able to
secure, to our great relief.

The Captain was in charge on board of course and he had seamen
arranged on deck to pull on the line attached to the lifeboat. A pilot

ladder had been lowered out of the gangway door amidships and the idea was to haul the lifeboat to that level, get us on board and hoist the boat. However before reaching the ladder we had to pass under the main engine cooling water discharge which was well above sea level as the ship was empty. Through a slight misjudgement of orders to the crew, and the rage of the Old Man, the lifeboat ended up underneath the discharge instead of the ladder. We in the boat were not amused and nearly drowned alongside. When we finally got on board we were greeted by the chief steward, who by this time was overcome by emotion, offering us first aid! Needless to say he was swept aside so that we could have a warm shower. An evening to remember and no survivors of the fishing boat were found as far as we knew but we did our best. I am still in touch with the third engineer – a shared experience not easily forgotten.

Tanzanian Independence Day

In 1961 Tanzania was granted Independence. I was Chief Officer of a cargo ship, *MV Clan MacInnes*, and we had arrived at Dar es Salaam three days beforehand. Our agents in the port advised us of the requirements leading to the big event. This included dressing our ship overall with the International Code Flags on Independence Day. There would be no cargo work on that day either. At the time there were other vessels in port including three under the Red Ensign.

The day before Independence Day *HMS Belfast* arrived to take part in the event and moored in the harbour. All merchant ships in port then received a memo from the First Lieutenant of *HMS Belfast* instructing us in our duties on the day. We were all to watch *Belfast* on the morning who would raise her dressing pennant at 07.50 and on lowering it at 08.00 all other vessels were to raise their overall dressings as smartly as possible. This message was not taken well on merchant ships priding themselves on their smartness.

The evening before, in the stadium, where the handing over was to take place, a dress rehearsal was held and some of us lesser mortals were invited to view. Our agent invited the captain, chief engineer, second, engineer, purser, chief steward to join him at the event. The main march past parade was to be lead in by the Band of the King's African Riffles, with following detachments of the Coldstream guards, RN and RAF then by the other various organisations represented at such an affair. It was an interesting and jolly event but the highlight was the march past. It started off well and then we were aware that, instead of marching in a straight line, it was becoming a somewhat wavy line across the stadium. The band was following the Drum Major who was steering this somewhat curving route followed by the disciplined troops behind. This was highly interesting to the audience and we gathered afterwards that the Drum Major had fortified himself with a couple of beers and then was somewhat overcome by the heat and the occasion. However, on the day all went well.

The day and we were all ready to obey *Belfast's* orders. At 08.00, on signal, our serang blew his whistle and our crew did an excellent job raising our flags. Then on turning to *HMS Belfast* we had the wonderful sight of their flags getting tangled up in a slowly rotating radar scanner. I have to say we rather enjoyed that and the sight has remained with me always. Life returned to normal the following day.

It is of interest that about six months later, the President of Tanzania had to call in the Royal Navy to restore law and order.

Football Matches

In the days when more time was spent in port the younger ones were usually keen to have a game of football. All claiming to be experts as you would expect. The local Seaman's Mission were normally able to organise these, usually with a team from another vessel in port who were equally unfit. Two occasions come to mind. In Madras a match was arranged with a local youth team and our boys were initially unsettled in that the opposing team played with their bare feet, no such things as boots or shoes. Our excuse for losing was put down to being unable to tackle in case the bare feet were damaged!

The second occasion took place in Port Louis Mauritius where a match was arranged to play a team from the local Reform School. I was fortunately a spectator, one of the few from the ship. Most of the school were there to watch the match but under supervision. They supported their own team in style and at half time the score was 6–0 to them. At the interval they were ordered not to cheer their collegues and our team was 'allowed' to score near the end to a tremendous cheer from the crowd. Final score 10–1. It was an amusing outing for me. The following morning the chief engineer was not so amused when most of his squad could hardly reach the engine room for essential repairs.

Voyage to Remember

I was chief officer of a ship called the *Clan Macinnes* in April 1962 when we were loading a general cargo on the South African coast for discharge at the Western Mediterranean ports. The vessel was running behind schedule due to a cyclone in the Mozambique Channel and later bad weather off Port Elizabeth. The ship finally docked at Cape Town early on a Monday morning in May; fourteen days late and due to sail again that evening on completion of loading our cargo.

During the vessel's stay our twelve passengers boarded who had been waiting patiently, for our arrival. I had invited the wife of an old shipmate on board for lunch; I was Godfather to their son, and another lady friend joined us whom I had met on a previous Cape Town call. The passengers were scrutinized as they came abroad and it was decided they were all unremarkable and would cause the ship no trouble. Little did we know!

The ship sailed that evening and when I came down to dinner there were two young ladies sitting at my table. The other passengers were at the captain or chief engineer officers' tables as was considered more suitable. I might add now that, of our twelve passengers, most of our guests were over sixty-five. Here I was sharing my table with two young ladies who were good friends. Their names were Carol Squires and Pamela Richmond and from then on they entertained themselves, forever wondering whatever they would think up next, as a means of keeping me on my toes. There was one other couple on board who were middle aged and the others were all enjoying their retirement. The chief and second engineer officers also had their wives on board for the voyage who were both very pleasant ladies.

The vessel called briefly at Walvis Bay to load wet hides for the shoe industry in Italy. Fortunately these were stowed in a ballast tank which was sealed after loading to prevent the rather disgusting smell reaching the accommodation. There was also a brief call at Dakar in Senegal for the ship to replenish the fuel oil before proceeding to Barcelona, the first discharge port.

The sea passage passed agreeably with social evenings in the passenger lounge, helped by my long playing records which were somewhat more varied than the ones the ship provided. The second engineer was an accomplished piano accordion player who was much in demand and the captain would sing if asked but this was not encouraged. With the occasional rolling of the vessel, dancing could be quite exciting in more ways than one. On one day during this sea passage I gave the two cadets the afternoon off working on deck, to do some studying to complete their correspondence course. However they had assumed that I would be taking an hour's siesta before going on watch at 4.00 pm. The crew were carrying out a particular job that I felt needed my presence and in walking along the boat deck I discovered the two cadets serenading the two lady passengers with their guitars and the said ladies relaxed on their deck chairs enjoying the entertainment. My appearance of course put an end to this little gathering to the irritation of both parties as I was later informed over dinner that evening.

The ship passed the Rock of Gibraltar just after sunrise one lovely morning and passengers were called if they wished to enjoy the view from the bridge. The vessel entered the Med and arrived at Barcelona where seven of the passengers left; leaving the middle aged couple, the two young ladies who were leaving at Marseilles, and our oldest passenger who was doing the round trip.

A pleasant stay was had at Barcelona with the city explored and even a bull fight visited at the big bullring – an interesting experience but not one that was to be repeated. I managed one evening off and invited Carol Squires to a meal and ended a very enjoyable evening at a highly recommended night club. I had to remember that the unloading was to commence at 6 o'clock the following morning which meant having to leave early.

The vessel then proceeded to Genoa where the dock labour went on strike resulting in the ship having twelve days in port instead of two. This was an opportunity to catch up with ship maintenance both on deck and in the engine room, and of course allowed the ship's company and passengers to enjoy a few days in an interesting port in good weather.

There was at that time a very good Mission to Seamen at Genoa, the only one, I understand, managed by the Church of Scotland and supervised by a rather timid padre by the name of McVicar. Among other activities they held a dance twice a week with a small band and lady vocalist no less, and very well attended. The *Clan MacInnes* officers, two wives and the four passengers made a sizeable group. With Asti Spumante at 60p a bottle a jolly evening was assured. Our second engineer also brought his piano accordion to play when the band took a break. All our ladies were reminded that they would have to dance with everyone who invited them. Carol Squires was invited to dance the twist, very popular then, by a tiny Japanese gentleman which her friends found very entertaining. All in all a good time was enjoyed in Genoa and prior to the ship departing a party was held on board to which the girls from the Mission were invited. It was very successful and was brought to an end around 1 o'clock with all concerned having work to attend to later that morning. I have to say a bit of culture came my way as I was persuaded to take the lady passengers to the opera.

On our arrival at Marseilles our four passengers had reached the end of their passage with us, having had an enjoyable extension of their voyage, at no extra cost, thanks to the docker's strike. The two ladies booked their passage on the overnight train to Calais and then by ferry to the UK to their respective parents. On the evening of their departure a group of officers including the captain, accompanied the ladies to the station. On leaving the ship the duty officer played *Will Ye No Come Back Again* over the ship's loud speaker system. At the station, the captain was quite emotional, due to drink, and the train's conductor made sure all the ship's party were back on the platform, before the train left the station.

Our passage back to Cape Town was very quiet and our only passenger was fortunate in having the wives of the two officers for company. The voyage had implications for me as when I eventually went on leave,

Carol Squires and I met up again. We were married on the 5th January 1963 in Shrewsbury in the terrible winter when the river Severn was frozen over at the time of our wedding. A special licence had to be obtained from the Archbishop of Canterbury as we were to be married out-with our home parishes – at a cost £25. I have to say it was money well spent.

TSS *Clan MacTavish*
Honeymoon Voyage 1963

On 5th January 1963, Carol and I were married at Shrewsbury in St Chads church. This was at the beginning of a very severe spell of weather which lasted nearly three months. Carol's parents, at that time were living in London and my parents resided at Elgin. The venue was chosen as my sister and her husband were living in Shrewsbury where Keith was a registrar at the Royal Salop Infirmary. This enabled my sister to help co-ordinate the wedding arrangements.

The majority of guests managed to make the wedding despite the severe weather and the distances to travel. The bridesmaid had to be helped out of her house by a farm tractor. Due to the appalling conditions we were unable to have a honeymoon and so we returned to Elgin.

Shortly before our marriage my company the Clan Line, had announced that chief officers and second engineer officers would be allowed to take their wives, deep sea one voyage, every two years. Carol thought this was a great opportunity for us though I was not so sure. I would be joining a ship new to me and a captain I did not know and I knew from experience that some of the older captains were not in favour of wives travelling. However I was persuaded and received permission for my wife to join me for the voyage.

I joined the *Clan MacTavish* in Glasgow on the 7th February as chief officer. It was a good ship, twelve years old, and by the standards at the time very comfortable. Each cabin had running hot and cold water to the basin but common toilet facilities at the end of the accommodation alleyway where there were also square baths and showers. We loaded in Glasgow and proceeded to Birkenhead to complete loading for South Africa and Mauritius. The ship carried seventeen British officers and about forty-two Indian seamen who came mainly from Chittagong. At Vittoria Dock, Birkenhead the captain C Rodger joined, and shortly afterwards Carol joined and was duly introduced to the sailing crew. The carpenter who had been on the *Clan MacInnes* when Carol was a passenger when we met was now introduced to my wife as he left. He was a fine man from Loch Maddy and a staunch Wee Free, though he did mention to a shipmate "Does he know whether she can boil and egg?"

We sailed once all the cargo had been loaded, at the time when, as a country we still had a big export market. The ship settled down quickly to the seagoing routine and the officer's steward called Emau Bux was very anxious to please Carol. I was keeping four–eight watch morning and evening and he would arrive with morning tea for memsahib at 06.30 hrs. This was not really appreciated at that time and he kept returning with fresh tea until memsahib drank it. A compromise was duly reached and Carol fitted in well with the ship's routine and we had a good crowd on board. The chief engineer was a very nice, quietly spoken man called James Smith who was known as Whispering Smith behind his back.

Our first port of call was Dakar where the ship filled up with fuel oil and fresh water and then proceeded to Cape Town. Carol had worked in the British High Commission office before coming to the UK and so on arrival was greeted by many old friends. We had a very jolly party on board one evening. Carol in the meantime had booked a flight to Joburg to visit her two married sisters and was taken to the airport by two of my friends before we departed.

The ship proceeded to Port Elizabeth and East London before arriving at Durban, when I heard that Carol would be arriving the following day by car with her two sisters and their husbands. As the family car arrived alongside the ship around lunchtime, there was quite a reception committee. Everyone was suitably impressed that it had held five adults and two baby boys! I was introduced to my new in-laws and found them very agreeable and the babies were made a great fuss of by the Indian crew members. In due course the family set off for the drive home.

When the ship completed unloading the Durban cargo we proceeded to the dry dock as one of our propeller blades had been damaged when leaving port in the UK. Whilst in the dry dock other repairs were undertaken and the under water part of the hull painted with antifouling paint. We had to use shore lavatories and the Zulu gangway watchmen held the key. The lads used to enjoy when Carol went ashore to use the facilities as the watchmen always gave her a big salute and ceremoniously handed over the key which was attached to a large wooden ball to prevent it being lost. Our radio officer who had some time on his hands decided to take a city mystery bus tour and to his surprise found himself being driven around the dry dock. He managed to keep a low profile and none of his mates on board saw him.

With the repairs completed we left the dry dock and departed Durban for our final discharge port, Port Louis Mauritius. Once clear of Durban the ship entered a heavy swell and when I was on watch the books came out of the bookcase in my cabin and landed on top of Carol. She was not best pleased.

On arrival at Port Louis we had to anchor in the middle of the harbour and discharge our cargo into barges since there were no quayside berths for larger vessels. A small launch and boatmen was made available to the ship for going ashore. By this time Carol and Captain Rodger were good friends and when in port, if he was going ashore to the agent, he would always offer her a trip to town. On one occasion in Port Louis they both went ashore and went their own ways. Carol as I remember to the Seaman's Club run by a very pleasant couple. Captain Rodger came back to the boat to take him back to the ship and the boatman told him he would have to wait as he was waiting for Mrs Mate as he called Carol. Needless to say, the boatman was over-ruled! On another day the ship was working late at night to land heavy cargo and no way could I go ashore that evening. The radio officer and a couple of others were going up to the Seaman's club and invited Carol to go with them which she accepted with pleasure. The ship finished cargo work about 22.30 hrs and after a pretty long hot day I had a shower and turned in. I was suddenly awakened by an indignant wife who had expected me to be awake and worried that she was still ashore. I pointed out that she was in the company of responsible young men but this was unacceptable though she did concede later than she had had a very pleasant evening. Port Louis harbour was known for its sharks among other fish and at night you could see them occasionally in the flood lights. One evening, unknown to me and any other more senior officers, one of our cadets tied his clothes to his head, and with another as witness, swam from our gangway to the shore and then returned by the launch. This came to light the following day when he required a signature as he was taking part in the Duke of Edinburgh's Award. Needless to say he was reminded of the risk he had taken with the sharks and in future told to consider all the implications before embarking upon such a venture.. I am sure he had learned a lesson and he obtained his signature.

The vessel left from Mauritius bound for Dar es Salaam in Tanzania to start loading in East Africa for the UK. Dar es Salaam is a very attractive harbour. As you approach you see the reef and the palm trees and inside it is still attractive if you overlook the dock area. The Mission to Seamen Club had a nice swimming pool made use by the ship's company. From there we proceeded to the island of Zanzibar which reminded you of its past and was a main trading port for India and the Persian Gulf. The harbour was then busy with Arab dhows ,some of which were very ornate and impressive with many fierce looking dhow captains with their swords. You can smell the strong aroma spices which are grown on the island and exported worldwide. Carol was taken by the agent to the Country Club where she settled for a fish curry which nearly set her on fire. It took her some time to cool down.

Our next port of call was Tanga where we anchored in a very attractive bay to load sisal. There was no work on the Sunday and through the services of our agent, an Anglican nun brought a group of teenaged African school children on board to have a look around a ship. Carol had an aunt who belonged to that order and had taught in Tanzania for a number of years. Tea and tab nabs were served and they had a jolly time.

Our final and main port was Mombassa where we had to anchor and wait for a berth to become vacant for us. At this time Carol developed a very sore throat and, referring to the famous Shipmasters Medical Guide, I thought had tonsillitis and the captain sent a message ashore saying he wanted a doctor to come out. One appeared in torrential rain, quite quickly I think expecting to treat the captain's wife, who turned out to be the chief officer's wife. On the way up to my cabin I made the mistake of telling the doctor that I thought it could be tonsillitis. He examined her and said that she had two very swollen balls in her throat and was running a temperature and was able to provide antibiotics for the patient. He then retreated to the captain's cabin to have a beer as they knew each other from previous calls.

Prior to leaving Dar es Salaam we had taken on board a young Alsatian dog to take to the UK. The owners were returning permanently to the Britain by air but did not even give us the dog's name. He would have to go into quarantine on arrival in the UK for six months and by the end of that time I would doubt if he would remember his owners. Initially he lived in a kennel on the boatdeck but his wailing at night kept the captain awake so that he spent most of his journey in our cabin.

When we finally berthed Carol was now feeling a little better and the agent and his wife, whom I knew from previous calls, came on board to meet her. Also an old seafaring friend who was now a harbour pilot in Mombasa. He and I had sailed together when I was a cadet and he was the second mate. He took us on a tour round the area on the Sunday along with his young son. The boy enquired of his father, as we passed Mombasa prison, if he had been in jail his father said, "No". However, I knew that he had spent part of an early Christmas morning in a police station in Cape Town when we sailed together. He had been ashore at a party on Christmas Eve and on the way back to the ship he had felt tired and weary and found an unlocked car and fell asleep in the back seat. Unfortunately the owner of the car found him when going to early church and took him to the police station still asleep. The agent came to speak for him as a respectable person. My lips were sealed. Sadly this friend, by now harbour master at Dar es Salaam, died a couple of years later leaving a wife and young family.

When still in Mombasa the agent and his wife invited us to a dinner dance at the new Oceanic Hotel along with our Captain Rodger. The captain of another vessel in port was also invited with his lady who was a lion tamer with a local safari company. Carol still not fully recovered and our captain, normally a very abstentious man helped her out by drinking her gin and tonics. It was a jolly party but I was anxious to return to the ship as we were to commence loading at 06.00 hrs. The party only broke up when the air conditioning was turned off. Our captain left with the captain of the other vessel to have a night cap on his ship having danced down the hotel steps and into a sports car driven by the lady lion tamer. We returned to find drama on board. During the evening our Alsatian was lonely and started to howl and our purser/chief steward decided to take him for a walk on the quayside on his lead. However, in his excitement he managed to pull his walker down an internal stairway. The chief engineer returning from shore found the purser/chief steward lying at the bottom of the stairway with the dog licking his face. The kindly dog walker had broken his arm and so an ambulance was called to take him to hospital. We returned as he left for the hospital. The dog had to forego his walk and remained in our cabin instead.

The following morning I instructed the third mate to attend to anything with regard to the catering on board. This meant he had to type the day's menus for the officers and in doing so added a few phrases of his own, The next thing, I heard the captain shouting at me and waving his menu and wishing to know who the joker was. I then had to tell him of the accident as all was quiet when he had returned to the ship somewhat later. He was not best pleased, suffering from the jollity of the previous night. He and my wife visited the casualty in hospital that afternoon and the chief steward returned to the ship before we sailed to resume his duties with his arm in a sling. Shipboard life did not encourage time off for recuperation from illness or injury unless really serious.

The ship departed from Mombasa with a full cargo. Sisal, coffee, tea, oil cake and various other commodities for the UK. By this time the captain and chief engineer were keen for a game of bridge and Carol offered to make up a foursome, dragging me along. I was not a bridge player and had my misgivings especially when she lightly doubled the captain's bid and won. I did feel it would affect my end of voyage report.

The ship called at Aden and it was as hot and barren as usual. The one compensation was being able to buy duty free goods. Long playing records were a very good buy forty odd years ago. We then proceeded up the Red Sea to Suez Bay where we anchored to await a place in the next northbound convey. Our dog came into his own then as I walked him round the deck which quickly cleared uninvited Egyptian traders or bum boat men as they were usually called. We entered the Canal just before dawn and had an uneventful transit. There is always something to see as well as the desert sands. We landed our pilot at Port Said with his usual gifts and then proceeded to sea without stopping and now really feeling homeward bound.

We had a very pleasant passage through the Med and docked at Avonmouth, our first UK port of call. Carol's parents came down from London to see us which was very nice. It was also a chance to catch up with all the news of the families in South Africa. The vessel then proceeded to Liverpool where I was relieved for the coastal voyage. Time to say 'cheerio' to fellow shipmates and especially to Captain Rodgers who was leaving the vessel having been appointed to one of the new ships in the fleet. He had been very kind to Carol during the voyage.

RHMV *Stirling Castle* 1964

The Clan Line and Union Castle Line merged in 1956 and became known as British and Commonwealth Shipping with the top management principally from Cayzer Irvine service managers of the Clan Line. In the early '60s a decision was made to fully integrate the seagoing personnel. A retired Royal Navy captain was appointed to head up this operation of the Marine Department with no company allegiance.

In 1964 I was one of three Clan Line Chief Officers who were appointed to Union Castle passenger vessels which like any mergers caused a certain amount of resentment, especially from the passenger ship officers. I was appointed to the *Stirling Castle* at that time one of the oldest passenger ships in the fleet. I joined the vessel on its arrival at Soton for the ten day turnaround to familiarise myself with the ship. The officer I relieved just wished me luck and departed. The officer in charge during the in port period was a passenger ship master who through ill health, could no longer go to sea, Captain Wilford by name. He took me under his wing, so to speak, and made me familiar with the ship and the various procedures and situations that could and did arise. It would also be the first time I had sailed with a European crew rather than an Indian crew, quite a change.

The seagoing ship's company joined and all were new to me. At the Board of Trade inspection of safety procedures the day before sailing, I was introduced to the other deck department officers by the captain, as the Clan Line officer and to be wary of me as possibly a head office spy. He was only half joking I realized but it did little for my confidence though I soon found more help and friendship from the junior rather than the senior staff at first. I sailed four voyages on the *Stirling Castle* and adapted quickly but cannot say I enjoyed it at first.

One voyage in particular came to mind. Every week, prior to leaving Durban, the mail ship would load gold bullion into a strong room on board. It would be brought to the ship in a special railway wagon with armed escort and shipped on board. There were two gold ingots in each wooden box, each with its own serial number which had to be individually checked in by the chief officer and purser and of course checked out the same way at Southampton with a policeman in attendance. On this particular voyage most of the passengers accommodation had been booked by the MOTHS, the Memorable Order of the Tin Hats, an association similar to the British Legion who were going to the UK and then a tour of the World War I battlefields and war graves. There was a big send off for our departure time of 4.00 p.m. with a pipe band and singing by a lady known as the Lady in White. She was well known to many since she had sung at the departure from Durban of every troop ship during the second World War. Unfortunately the gold bullion was late on arrival and so by the time the ship sailed the band had run out of breath and the singer had lost her voice. It was quite a social voyage to the extent that the ship had to restock with beer at the Canary Islands when we called at Las Palmas. One veteran died at sea and he certainly had a bigger funeral then he would have had ashore.

Incidentally, in January 1965 some gold bullion was stolen when in transit on the *Cape Town Castle*. It was found when checking the boxes ashore at Southampton that ten boxes were missing – about £100,000. As you can imagine, an immediate sealing off of the area took place and an intensive search of the ship carried out. There had been extra gold carried that voyage, and an overflow from the strong room put in another locker and sealed up. It turned out that the thieves had entered through a ventilation trunk and had to be very agile to do it. Despite a thorough search no gold was found and all sorts of theories put about. I was on the *Transvaal Castle* the ship sailing one week ahead and on returning from leave had to check out every key on the ship. No mean task. Six months later, as some routine maintenance was being carried out at sea on the *Cape Town Castle* one deck locker was found to have a cement floor instead of a steel deck and in this concrete floor was found the ten boxes of gold. It turned out that it had been stolen by two enterprising members of the crew who were then unable to land their ill gotten gains. They were arrested. All stories of international criminals gone up in smoke!

TSS *Kenya Castle,* Royal Docks 1965

When I joined the *Kenya Castle* in the Royal Docks in 1965 it was my first experience with London seamen who were a little different from the Southampton men. I discovered from the Bosun that one or two of them made a habit of signing on the vessel two days before sailing and then disappearing until the vessel was due to sail with no one knowing whether they would turn up at all. They were usually the most disruptive.

At that time all UK passenger vessels were required to carry out the pre-sailing emergency drill in the presence of a Board of Trade Nautical Surveyor who inspected the whole procedure. No crew member was exempt without the express permission of his or her departmental head. At the end of the crew check all absentees were listed. On this occasion two men were missing the same two as on the previous voyage. I checked with the Shipping Master, the civil servant in charge of crewing regulations, and discovered that any crew man absenting himself without permission from the emergency drill could be dismissed in his absence. I took this information to the captain, who surprisingly did not know that this was the situation and told me to go ahead and deal with it.

We sailed on the tide on a lovely summer afternoon and entered the lock through which we would have access to the river Thames. As we secured in the locks our two missing seamen appeared on the lock expecting to board watched by their shipmates on deck. I went down the pilot ladder to the lock and had the two men's gear lowered as well. I then told them that they were dismissed and why and that their seamen's documents were at the shipping office in the docks to be claimed. I was then subjected to a torrent of abuse and was suddenly aware that every space on deck was taken up by passengers not wanting to miss their first entertainment on board. No one had their ears covered to avoid the language. I boarded the vessel and we sailed into the river.

I am pleased to say that we did not have any member of crew out of line all the way to Mombasa. Even the captain commented on that!

SS *Rhodesia Castle,* 1966

I was transferred to the above vessel after the *Kenya Castle.* They were sisterships in the same East African trade service. This was at the time when Rhodesia, with Ian Smith as prime minister, declared UDI. The development gave us rather irritating problems at the East African ports of Dar-es-Salaam and Mombasa. On one occasion in Dar-es-Salaam, just as we were getting ready to depart, a young man, a member of the US Peace Corps, arrived at the Pursers Office to book a passage out of the country. He had no money and his passport was held by the Consulate and so he could not be taken. He then lay down on the floor and refused to move. I did have some sympathy for him but I could not get him to co-operate. We had the agent contact the US Embassy there and very soon two US Marine embassy guards arrived and with little finesse hustled him down the gangway witnessed by many, and then we sailed.

At this time sanctions were imposed against Rhodesia which had a considerable effect on British flag shipping and our company in particular. As the principal carriers of Rhodesian tobacco to the UK and North Europe the Company ended up having to sell six Clan Line cargo vessels. On one occasion when loading in Lourenco Marques, now called Maputo, in Mozambique, the British Consul came on board to inspect our loading list and make sure we were not carrying any Rhodesian exports. As it was we were not loading any Rhodesian cargo and as a result our lifting was very much reduced. I pointed out to him at the time a Dutch vessel ahead of us on the quay, and a French vessel astern of us were loading what would have been our cargo even if both their governments had agreed to sanctions. He said that was not his concern and we parted without any offer of hospitality from me.

By this time the Royal Navy had what was called the Beira patrol off Beira the principal port for Rhodesia. All commercial vessels were reported in and out and booked on occasions. At this time an aircraft carrier was on station – whose name I cannot now remember. As we were approaching the Beira pilot vessel at about 4.00 am on a beautiful still morning, those of us on the bridge were left in shock. Two jet aircraft from the carrier came up behind us at low level, unnoticed, and we were deafened by the roar of them receding and possibly enjoying the effect.

To crown it all we then received a message from the aircraft carrier asking us to take his mail into Beira which they had put on board the pilot boat. At the time there was a temptation to say 'Get Lost', but knowing how much mail meant to seafarers we did our duty and handed it over to the British Consul in Beira.

At around this time the company was closing the East Africa service and we were the last vessel to be withdrawn. The other two sister ships, *Kenya Castle* and *Braemar Castle* had been laid up prior to sale. Last voyages are not easy and especially with a dwindling fleet most of the crew knew they would be out of work when the ship reached the UK. However we had a nearly full complement of passengers, in part due to this being the last sailing. Also these ships had been popular with the Europeans in the various ports where they could board for an evening and enjoy a glass of draught beer and even a dance. At our final port, Mombasa, there was considerable interest in our departure. We had been scheduled to sail at 4.00 pm. and prior to that many visitors had boarded. Cargo was our principal earner and the loading was running late.

Many of our visitors were determined to see the ship sail away and we departed at 11.00 pm. Prior to that our biggest problem was seeing that all our visitors left the ship – otherwise Aden was their next stop. Many had been overtaken by emotion and in a number of cases had to be assisted or even carried down the gangway and deposited on the dock side. As we departed we reflected on a very exhausting day one way or another. As it happened, two days after we transited the Suez Canal in 1967 it was closed again by war. Did our owners know or was it just a coincidence that we arrived safely at the Royal Docks, London for the last time.

Dealing with the Ladies –
SA Oranje 1967

I was first sent to the above vessel in 1967 as staff commander and it was the first ship that I had been on with a number of female crew members whose discipline would come within my jurisdiction. On this ship the majority of staff in the tourist dining saloon were female as well as the usual number of cabin stewardesses. On the first occasion that one of the young ladies was brought before me by the master at arms, the ship's policeman, she burst into tears. As one knows this does not help in dealing with the matter in hand and she was warned and left. I decided that I was on new ground and so asked the chief purser to muster all the female staff to a quick meeting prior to going on duty. When the ladies were gathered I introduced myself and then pointed out that the rules of the ship had to be maintained and in future, if any female staff infringement caused the onset of tears of remorse or otherwise, it would not be accepted as reparation or apology. After that we had a very agreeable working relationship.

Some years later when I was captain of a large container ship I had, for the first time, a lady second navigating officer. At this time there were not many at sea on British ships in that capacity. We departed Rotterdam bound for the Panama Canal and this lady was officer in charge on the eight–twelve watch morning and evening. In the evening watch we had just rounded the Channel Islands in good clear weather. I had written up the night order book which each officer had to read and sign on taking over the watch. The watch keeper was happy with the current situation and with the usual reminder to call me if in any doubt I said I was off to bed. This was followed by the lady saying 'night night captain' and I was aware of the seaman lookout on the bridge trying to suppress his mirth. No doubt when he met up with his mates he would be saying 'she will tuck him up next'. I have to say it was not easy being the only woman on board and she had to be good at her job as some men would be looking to see if allowances were being made because of her sex. The number of men who suddenly had an interest in navigation was notable and had to be curtailed. This lady was good at her job as she had to be, surrounded by men who would, in some cases, take advantage of her if they could.

Our calls at Las Palmas outward and homeward bound were always of concern on our ships. The duration of stay was about four hours allowing off duty personnel to go ashore. There was always the temptation of crew members to try and bring liquor on board which caused problems. When I was staff commander I would always be near the gangway to give back-up to our master at arms with the removal of alcohol. Bottles would be labelled and put in the bond and returned to their owners when they signed off in Southampton. On one occasion I had reason to believe that some of our female staff were going to smuggle bottles on board for a party before Southampton. I had the nursing sister on standby if necessary. In time, a group of our stewardesses climbed the gangway in high good spirits and full of banter and denying having any liquor to declare. However, once on board I noticed two characters with an unusual gait so invited them into an adjacent spare cabin and had the nursing sister search them. Each had four bottles of spirits hanging from a belt round their waists! It was a fair cop and as they said at the time worth a try. Though how they thought they could walk normally beats me. Their bottles were returned in due course but I did not know how they fared with the customs in Southampton.

Captain's Wives

In my earlier days at sea I had no experience of wives travelling, other than wives of senior officers going round the UK and North European coast. Only from the late '50s were senior officers wives allowed to accompany their husbands foreign going and not all wives could join their husbands due to family commitments and the like. The company did not allow families to travel except on the passenger ships on limited occasions, when there was a doctor on board.

I was on the *Cape Town Castle* when the captain had his wife travelling and he called her 'Treasure' to which obviously she became known to the ship as a whole, if not to her face. Despite being on a passenger ship the Captain was not very socially inclined in the evenings after dinner and she was a very pleasant lady who enjoyed company. He would decline all invitations to big crew social evenings and I would have to stand in. Nothing remains a secret on a ship for long and the crew discovered the captain's wife would be having a birthday on this voyage. It was the general practice that the crew would have a social evening with various acts and with a complement of around 270 there was plenty of talent wishing to perform. In due course I was approached with an invitation to attend for the captain and his wife and a present had been bought for her birthday. I reminded the social secretary that the captain would be unlikely to accept but would pass on the invitation. I duly informed him and had the usual reply but when I mentioned the gift was told I should accept. Unknown to me, his wife had been in the bedroom and appeared and said she would like to go. I did wish at this stage that I could leave. In the discussion that followed it was decided I would escort the captain's wife to the concert as neither side would give in. I left with grave misgivings reckoning I had been handed a poisoned chalice! I sent for the social secretary to tell him the news and to warn him to make sure the various acts were toned down accordingly because if not, his life would be as miserable as mine for the rest of the voyage.

In due course the evening arrived but meantime I was reminded that at these occasions it was beer and soft drinks only. But the captain's wife, we knew drank gin and tonic with ice and lemon, so I had to grant a limited issue of gin. I picked up the captain's lady who had dressed up for the occasion and was obviously looking forward to it and I was warned by the captain to have her back to his quarters no later than 10.30. It was now 9 p.m. We descended to the bowels of the ship to the Pig and Whistle bar and recreation room. No air conditioning on this old ship and heavy in the smell of beer and tobacco. We were shown to our table, given a very warm welcome and the guest given a large gin and tonic. The show commenced and was very good and toned down in places, though on occasions I thought they were pushing their luck. I was watching the clock and had to remind them of their presentation which they duly made and was graciously accepted. I now reminded Mrs Captain that it was time to go, but she announced she was so much enjoying herself and of course the host assisted by saying there were two more acts she had to see. I meantime decided the forecast for me did not look good. I managed to escort the not a happy lady away reluctantly to a fond farewell and arrived outside the captain's quarters at 11.30, an hour late. As I had expected he was pacing up and down. I was dismissed with a curt "I will see you in the morning" and the door closed. I withdrew to my cabin, drew the curtain and sat down to contemplate my future. I then heard footsteps and immediately assumed it would be the ship's Master at Arms to report a minor disturbance at the crew bar. When the knock came I invited the caller to enter and there stood the captain. He said through gritted teeth to come in to his place for a nightcap. I tried to decline by saying it was late, but he swept this aside by saying his wife would be upset if I refused. When I arrived, there obviously had been words, and I was handed a beer. The conversation was somewhat stilted. When I finished my drink – as quickly as was seemly so as to make my withdrawal. The captain's lady thanked me again for a most enjoyable evening. Next morning the captain and I reverted to the usual ship's routine.

On another voyage on a Cape liner the captain's wife was travelling and she was known as 'Honey'. This was the captain's first marriage but his lady had been married before. However, he had never danced until now and his wife enjoyed dancing so when she was not travelling with him, he took lessons from the professional dancing couple we had on board. His favourite dance was the cha cha. Every voyage we held a dinner dance south and north bound and if the captain's wife was travelling he rather enjoyed leading off the cha cha and we made sure they had a round of the floor before others joined in. On one occasion we had a bumptious junior purser who, overcome by a need to show his prowess at this dance, took to the floor before the decorous first round was complete. His dancing was sensational. This, to us onlookers was the best show of the evening, especially as the chief purser would be in for an uncomfortable morning to follow. The culprit kept a very low profile from then on to the end of the voyage.

On another occasion, when the captain's wife was travelling, we were to be in Cape Town for Christmas Day. We were full of passengers but the captain announced that he and his wife were going to have dinner ashore and spend the night at a hotel away from the hurly burly of the ship. I reminded him that the children's Christmas party was to be held in the afternoon and that Santa Claus would be presenting gifts to about eighty children and I knew the last one was for the captain's wife. I have to say he agreed to attend with little grace. They both arrived dressed for the shore in time for Santa's arrival. Santa was a very tall good looking chief officer and had a suitably deep voice. He also enjoyed these roles. The entrance to the lounge had been fitted with a large paper screen on which had been printed a very large fireplace. Santa leapt through the screen to the delight of the children gathered there and after his greeting started to give out the presents, assisted by the children's hostess. The captain with his wife and I stood at the back of the lounge enjoying the spectacle. Then the very last gift was called out for Mrs Captain and she walked up to Santa to the cheers of the children. When she arrived at Santa and expecting to shake his hand he instead opened his cloak and she disappeared from view inside as he closed it. I had known nothing about this but I thought the man standing beside me might have a heart attack. He was demanding that I do something about it but have to confess I was enjoying it. When Santa released the lady she appeared somewhat dishevelled and flushed to say the least but not displeased. She accepted his gift to loud cheers while her husband was leaping around with rage. As soon as they met up he whipped her away ashore as quickly as he could while we carried on with our duties. It was the highlight of a very busy day for the ship and I am pleased to say it did not affect the chief officer's career.

A voyage later on the same ship and with the same captain and his wife, we again were to have a big event in Cape Town. The day after we arrived there was to be a ceremony on board when the ship changed from British registry to South African flag. At 2.00 p.m. that afternoon one flag, the Red Ensign, would be lowered and the South African flag raised. This to be carried out in front of invited guests with the South African Prime Minister as guest of honour. It would be followed with a reception for about 1,000 then an evening dinner for 150 guests. A big work up for the ship. For the flag ceremony I had managed to muster eight officers to take part at the flag exchange and they drilled for three days beforehand in front of the ship's funnel, saluting the flags as appropriate. We were pleased with the effect and timing and so ready for the occasion. On the morning of the big day the captain came out to see me and to enquire that all was in order. Somewhat hesitantly, I like to think, he said the saluting party performance could be somewhat improved by some suggestions his wife had made! For a moment I could not believe what he had said, but recovering my speech I told him that with the time and practice given by these men no way would I change anything, but if he so desired he could approach them. On the strength of that he withdrew to his quarters having decided to leave well alone. I had the impression in the following few days that Mrs Captain was somewhat distant towards me. However, the day in question was a great success and the ship's company in general came up trumps.

Later on board the same vessel we had a change of captain and this man had never been on passenger vessels previously. We had sailed together on cargo ships and I was instructed to keep him posted on the usual procedures on board. Not the easiest of positions to be in with a man who could be a trifle stubborn. The ship sailed on the Friday and among other items I discussed with the captain was the church service the following Sunday. I gave him the standard draft of the service which he accepted but when I put forward the hymns that were considered suitable he objected. His wife had decided before he joined which hymns she thought would suit the occasion. I tried to explain to him that the ship's little band of older musicians were used to the older familiar hymns; different ones outbound to homebound but he was not to be moved. The band was informed and went to pieces saying they had no time to practice. As for the form of service the captain decided to put each page into a separate cellophane envelope. When the service commenced, it was obvious that the band had not mastered the music and the bright sunlight through the lounge windows reflected off the cellophane wrappers, resulting in the service becoming somewhat disjointed. When he and I withdrew he graciously admitted I had been right and would take my suggestions more seriously in future. Incidentally he had a charming wife and when she travelled later we had a good laugh over the choice of hymns.

I have to say when my wife travelled I like to think she was an asset to the ship. She enjoyed the company and talking to folk. They I am sure enjoyed chatting to her. She was a great admirer of the tales they had to tell, especially when they were supposed to be carrying out their duties! Only when I appeared on the scene were these occasions spoiled! On one occasion we left Rotterdam bound for New Zealand via the Panama Canal. On arrival at our first call, Port Chalmers in South Island, we were met by a number of Customs Officers and the Officer in Charge told me that they had been informed by Interpol that a consignment of drugs had been smuggled aboard in Rotterdam. As a result the vessel and ship's company were to be thoroughly searched and investigated. Not the situation in which we wished to find ourselves . At the time my wife commented on how good looking these New Zealand men were. As well as searching the ship, Customs Officers were body searching any of the ship's company who were going ashore. This took place at the gate house to the container terminal. After the evening meal my wife and I went ashore to telephone the family from the Seamen's Club which was just outside the gate house. By this time it was dark and as we approached the gate house we were met by two Customs Officers who invited us inside to be checked and searched. Having identified ourselves to the two men they told us we could carry on as they would not require to search us – to the great disappointment of my good lady. She decided it would have been better if she had gone ashore by herself!

By the end of our two-day stay no drugs had been found, to my considerable relief, but our one lady crew member complained to me that her cabin had been searched three times by different Customs Officers! The novelty of an attractive female crew member rather influenced this call of duty.

Yachts and Yachtsmen

From the time I went to sea until I retired in 1990 the number of yachts has greatly increased bringing with them their own problems. The international rule of the road at sea has not changed and one of the rules is that steam always gives way to sail. In other words any vessel under power of any kind gives way to sail which means only sail and wind power. With all the advances made at sea there is a tendency to assume that any object will show up on the radar screen and elsewhere. This does not always follow and I have always urged any yachting people I have met, to use a radar reflector on their craft. Especially in bad weather the target from a yacht can be lost in the reaction from waves. With modern communication systems it is much easier to keep in touch but the number of yachts that go missing worldwide is much more than people realise. They only make news when there is a newsworthy story to tell if they survive.

One event with which I was involved did not make the news as there was no loss of life but in its own way was interesting. I was chief officer of the *Cape Town Castle* when we departed Southampton bound for Cape Town, South Africa with around 700 passengers on board.

Late that evening the vessel was off the Channel Islands heading for the Bay of Biscay in a lovely clear night with little wind but a low swell and a number of other vessels around. I was called to the bridge by the officer of the watch since what appeared to be a small craft in the distance was flashing SOS on a signalling lamp. The radio room had not received a distress message and we called on the radio telephone and received no reply. I called the captain, warned the engine room and headed to the craft. When we approached we realized it was a yacht of medium size with the sails down and rolling a bit in the swell. We stopped and hailed the craft but got no response; neither could we ignore the SOS signal. We launched our accident boat with the second officer in charge and the ship's doctor among others and carrying a portable VHF set. We were close to the yacht but still getting no response. The boat party boarded the yacht and found a couple on board. The man was suffering from sea sickness and had broken his glasses. The lady was physically alright. They did not want to be taken off as obviously the yacht would be left behind. They just wanted a course to the nearest UK point of land and the distance away. This was reported back to us and they were given a course and distance to go to Portland Bill, which light we could see from our bridge, and also a RNLI station close to hand – but they did not want to be reported! The boarding party started the yacht's engine put them on the required course and left. We then took nearly an hour to lift and secure our accident boat and in all, lost three hours steaming time which we had to try and make up to arrive in Cape Town on schedule.

When the boarding party reported back it appears that the yacht was chartered for a romantic weekend though the man had no real sailing experience. Neither party would give a name as they did not want any publicity. However the incident was recorded in the ship's Official Log Book as an answer to a distress call and that the party involved required no further assistance from the ship. We could have had a charge against us in missing a distress call. I assume they chose us for help as we were lit up in a way that other vessels equally close at hand were not.

Some years later when I was master of a container ship, again en route to Cape Town but on this occasion not far from St Helena in the South Atlantic, the officer of the eight–twelve evening watch called me that he had picked up a distress call from a yacht requiring assistance. We proceeded to his approximate position, picked it up on the radar screen and then sighted it. Now in good response from their radio telephone we learned they were en route from Cape Town via Saint Helena to the West Indies. They had been dis-masted in a gale a couple of days earlier and there were six people on board. I advised the skipper to whom I was speaking that I could take them on board but could do nothing for the yacht as we had a schedule to keep. He asked where was his nearest port of refuge and I told him Walvis Bay in Namibia which was about 200 miles nearer than Saint Helena. I then asked if he had sufficient stores, food, fuel and water to reach Walvis Bay and he assured me he had and his auxiliary engine was in good order. I told him I would radio the Port Captain at Walvis Bay and pass on his details and a very approximate time of arrival. I also radioed the Port Captain of Cape Town, to say we had been in contact, with details. Having wished them well on the yacht, which by now was five miles distant, we resumed our passage to Cape Town having lost about two hours steaming. The incident with details was entered in the Official Log Book.

When we arrived at Cape Town the Port Captain informed me that the yacht had not yet arrived at Walvis Bay but was expected in the next couple of days. We proceeded to Port Elizabeth and Durban where we turned round loading for UK and North Europe and headed back to Cape Town. We docked there at 6 o'clock in the morning and when the agent boarded he gave me a copy of that day's newspaper. The front page headlines was a report of our yacht arriving at Walvis Bay and a story given by one member of the crew to a reporter. It was said that a large container ship had responded to a distress call sent by the skipper of the yacht but when close had refused to help or give them assistance. I immediately had our agent contact the newspaper and to contact the Port Captains at Cape Town and Walvis Bay for the true story.

It turned out that the skipper was the owner of the yacht and with his son advertised for four people to join them as crew to the West Indies and pay for the privilege. The four crew had not heard the conversation between us and the yacht and were told as we departed that we had refused to take them on board These passengers would have taken the offer had they been told leaving father and son to manage on their own. It just indicates how easily stories to papers can be untrue and lucky for me that I could correct it in good time and put the record straight.

NV *Nina Bowater*
Great Lakes 1970–71

My first command in 1970 was the *Nina Bowater*. It was one of the last vessels to be built by the Caledon Shipyard at Dundee in 1961. These ships were built to carry newsprint and pulp wood for paper making, and strengthened to operate in ice. The ship was very well appointed and had two double passenger cabins for customers of Bowater paper operations who were usually owners or executives of American newspapers. My first three months on the vessel we were trading from the paper mill at Liverpool Nova Scotia to Alexandria, the river port for Washington DC. We were carrying the weekly supply of newsprint for the well known *Washington Post* newspaper. It was an interesting but hardworking schedule and as it was spring time the sea passage was usually in fog. There was also a ten/twelve hour run up the Potomac River to Alexandria which, if in daylight, was very interesting. However, our time in port at each end was very short. It was during this time that our daughter Nicola was born in Stirling and the American passengers who were on the ship at the time sent my wife Carol very nice gifts. The vessel then had a spell carrying newsprint to Spain and pulp wood to Sittingbourne in Kent. This was winter time and we experienced our share of bad weather courtesy of the North Atlantic.

During one passage from Newfoundland to the UK we encountered very bad weather over a period of days. On the evening when conditions were improving I told the watch keeping officer I was going to turn in. I was not amused to be wakened by a seaman who advised me of an incident and could I go to the chief steward's cabin. There I discovered the chief steward and others with one of the seamen bleeding badly with a cut up face. Apparently another rating had broken a sauce bottle in the mess room and slashed the victim's face. If nothing else this required immediate stitching. I sent word for the chief officer to be called and to find the culprit. The motion of the ship was still quite violent and so I had to sit the victim in a chair and I sat astride him. He had a very big gash from just below his eye across his cheek to under his chin. The only anaesthetic we had was a local spray and with the chief steward supplying the materials I stitched up the wound and also managed to stop the bleeding. In the meantime the chief officer had found the guilty party and had him at the cabin door when I finished. When the chief officer let him go he promptly fainted. The patient was made as comfortable as possible in his cabin and we radioed ashore for further advice as we were mid Atlantic at this time. We were advised what drugs to use to guard against infection and the weather was showing improvement. With this being a very serious incident I decided it should be a police matter on reaching port which involved witness statements investigating the cause of the incident and other pertinent information. All had to be entered up and witnessed in the vessel's official log book – all this while we proceeded on passage. Fortunately there was no sign of infection and with the patient improving the company informed me that we would continue to Ridham Dock, the port for Sittingbourne, unless the patient's condition deteriorated. We reached Ridham Docks and were met by the police and a doctor as requested.

I was less than pleased when the police inspector came to my cabin to say there was little he could do. The two men had made it up and the victim had refused to press charges. As the inspector pointed out to me he could charge him on my behalf but it would not stand up in court. Meantime the doctor had examined the patient and informed me the wound had stopped just short of the jugular vein. A fraction further and it would have been fatal. I handed all the relevant paperwork to the police and the company which took it up with the maritime authority ashore. From the records the assailant had been involved in two serious incidents on ships previously. At least this time all his seaman's documents were taken off him and he would not be able to serve on a UK vessel again.

The victim returned to the vessel a few months later and was anxious to show his scar which was not at all noticeable considering that at the time it was not precise needlework, more likely rolling home, a seaman's expression for sewing canvas.

Once spring set in we were one of the first ships to enter the Great Lakes when the St Lawrence Seaway opened in March 1971. Prior to that I had my first experiences with ice at sea which was entirely different, I saw icebergs for the first time.

Four round trips from the Corner Brook paper mill in Newfoundland to the different US ports took about two weeks and long hours which the crew liked as there was plenty of overtime. Going up in the spring and finally leaving in the fall made the changing seasons most interesting. I obtained a Great Lakes pilot's licence which saved the company quite a bit of money. I had to undergo an oral examination with a Canadian marine surveyor which took place at midnight in Montreal while the ship was taking on fuel. Time was money so ordinary office hours did not apply.

In our various trips into the Lakes we called at Rochester , Buffalo, Cleveland, Detroit, Port Huron and Muskegon. It is quite an experience to be out of sight of land, in the middle of a continent, in a giant lake.

On one occasion when we were unloading newsprint, for some exercise I decided to walk up the main highway to the city along the riverside. I was aware that I was the only person on foot when a police car drew up beside me. The policeman enquired what I was doing and I told him. I was told nobody walks in Detroit. I told him I was aware of that being the case after dark but assumed daylight alright. He agreed grudgingly and told me not to make a habit of it!

On another occasion we were in Muskegon, a town on Lake Michigan. Unexpectedly we did not finish unloading cargo until an hour after dark, and as the harbour had no navigation lights we could not sail until morning. As a result the majority on board took advantage of an evening ashore. I was sitting in my cabin reading and enjoying the peace and quiet. There was a sudden very loud knock at my door and when I reached it I found the local sheriff, with his revolver in hand using it as a door knocker, he then introduced the police doctor and two patrolmen. I was a bit taken aback when he told me that they had been advised there was an under aged girl who had run away from home on board. I said I was surprised as I was very strict in that visitors to the ship had to have passes issued by me or the chief officer. He then said he would search the vessel and if a girl was found I would be held responsible and arrested. I arranged for the duty officer to show them around and awaited the result with some misgivings. When they returned to say no one was found and that most personnel were ashore I was greatly relieved. Once the ship sailed the bosun said he wished to see me and we had a talk. Apparently the day before one of the dockers or longshoremen, as they are known in the US had approached him and a couple of other crew members to say they had found a young girl hiding in the cargo shed who was cold and very hungry and could the ship do something for her. (By the by, in my opinion seamen are really very soft touches to use an expression.) The girl was taken into the galley and given a good meal by the cook. She was allowed to use the crew showers to clean up supervised by the bosun, and sent ashore again with a packet of sandwiches. Thank goodness I related what had happened the night before. One always had to bear in mind how the best of intentions can be misconstrued. The point also was who informed the police? Another longshoreman or who?

On two trips into the Great Lakes we carried passengers, guests/ customers of Bowaters. They all said upon leaving the ship that it was the best holiday they had had and two of the men never missed a locking transit even in the middle of the night. The ship was also blessed with a very good cook and on galley inspection one day I asked him where he learned his skills. He pointed to a butcher's hook from which hung a large number of recipes from *Women's Weekly*! But he had a special touch.

We undertook an unusual voyage on the Nina when I was there. We were sent to Charleston, South Carolina to load a cargo of wood pulp for Durban, South Africa where a new newsprint mill was to be opened and we would carry the first consignment of raw material. As we prepared to sail, the weather report was not too good but a hurricane in the vicinity was forecast to miss our area. As we were about to leave, the harbour pilot had just been advised that the port was now closed as the hurricane had changed direction and heading for Charleston. Had I been informed earlier I would have remained in port. Once outside and having battened down the ship we had no choice but to get as far off shore as possible which meant heading straight into the centre of the storm. We had two very unpleasant days where the ship was virtually awash, being deep loaded and no one ventured on deck. For the first time I went through the storm centre where the wind died away for a short time and we saw the sky and the US coastguard plane circling the centre and keeping track of the direction. Then back to overcast sky, very heavy rain and wind blowing again at hurricane force from the opposite direction making for a very confused sea. We were much relieved when we were through the storm and back to calmer waters and very grateful to be sailing in a very strong, well found little ship.

The St Lawrence Seaway was due to close for the winter in December 1971 and my wife was able to read this in the *Dundee Courier* before hearing it from me by letter. We loaded a cargo of newsprint for Belfast and Newport S. Wales.

We arrived at Belfast in November 1971 at the height of the troubles. Bombs were going off in the city and the docks were probably the safest place as they were well guarded. I had a visit from the senior Customs Officer soon after arrival with an interesting request. Because of the troubles we were the first foreign-going ship to visit Belfast in months and his boarding officers had been unable to purchase any bond. Did I mind if some purchases were made? I had no objection provided there were supplies left to give the ship's company their full issue. He then offered to check the crew's individual customs declarations, thus saving them time when we paid off in Newport. I said that I did not mind provided it did not cause any problems at Newport our final port of call. He said there was no problem with this as the ship would not be outwith UK territorial waters.

This clearance was carried out and having been away a long time most men had presents to take home. I have to say we were all treated very decently and all well pleased. However when we reached Newport I was visited by the senior customs officer there who was furious that the ship had been cleared in Belfast. I explained what happened at the advice of Belfast customs and asked whether I had broken any regulations, He admitted I hadn't but this was not normal procedure, More a question of someone's nose being put out of joint.

My wife joined me in Belfast as I had been away for 13 months except for seven days in dry dock. In that time my wife had sold our first home in Dunblane and bought a larger house in Cupar, Fife, and our daughter Nicola was a baby when I left and a little girl when I returned.

One other incident is worth recalling from my Bowater days. We carried one cargo of newsprint from Newfoundland to Spain. It was a new contract for Bowaters and the company was anxious that everything should go smoothly and make a good impression on our new customers. We arrived at Barcelona in the late afternoon and completed all the formalities. I had earlier been advised that a reception would be held on board the following evening for invited guests. The agents then advised me that the labour would start at 8 a.m., and that they would require the crew to open up the holds beforehand so that surveyors could check the condition of our cargo.

The chief officer was instructed to make the crew ready for a good start the following morning as I was sure the majority of the crew were looking forward to an evening ashore. As was my habit I was up and about early next morning and at the time I expected signs of activity. All was quiet. I went to the chief officer's cabin to find him still fast asleep in his shore going clothes in his armchair. I was not amused and brought him awake quite sharply to get things moving. I found the night watchman who allegedly had called everyone. I withdrew to the boat deck to the sound of fire alarm which the chief officer had used to alert every one he was up. I was aware of him then in vehement discussion with the bosun. I went for breakfast and met the chief engineer, a big man, naked demanding to know where the fire was. I suggested he ask the chief officer and continued to my breakfast in solitary splendour. However everything was ready on time for the surveyor's inspection. It took time for the dust to settle on board and I suggested the chief engineer take the chief officer to the café on the quay to settle his nerves before I had a few words.

On one voyage we went to Richmond, Virginia and we berthed close to the city centre. I was needing to buy presents to take home and the agent took me to a suitable shop. I remember buying a Red Indian outfit for son Bruce and a Reggie doll for daughter Nicola, both I recollect a great success. I also wanted crochet thread for my mother in law. Unfortunately the shop was quiet and when I made my enquiry for thread I was surrounded by middle aged lady assistants anxious to offer advice and convinced I was the needle worker and using mother in law as a disguise. In the end I bought too many balls of thread to facilitate my escape.

Hector Heron Incidents

During my time as Master of the *Hector Heron* an 18,000-ton tanker which carried products on charter to BP we had many moments of drama and amusement too. She was a vessel showing her age and everyone had to work very hard to keep her going and this created quite a bond with many who sailed on her.

The Chief Engineer with me most of the time was Jim Shepherd from Dundee and the Caledonian shipyard, another good friend and excellent engineer. He was also a very accomplished embroiderer which I had also taken up. It took our minds off the problems of the ship and you had to concentrate on the stitching. One evening we were in my cabin working away at our tapestries when there was a knock on my door. It turned out to be one of the cadets sent up by the others who were watching a film, to obtain ice cream alleged to be in my fridge. When he came in his facial expression was classic. Here he was confronted by two old duffers doing their needlework and he had to avert his eyes. This was not the adventure of life at sea and no ice cream either!

On the same ship, in a port called Bander Mashour in Iran, we had just completed loading our cargo at 2 o'clock in the morning and were ready to sail once the quantity of product loaded was agreed by ship and shore. The Chief Officer's figures had us loading 2,000 tons of aviation fuel – less than the terminal stated. This tended to be the norm and I had a very efficient Chief Officer. The terminal official and Chief Officer departed to check figures. On return the terminal figure was 300 tons less and the ship's only a few tons different from the previous figure. I said I would not sign the terminal figures until agreement was reached. It happened that on my office wall, there was a calendar given by a ship's chandler somewhere and all the pictures were playgirl photographs. The terminal official then announced if he could have the calendar he would agree the ship's figures! This was before the revolution.

Another occasion comes to mind, this occurred in Mossamedes in Angola when it was still a Portuguese colony. Ever since India annexed Goa, the Portuguese enclave south of Bombay, Portugal stipulated that any ship having an Indian crew, as we had, required a policeman at the bottom of the gangway to prevent any Indian crew members going ashore. This was the case in both Angola and Mozambique and was really very petty and frustrating for any ship with an Indian crew. On this occasion, we had a very awkward, very fat policeman on duty. He would not even allow the seamen on the jetty to paint the ship's side. However as we were obliged to feed him he saw no reason to refuse good Indian food. Since the terminal was well away from the town, his mode of transport was one of these small utility French cars. As our discharge was coming to an end, again of aviation fuel, a single leak had developed in the discharge hose and some of the liquid was lying on deck and a seaman was transferring it to an empty drum. Health and safety in many of these overseas terminals were non-existent. Our policeman then asked if he could have the fuel for his car and we agreed, seeing that this could be amusing for us but not for him. He waved to us as we departed, having filled his tank, but sadly he had not started the car before we left. So we could not see whether he took off to town by air or did not start at all

On another occasion on the *Hector Heron* we called at Port Wyndham in North Australia. The little port up the river is access to the small town of Wyndham where there was a very big abattoir for the cattle industry of the territory.

We were in again discharging a six months supply of aviation fuel for the airport and Flying Doctor Service among other things. It is a very barren country there and literally hundreds of miles from any other town. As there were no navigation lights as such on the river our arrival and departure had to be in daylight. We were not going to finish our discharge before dark and so the chief and I were looking forward to a night in bed, when we saw our junior engineer going ashore. In tankers there is little chance of shore leave but he was going to take a chance. He was a Glaswegian and a snappy dresser for the early 1970s. There he was, winkle picker shoes, ducks tail haircut, wide jacket lapels the lot and a two mile walk to town. The chief and I wondered what effect he would have at the saloon bar in Wyndham. Next morning the officer of the watch told me he was brought back in a buggie by locals, somewhat dishevelled and had not had to buy a drink all night. To the locals he must have looked like someone from outer space.

We had our moments of light entertainment during a demanding voyage.

Lagos

I joined the *Hector Heron* in Lagos in 1972. The chief engineer and I joined together and we were old shipmates. The first night we spent in a new hotel waiting for the vessel to arrive. We discovered that though the rooms had en suite there was no water out of the taps! A sign of things to come.

The vessel was now to do five trips, on charter to BP from Port Harcourt to Lagos with the weekly supply of fuel for the area, especially the airport. There was an acute shortage of fresh water in Lagos and Apapa. At this time all ships in port were on rationing. It was the one benefit we had in getting all our fresh water needs otherwise the fuel would not be pumped ashore and so no flights to foreign parts especially for the 'fat cats'

Safely at the terminal was not a priority and we discovered that when we changed the different grades of fuel we were discharging, the terminal officials just uncoupled the pipe line on the jetty and allowed the residue drain into the harbour. The standard procedure was to flush the pipeline with water into a special tank ashore. Our objections to this current procedure were ignored and we had no control once the cargo left the ship. We pointed out that welding was being carried out on a ship close to our jetty, and our residue was floating past. Then the other ship on this shuttle service, a modern BP vessel had a serious fire at the jetty after we sailed. At 02.00 hrs the line had been broken and unfortunately a local fisherman in his canoe was under the jetty where he lit his cigarette and the jetty caught fire. The ship alerted the fire service who failed to turn up and the ship's crew went ashore and succeeded in putting out the blaze. We were so lucky it was not us, as being an older vessel, we did not have the inert gas system which prevented the BP vessel catching fire. When we returned and hoped that procedures were improved, we discovered the only change was that the shore staff looked under the jetty before disconnecting the pipeline!

During this time we never left Nigerian waters and our bond was sealed by customs. Each time we returned to Lagos the customs would search the ship, check our bond and help themselves to what they wanted. I raised this with the agent who advised me that if I objected the ship would not be allowed to unload. I had the agent countersign for all the bonded supplies and food stuff taken by officials. When we received orders to proceed to the Persian Gulf to load we heaved a great sigh of relief. On departure, I advised our London office that we would have to make a call at Cape Town to replenish our stores as we would not be able to obtain supplies at our loading port. On receiving the reply "that they failed to understand our need for stores" I referred them to our Lagos agent. We made our stores call.

On my last passage on this vessel we were cleaning the cargo tanks in the South China sea as the ship had to be gas free before arriving at Singapore for repairs. Tank cleaning is the most dangerous time on a tanker with inflammable vapour around. This particular morning the chief engineer and I were on deck viewing the progress being made by the crew. There was a sudden loud bang sounding like an explosion and everyone froze expecting the deck to fracture, followed by a second bang. It seemed a long time but when nothing serious developed we suddenly realised that it had been two US fighter planes breaking the sound barrier above us. Our relief showed when fists were raised at the disappearing planes. The Vietnam war was going at that time.

Brisbane Call

Again from my time on the *Hector Heron* we called at Brisbane to discharge fuel products. We had old friends living there who went back to 1954. We were required to discharge first of all at an oil jetty half-way up the Brisbane river which would take about six hours so I invited my friend Judy to come down to the ship with her son Tom aged ten. They could have lunch on board and then sail up the river when we moved to our next discharge point in Brisbane port – which they did and enjoyed a curry lunch. As the ship was to be in overnight I would then go to their house for a meal in the evening. On arriving at their house I discovered that my hostess was laid up with a stomach upset due to the ship's curry but I was entertained by her husband Bruce and his two attractive late-teens daughters. They insisted they drove me back to the ship but Bruce could not drive because he had forgotten to renew his licence and in Australia it meant him having to re-sit a driving test. As a busy GP he was dependent on his daughters driving him around until he re-sat his test. We left Judy in bed and proceeded to the ship which was still pumping out the cargo.

When we arrived, the duty officer was at the gangway and so I asked Bruce to remain in the car until I had entered my accommodation with the two girls. Once the officer had left the gangway he could follow us up. As expected the reaction of the duty officer was rewarding. He could not believe his eyes seeing me escort these two young ladies to my cabin after he told me all was in order. I knew the news would be around the ship in no time. The next morning I had the feeling I was treated with some admiration. We sailed at daylight the following day and in due course I had a word with the chief engineer. He told me he had walked ashore for a beer at a public house well known to seafarers called the Hamilton Arms. He was disappointed as it had been modernised since he was last there and instead of sawdust on the floor there was chrome everywhere and cushioned seats with carpets on the floor. But the landlord told him the atmosphere had not changed much and the carpets soaked up the blood when they had a lively evening!

Bombay Calcutta

On another voyage on the tanker we had cargo to deliver at Bombay, Madras and Calcutta. At Bombay the traders, with their various skills, were on board almost before the ship was secured. It had been some time since I was last in India so I ordered shirts and shorts for tropical wear and a light weight navy blue uniform. The ship would only be in port for 36 hours but that was no problem to these business men. However, when the tailor returned with my order for fitting I discovered that I had gold braid on my sleeves almost up to my elbows. I looked more like a cinema commissionaire and could hardly bend my elbows with weight of the braid. I had told him when ordering that the braid had to be the correct size but his excuse was that his style looked better, he was disappointed to have it removed.

When bound for Calcutta we took on board the Hooghly pilot at Sandheads which was quite some way from the river mouth because the sea there was very shallow. Once on board the pilot informed me that it would take two days to reach our berth at Calcutta as the ship's draught meant we could only transit sections of the river channel at high water. Consequently he would advise the port authorities and our agent. When we anchored on the first evening the pilot enquired if we had any films on board and if so could he watch one. He chose *Cabaret* as I remember and one of the cadets was summoned to show it. Early the next morning when we were under way again the pilot told me he had enjoyed the film very much and that he could possibly get us to our berth earlier than first thought which was fine, provided he advised the port and I informed the agent. We were also due to change about half of our Indian crew when we arrived. At last we were secured, a long tedious job since we had to use chains because of the tidal bore that came up the river at the change of tide. The crew change took place with temporary crew taking over, all organised by our agent. But, due to a breakdown in communications, neither customs nor the local seamen's union had been advised that the vessel was arriving earlier than originally expected. This meant that the men leaving had no duty to pay on their possessions or back handers to the customs men, The same with the union representative who expected some gratuities irrespective of them all having paid their dues. As can be imagined, both parties were somewhat put out, but nothing the ship could be blamed for but they had to take it out on someone. When the seamen's union representative boarded he was under the influence of liquor and was rather upset to find the members had already been paid off and left the ship. He then accosted the chief officer who was engaged in discharging the cargo and who could not spend time with him so he referred him to me.

The official arrived at my door to say that the chief officer had assaulted him and demanded an immediate apology. I pointed out that the chief officer would not assault him and when questioned the chief officer informed me that the union man tried to prevent him from closing an essential cargo valve and had moved him aside. The union man then threatened to bring the crew out on strike but they had made themselves scarce. The agent was witness to this and eventually the official departed. The following morning our agents were informed that our new crew members, numbering about thirty, would not be allowed to join. This was serious as the ship would finish discharge the following day and sail. A meeting was held aboard the vessel with other officials and it was obvious now the issue was about loss of face and they required something from the company if the question of assault was dropped. In the end we made a minor concession in the supply of cold weather clothing to the crew and our new crew joined. I was rebuked by our London office for conceding this concession without their permission, but in defence, pointed out the vessel would have been delayed in the time taken to get their clearance.

Incidentally; some years later when the company's employment of Indian ratings came to an end the same union tried to gain control of the company pension for their Indian ratings. The company had to go to court to prevent this happening to be sure of delivering the pension.

Another chief engineer joined the vessel as we returned to the Persian

Gulf to load. While there the current chief would leave, having had time to hand over properly to his relief as the ship was a one-off in the fleet. On completion of loading in Iran and the new chief had taken over we sailed – and within hours our new chief engineer collapsed in the engine room with heat exhaustion and dehydration. With difficulty we took him to his cabin put him in his bath, obtained all the ice possible from our refrigerator rooms and packed the water with ice. It turned out that he had not been eating properly, not taking his salt tablets and drinking beer rather than water. It was August in the Gulf, the hottest time of year. It took us three days to get him back to near normal under close supervision – he was lucky.

Final Voyage of TSS *Oranje* 1975

In the spring of 1975 the managers of the joint passenger and mail service, Union Castle and Safmarine, between the UK and South Africa announced the withdrawal from service of the SA *Oranje*. It would be the first of the five ships to be withdrawn leaving Southampton for the last time on the 19th September. The last passenger ship in the service was withdrawn two years later, the *Windsor Castle*. Safmarine also stipulated that the SA *Oranje* would carry passengers on its last voyage as far as Durban, prior to proceeding to Taiwan and the ship breakers yard.

On the penultimate voyage when in Durban, a meeting was held on board to discuss and finalise arrangements for the return to the UK of the majority of the ship's company once the last passengers had disembarked. Attending the meeting were the Officers in Charge of Customs and Immigration, the Port Captain, the company's marine superintendents, a representative from South African Airways and the agency manager. Also attending were the heads of the departments on board ship. It was agreed that the ship would berth at the Passenger Terminal at 06.00 Monday 6th October and disembarkation of the passengers would take place after breakfast from 09.00 and be completed by 10.30. For the crew members leaving the vessel at Durban to fly to the UK, it was agreed by Customs and Immigration that no check was necessary provided no shore leave was allowed and transport arranged from the ship's gangway direct to the airport by buses. It was agreed with the SAA and airport officials that the buses would take the crew members directly to the jumbo jet at the runway and so no official check was required. The airline representative emphasised that the departure of the plane on time was essential as it had to refuel at Windhoek and make its slot at Heathrow. The meeting finished in agreement and members had a good lunch on board.

On the homeward leg a timetable with all the arrangements was made up for the final voyage to Durban and then distributed to the ship's company. Departure of the plane on its scheduled time was again emphasised.

The day of departure for the final voyage of the SA *Oranje*, formally *Pretoria Castle*, Friday 19th September 1975 was full of activity. Passengers embarking and the completion of loading of cargo and mail, officials from the National Union of Seamen were in attendance to answer any requests, queries from their members. Prior to sailing Mr Bernard Cayzer came to wish us well together with Southampton senior management and the senior official of the National Union of Seamen. He informed me that he was well satisfied with all the arrangements made with regard to his members. This was what I was hoping to hear before we sailed. We had embarked ninety-six first class passengers and 505 tourist passengers and a good cargo load and departed at 17.00 with a few well wishers seeing us away. The attending tugs and adjacent vessels gave us a farewell whistle which we returned. Recently a number of older passenger vessels had said farewell to Southampton and so it was no longer an event.

The following day at sea it was brought to my attention that one or two trouble makers were trying to cause dissent and I have to say, not unexpectedly. I mustered the crew in recreation rooms for 18.30 when many would be off duty, with the Chief Engineer, Staff Commander and myself attending. As I had anticipated the usual individuals raised the usual questions and had not met or even seen their union officials. I was able to point out that two of those raising the points were known to have deliberately gone ashore at lunchtime when the union meeting had been held and any genuine query was dealt with . The meeting had ended with no ill will and had successfully dealt with those few to whom trouble was their aim. I had in due course spoken to the crew to say everything had been done to clarify things.

Our next call was Las Palmas arriving at 21.00 to sail at 01.00. The principal reason was to replenish our fuel oil and fresh water before the long voyage to Cape Town. Passengers and crew could go ashore but were required back on board by midnight. During the time in port I was in my quarters where I had a visitation from the ship's union spokesperson. He informed me that some members of the crew were going to hold a strike meeting on the quayside at sailing time. I thanked him for his information and would have the agent notify the police that every crew member ashore at sailing time should be considered deserters and to deal with them accordingly. Their duties on board would willingly be carried out by the others anxious for the overtime pay. At the time of sailing our agent and the harbour staff were there to deal with our moorings and no one else.

On the passage to Cape Town I had a request for permission to have a crew dance as this would be the last occasion when many would sail together. and we had about forty female crew members. Permission was granted with the usual conditions with the gathering starting at 21.00 hrs and finishing no later than 23.30 hrs and it would be held in the crew mess room which had to be ready for its normal function the following morning

The arrangements were made to coincide with the ship's five piece band's night off and they had been sweet talked into providing the music that evening. One or two of the senior officers were invited, including myself. On the night, the ladies were all dressed up and the men attending had made considerable effort too. The crew mess man who was very good at his duties had decorated the large room and was one of the members of the catering staff who was gay. He turned up on the night with his wig and make-up on and a long dress. I attended for a short time and enjoyed a dance with the lady with the longest service on board. Prior to taking my leave I invited the crew mess man for a dance in his finery as a way of raising spirits which did just that plus a photo opportunity for some which I had not expected! Next morning all was back to normal and no defaulters.

I was aware that much would be made of the ship's last voyage at our ports of call. Being the first to be withdrawn from service, sailing latterly under the South African flag and launched by Lady Smuts by radio telephone from South Africa as *Pretoria Castle* in 1947. We had many long service crew members on board including our first class stateroom steward John who had joined the vessel on it's maiden voyage and been there ever since. I arranged for all those who had been on the vessel when I joined it as Staff Commander in 1967 to join me on the bridge when we finally departed from Cape Town at midday on 3rd October. The crew's social club gave their final donation to a Cape Town Primary school which they had adopted years before and the press boarded for stories. A party of about twenty belonging to the World Ship Society boarded as passengers to Durban and we flew their pennant along with our overall dressing flags on the morning of sailing. A large crowd assembled to see us depart on a beautiful Cape Town day standing all the way out on the breakwater. There were in the end thirty-six crew members on the bridge and it was very emotional as all the ships in port and tugs sounded their whistles as we cleared the breakwater.

We had a pleasant run round to Port Elizabeth and a nearly full passenger complement as many had joined at Cape Town to enjoy our last coastal voyage. We arrived at Port Elizabeth mid morning and had many visitors as the ship would not be in overnight. Again local children's charities benefited from the last call of the ship. Our departure in daylight did not take place as we were still unloading our cargo and it was now blowing a gale. When the harbour pilot boarded we discussed the weather conditions and he was prepared to take us out providing he could have maximum power when he needed it. I assured him of that and warned my very good friend the chief engineer. A few brave people turned out to see us off and, having dispensed with the tugs, full power was requested to get us moving. The pilot was taken aback by the response as we covered the city in a cloud of black smoke to remember us by. I urged the pilot to leave otherwise he would be with us to East London and he bade a hurried farewell as I slowed the ship down.

Early the following morning, as we arrived off East London, it was blowing a full gale. We embarked the harbour pilot with difficulty and stood off to discuss the situation. East London has a small harbour with little room to manoeuvre. The pilot said we could berth but more important to me was the ability to sail that afternoon with our date the following afternoon with the jet plane at Durban. We obtained the latest information from the weather bureau who said there was no chance of the weather moderating before nightfall. I advised all the interested parties of our abandoning our East London call and apologised to the passengers who had hoped to disembark. We managed to land our pilot and again apologised to all at the shore reception for the last call.

We slow steamed to Durban giving our time for a pilot at 04.00 6th October. A very good farewell dinner and entertainment was arranged. Again I had a request from the crew to hold, which was called on these ships, 'the Sods Opera' when the on board talent do their bit and were usually very funny if a trifle crude at times. I was in a spot as they would do something anyway and up to now they had performed really well considering the circumstances. I reminded them of their duties and that the majority would be flying out the following day with their luggage. I agreed to attend for the first hour and it really was very entertaining. Meantime, the group from the Ship Society had been told they could come to the bridge when we would be picking up our pilot but to remember it would still be dark.

It was a lovely calm morning on Monday 6th October when the harbour pilot embarked. Admittedly the bridge was somewhat more crowded than usual but everything went smoothly and we were secured at the Ocean Terminal by 05.30 and the shore officials boarded at 05.50. There were no absentees from the various duties and all our passengers had a good breakfast and well served. Our passengers commenced disembarking at 08.30 and all away by 10.00. As previously arranged we would start disembarking the 250 odd members of the ship's company who were flying home. A crew of forty would take the ship to the ship breakers and about ten officers and leading hands would assist in the closing down before returning to the UK before we departed from Durban.

At 11.30 with the buses ready on the quayside the Purser and I stationed ourselves at the bottom of the gangway, he to check off each individual leaving and I to say cheerio, thank them, and wish them well. For many it would be their first air journey and a number had to be reassured. About halfway through, and everything going smoothly, I was approached by our marine superintendent to say there was a delay with the plane and could I stop or slowdown the operation. To say the least I was taken aback but as all the buses were there we would continue as normal and fulfil our obligations, especially as the pressure had been on us from the start to fit in with the airline. Our operation was completed smoothly and the buses departed for the airport. I then learned that the jumbo jet had been delayed on take off from Johannesburg due to an incident on the runway. This meant that the buses had to wait at the airport until the plane arrived before taking their passengers straight out to the plane. Some people were allowed out either for comfort stops or to stretch their legs and very soon an Indian was doing a good business with snacks and cold drinks.

On board we now started cargo work and the closing down operation. We were in touch with the airport and I was advised that the crew had now been safely embarked. There was also a message from the plane captain to say that he had permission on take off to fly over the harbour above the terminal and had I any message to pass on. Other than to wish them well I added that on the mail ships we always endeavoured to leave on time, not expecting it to be passed on but I heard later it was relayed to a spirited response from those on board. We were all out on deck as the plane flew over and it was impressive and as a group we were quite moved.

De-storing the ship commenced as the cargo was discharged. Safmarine had intended to pretty well strip the vessel and presumably sell off the fittings. However it was stopped by Customs as Safmarine had not applied for permission to do so and agreed on duty. Any items going to charities, e.g. bed linen and beds were allowed. Also ship's stores of foodstuffs etc. were allowed to be landed for other company ships. Fortunately this was something the ship was not responsible for and it seemed to have been mishandled as the Customs would not alter their position. Meanwhile Safmarine was using the occasion for publicity and there was much local interest. I was asked about sailing times and suggested departing in the early afternoon of Saturday but that the ship would be ready to sail by Thursday evening. The company decided on the Saturday sailing and advertised it widely. Saturday afternoon is the quietest time in the dock area as well. In the meantime many people came down to the ship for a last look. I also had a number of phone calls from the UK from crew members to say they had had a good flight home which was good to hear. On the Saturday people began to gather and a number of senior personnel gathered in my quarters for a farewell drink and I left them to it. The pilot who boarded to take us out had sailed with me some years ago as third officer. As we left the berth my very good friend Bob Gemmell, the chief engineer, joined us on the bridge and took over the engine room telegraphs! He decided they could take care of the job themselves down below. It was all very moving as we left the quayside and all the vessels in port sounded their whistles/ sirens and the harbour tugs dressed overall and fix jets in operation. I was quite amazed at the number of people mustered on both break-waters as we sailed out, having taken time out to see us on our way. Then back to reality, the pilot disembarked and away on our slow speed passage to Kaohsiung in Taiwan and the ship-breakers.

It took us twenty-two days to Taiwan via the Singapore Straits at a reduced speed. Those of the crew who wished changed their cabins and we were all gathered round. With so much empty accommodation it was necessary to have regular fire patrols and it was quite strange to hear the odd door, not properly secured, banging with the motion of the vessel. I visited the engine room one day and was amused to see the engineer's laundry hanging out to dry between two large steam boilers. The bosun kept the decks spotless washing them down each day as usual. We had a very good cook on board who enjoyed himself dispensing ice cream to those sunbathing on the boat deck. For the passage through the Singapore Straits we increased speed to give us more manoeuvrability which came in handy when a US aircraft carrier and escorts made some foolish moves off Singapore Port. Every effort was made to arrive at our destination with minimum supplies. This was everything from fuel oil to domestic stores and bond and so reduce paperwork and costs with Customs and the like. Each member of the crew was allowed his customs allowance of liquor and tobacco and any left was disposed of. We had to ensure as near as possible an even keel as in the harbour area where we were bound, the water was relatively shallow. The arrangements on arrival were that the crew would fly back to the UK the next day and I was to remain in Kaohsiung until such time as our owners had the agreed price for the ship paid into a London bank and then the ship could be handed over.

The harbour pilot boarded on 2nd November and as we entered harbour we touched bottom and stopped. When I suggested to the pilot that a tug boat might help he reminded me the vessel was going for scrap and no one would be prepared to pay the services of a tug! Fortunately, with much use of our engines we got moving again. I then asked the pilot where we would berth and he pointed out a huge collection of vessels of all types and sizes further down the harbour. I could see no space and again on enquiry was told that we would turn round and then force ourselves stern first into the bunch of ships until our stern was hard aground on the sandy shore. I was somewhat taken aback and again was reminded the ship was to be scrapped and any damage would not matter as this was where the ship breakers wanted the vessel. I warned everyone what was going to happen especially the engineers and to ignore all the noise and to give maximum speed astern when required. I can assure you it was not a pleasant experience. The noise and sparks flying was impressive as we forced our way between these other vessels until our propellers hit the beach and stopped. Then the only sound left was the steam from the boilers as the safety valves lifted. The chief officer told me later that the old bosun was in tears amid all the noise.

That night we turned on every light on the ship that still operated as an oasis as it were in the graveyard of dead ships.

In the morning all the formalities took place and I had a message from London to say the money had been paid out and I could return with the crew. By this time the ship was swarming with people and the agent informed me they were sub contractors for all the fittings on board, everything that could be moved, and our teak wood decks were much in demand. He reckoned that the money the ship breakers obtained for the fittings would be about what they had paid our owners and the steel structure of the hull would be their profit. They must been well pleased with their purchase because of fittings that the company could not land in Durban, and the price of scrap metal had risen since the sale was agreed.

We left the ship the next morning and flew from Kaohsiung to Taipei and an overnight stay. Unfortunately the agents at Kaohsiung would not take the cash remaining on board as it was all in sterling. Not only that, a considerable amount was in coin, and so I had this to carry back to London which was quite a considerable weight. The following day we had to fly from Taipei to Hong Kong, change planes and fly to Bangkok for another overnight stay. Then on to a flight to Copenhagen and change planes for London – this was the cheapest route home.

I don't enjoy flying at the best of times, and with a group men of whom you are normally in charge, less so. Officials prefer to deal with one person, in a group so it lands with the senior person. It is always the case that many mature people, once they find someone is nominally in charge, will then try and do their own thing. Drinking in the bar after their flight is called and not even bothering to check out the departure gate. I quickly developed a system of checkouts where I had my good friend the chief engineer round the strays like a good sheepdog but with a loud voice. In Taipei, I had to make sure they were all up for a flight leaving at midday. I did mention to the duty manager at the hotel that some of the rooms would be pretty untidy. He informed me that he had already checked and they were fine. He had some crews mainly American he said, who wrecked their rooms. At Bangkok overnight everyone was reminded that meals were provided but individuals paid in cash for refreshments other than water. Next morning as I completed the check into the bus for the airport the hotel duty manager boarded to say there were two outstanding room accounts to be paid. The bus would not leave until they were settled. One was for our radio officer for a number of gins by room service and the other a leading seaman who had phoned his wife for thirty minutes, helped by a couple of beers. I was not amused and the excuse of having no money was offered. I had to use money from the ship's cash for it being sterling. I reminded the culprits that this would be deducted from their salaries in London and then we were allowed to proceed. I was then taken aback when we boarded the SAS plane that drink in tourist class was free! Fortunately most of our party had been on the town in Bangkok and slept most of the way.

Prior to landing at Tashkent for refuelling I had a wonderful view of Calcutta and Kidderpore dock which brought back memories without the heat and smell. Tashkent was primitive to say the least with employees totally indifferent to one's needs. The toilet facilities had no roofing so the sub zero temperatures did nothing for one's well being! As our flight into London did not arrive till evening I had made arrangements for those who could not get home to have overnight accommodation, about half of us, with a bus to take us to a hotel in the city. We boarded the bus and found one missing, our radio officer, and it was then said that he had mentioned to someone earlier that he might just go straight home. Once settled in our hotel with the chief engineer and me sharing a room, and vastly different to what we had experienced since leaving the old ship, I was called to the telephone. This was our radio officer at Heathrow asking how he could get to the hotel as he had missed the bus because he had to refresh himself one way and another. It had been a long day, I gave him the address of the hotel and recommended a taxi for which he would not be recompensed and ended the call.

The next morning we all went our separate ways. I proceeded to the head office where I gratefully handed over my bundle of cash and dealt with any outstanding items. The management was pleased with the whole operation and I headed home happily to my family.

Three weeks later I was back in Southampton as captain of the *SA Vaal* for the Christmas voyage to South Africa. No rest for the wicked!

Passengers Carried

I first sailed on a ship with accommodation to carry twelve passengers in 1953. I was then a second officer. The biggest benefit to us at the time was the better standard of feeding. The passengers were mostly retired and of a certain age.

The next time I was sent to a twelve passenger ship was in 1958, by this time I was chief officer, and if twelve passengers were on board I would have three sit with me at meals. It certainly made life more interesting. These vessels suited retired people in general who had the time to accept a cargo ship itinerary and be away from the UK up to four months if they were on board for the round trip. Others would be there just for the passage to India, South Africa or Australia. With an Indian crew they were made very comfortable and well looked after but without the amenities and space of a passenger vessel.

A particular voyage that comes to mind was when we had ten passengers doing the round voyage when we left the Mersey. At my table I had an elderly couple from Glasgow. They had just retired in 1959 having run a sub post office all their married life and had never had a proper holiday. The husband lost one arm below the elbow in the Great War and before artificial limbs were common place he had adapted very well. They were a lovely couple and everything was new and exciting to them and reminded me of how I felt on my first voyage to sea as a cadet. We called at Dakar, Cape Town, Port Elizabeth, East London and Durban in South Africa and Lorenzo Marques and Beira in what was then Portuguese Mozambique. They took every opportunity to see the sights and would tell me all about it at the evening meal.

At Beira we received instructions to proceed to India to load a cargo to take back to the UK. These days ships were not fully air conditioned and so it could become quite hot on board especially in port. Our first loading port was Calcutta where our agents arranged a five day coach trip away from the ship for the passengers if they wished. Kidderpore

Docks in Calcutta was no place to spend your time if there were other options. The ship then proceeded to Vizagapatam, Madras and Colombo where we completed and then headed for the UK. We called at Aden for bunker oil and then through the Suez Canal, passed Gibraltar and finally arrived at Tilbury Docks, London where my two passengers left the ship to return home to Glasgow. They commented on their wonderful holiday and I was able to say how much I had enjoyed their company which had brought memories back for me.

On another voyage on the same vessel bound for South Africa from the UK we had eight lady passengers and no males. The youngest would be about sixty and the oldest an American lady of around eighty and very sprightly. They were all strangers to each other and, as I recall all widows, and were all dining with either the captain or chief engineers at their tables. About two days after we had cleared the Bay of Biscay the purser/catering officer approached me to ask if he could borrow some of my long playing records, including some of Scottish dance music. He said the atmosphere in the passenger lounge was very subdued and the ships own selection of records did not help. This certainly had the desired effect and the captain allowed some of the younger officers into the lounge to partner the ladies at the dancing. I think they were quite sorry when we arrived at Cape Town where all but the American lady disembarked. Our only passenger was remaining on board until Beira but in Cape Town she went to the hair dresser and returned having had a blue rinse because she felt so much younger! The ship was markedly quieter on departure from Cape Town. On my last voyage on the ship in 1962 I met the lady who became my wife and the company ceased carrying passengers on their cargo vessels from that time, but not, I think because I married a passenger.

On the passenger ships which I was transferred to in 1964 I then met up with a wide variety of people which was very interesting. In the seven years I served on these vessels I can honestly say I never had a dining table that was difficult to manage. I found people of my own age or older much more interesting to dine and socialise with. I suppose they had more experience of life and a tale to tell.

One or two incidents come to mind. One voyage at our departure from Cape Town the purser informed me that a passenger had told him that his wife had gone ashore for some essential last minute shopping and had as yet not returned, which was unusual at sailing time. I informed our shore staff as the ship prepared to sail at our scheduled time. This man also had three youngish children with him and was unwilling to leave the ship with them. The gangways were landed and as we departed the harbour a message from our office informed me that the wife was in the office saying that she had no intention of sailing to the UK with her family. One felt very much for the husband and family. The children's hostess took the children under her care. Until the family left the ship at Las Palmas and flew on to the UK.

Another domestic incident occurred on a Christmas voyage which was always popular and the ship full. The couple in this case was doing the round voyage but leaving in Cape Town to spend the ten days there before the vessel came back from the coastal passage to Durban. On return to Cape Town the ship had a three-day stay during which time cargo was loaded, principally fresh fruit and wine.

Shortly after our arrival back at Cape Town the lady arrived on board to say she wished to join now rather than on the sailing day. This was arranged as her cabin had been used by coastwise passengers. She then announced that when her husband joined on sailing day he was not to be allowed to join her in their two berth cabin. It turned out that during their Cape Town stay the husband had met up with an old lady friend and gone to stay with her! This presented the ship with a problem as the accommodation was to be full on departure with no spare passenger cabins and the couple had paid for their passage in a twin cabin. Their domestic problems were of no concern of the ship. The ship had one spare officer's cabin at that time and when the husband boarded on sailing day this was what he was offered or he would be unable to sail, or they both would have to leave. He was happy to go along with this as his wife also had their house keys! The ship's doctor was now involved with the wife as she was taking it badly and did not wish contact with her husband. A week later the doctor reported to me that on his daily call he had found a strange man in the lady's cabin and asked him to leave. The lady intervened to introduce him as her husband and they were now reconciled. We were pleased it ended peacefully but could have done without the hassle – but they still had the doctor's account to settle.

Another of the many passengers travelling was the RAF Air Marshall called Bomber Harris. He travelled three times on ships I sailed on. He could be a bit demanding but his wife was charming. On one occasion, as they were leaving the ship at Cape Town, I called him to say good bye. By this time I was in a suit as I was on my way to the Company's Cape Town office. Bomber Harris to my surprise said that he very much liked the suit and who was my tailor? I informed him, much to his surprise, that I had bought it from Galloways, Gents Outfitters in Cupar, but that I could give him their address.

On another voyage we had three widows travelling in first class who were addicted to gambling on our Fruit Machine. Each evening after dinner the lounge steward would place three chairs around the machine and they would each have a turn at pulling the arm having put in the money, one evening when doing my rounds I arrived at the ladies playing the machine. When I was there one of them went to the cocktail bar to obtain more change for their game. During this pause in their play a small boy came along with some money from his parents which he put in and pulled the handle. Believe it or not he rang up the jackpot which overflowed on to the floor. Needless to say he was delighted with this shower of money but he was lucky I was there; otherwise these ladies might have thrown him overboard judging from the expressions on their faces.

Wedding from SA *Vaal* at Cape Town – December 1975

I joined the SA *Vaal* as the relief Captain for the Christmas voyage departing Southampton for Cape Town. We had a full complement of passengers both outward and homeward bound and also on the South African coast.

In due course I was informed that the second Radio Officer, W. Macintosh and the Passenger Hostess Agnes Marais were to be married at Cape Town on our homeward call there on 28th December. This of course had nothing to do with the operation of the ship. The bride's mother joined at Durban to sail down to Cape Town and we learned indirectly that she did not exactly approve of her son-in-law to be. Tell me which mother-in-law to be ever did! Invitations to the wedding were duly received which included myself and the Staff Commander and other friends of the couple from the ship's company as well as guests from the shore. Guests from the ship were requested to wear uniform which was not entirely to my liking.

On the day of the wedding, those of us from the ship were picked up by bus to take us to the little Presbyterian Church above the docks, one of the oldest churches in Cape Town. The hired bus was a tourist double decker for city tours and the upper deck was open. It was a lovely church service and the Chief Engineer Officer played the happy couple out of the church on his bagpipes. On rejoining the bus to take us to the Vineyard Hotel in Cape Town for the reception I discovered that part of the upper deck of the bus now held a band from Cape Town which had been used by our cruise ship in the past. They were playing merrily and joined by the younger guests from the ship while we senior personnel occupied the lower deck and endeavoured to be inconspicuous. To my further uneasiness I discovered that the conductor's locker under the stairs was in fact a well stocked bar!

141

We set off for our destination which took us right across the city around 17.00 hrs just about the busiest time and with the band playing, now the focus of some attention. To add to my understandable misgivings every traffic light we met appeared to be at red which allowed many passers-by on the street to jump on and off to enquire of the party. Eventually, we arrived at the hotel to enjoy the reception. Fortunately I had a dinner engagement with the company's Cape Town manager and he picked me up with his car quite soon. Having told the Staff Commander to endeavour to see that all those from the ship caught the bus back at the agreed time, I took leave of my hosts, and without a further thought for the Staff Commander. I had an enjoyable dinner and in due course returned to the ship where all was in order according to the officer on duty.

The next morning the Staff Commander came in to give our daily briefing and looked somewhat subdued. He had managed to get everyone on the bus the previous evening which included the band still playing – after a fashion! Then as they were approaching the dock gates where the Police and Customs are in control, the female vocalist was overcome by emotion and promptly started to do a striptease and had to be held down on the floor by many willing helpers until through the gates. Luckily there was no comment in the papers that day. What I missed by going to dine with Neil Sempill!

Doctors at Sea

I have to say that the duty I liked least at sea was the medical role. Under UK regulations, only vessels carrying more than 100 people, crew and or passengers were required to carry a doctor. When one sat for a master's certificate you had also to pass a first aid course which was pretty basic and from time to time attend further courses. Every British ship was required to have a medical chest to comply with Board of Trade requirements which could be checked by marine surveyors. Each UK ship was also supplied with a large book called *The Ship Master's Medical Guide* which was full of information and many sometimes lurid pictures. It was of great help on many occasions. In my time at sea you could radio in to a particular phone station for medical advice giving all the patient's symptoms. At the back of the volume was a procedure to follow for a burial at sea

On one occasion when I was Chief Officer of the *Kenya Castle* we were berthed in Mombasa, Kenya. On walking around the vessel I met the Purser who demanded to know what the doctor was up to as his men were lined up at the sick bay. On arrival there and enquiring of the doctor what his problem was, it turned out that the Mombasa hospital was running short of blood and a doctor from the hospital had approached our men hoping for volunteers. It was decided that volunteers would be unlikely unless there was an incentive and the hospital agreed to supply each donor with a quart bottle of good local beer called Whitecap. Hence the queue at the hospital. Having pointed out that this should not have been carried out without higher approval and warnings to department heads, I put a limit on the beer to be supplied at fifty otherwise the passenger services would suffer. I also reminded the hospital doctor that the quality of some of the blood donated might do more harm than good! As a result the majority of volunteers had to return to their duties while the chosen fifty had their bottles of beer and a recommended one hour's rest to recuperate legally. It was a worthwhile exercise for the chosen ones.

When on a twelve passenger ship with Indian crew, a seaman reported sick and had also come out in spots. This was when smallpox was still quite prevalent and we were due at Cape Town in three days time. On consulting the Medical Guide it was difficult to tell between chickenpox and smallpox and this man had the scars from a childhood attack. I informed the captain and he told me to ask one of our passengers if he would have a look. This gentleman was a retired Surgeon Rear Admiral who had been the surgeon on *HMS Vanguard* when the King and Queen had visited South Africa in 1947. He agreed to come with me and examine the patient. He too studied the pictures in the Medical Guide and then said that my guess was as good as his as the last time he had practised medicine was fifteen years ago but his fee would be a large pink gin! As a result, on our quarantine message to Cape Town, we played safe and stated that one man had spots. Needless to say a doctor and back up were first on board when we docked but to everyone's relief it was decided it was chickenpox.

On another occasion on this same ship when I was Chief Officer we had an accident at sea when an Indian seaman was struck on the side of the head when on maintenance work which knocked him out and tore his ear quite badly. I was able to stitch and dress the ear but the seaman was drifting in and out of consciousness. Fortunately one of our passenger vessels was within a day's steaming of us and we asked for medical assistance. We met in daylight, fortunately a calm day, and the ship's doctor boarded with his medical orderly and conducted a medical examination. As our destination was Walvis Bay five days away he said the patient should stay with us until help would be available, which we were not happy about. On arrival at Walvis Bay, the seaman still unconscious was hospitalised and after examination was flown to Cape Town, in the care of two doctors. I think the second one went for the ride. I am pleased to say the seaman survived and after six months was fit for sea again. Ten years later I joined one of our passenger ships as captain and in due course the doctor came to my cabin to introduce himself as according to him we had never met. I reminded him that we had and related the occasion and the transfer of the injured man care of two doctors. I have to say he was somewhat wary of me for the rest of the voyage.

Latterly most of the ship's doctors were young men between jobs or courses and right up to date. On occasions I had to remind them that they were paid by the company to look after the crew so they charged the passengers for their services and that ultimately on board ship it was the captain who was responsible for the well being of those on board. I made a practise of visiting any crew member who was laid up when possible, which tended to surprise the doctor on board at the time if he had not been calling on his patient.

It used to amuse me that the first drinks party held on board when leaving South Africa or the UK was held by the doctor for other medics travelling as passengers. It was useful to have back up I suppose. On one occasion however it did not help. We had a middle aged male passenger travelling who was making a nuisance of himself by pestering teenage girls at the social functions. Complaints were being made by parents and the man was warned about his behaviour and appeared to take it in. I enquired of our doctors if any of his fellow medics, a couple of whom were psychiatrists, if they would have a word with the man in question if he was agreeable,but none would offer. The next night our man was up to his old tricks and was assaulted by a male parent which caused a little excitement and the assaulted man threatened to throw himself overboard. At this point I had the man secured in a cabin and a watch kept on him. What slightly irritated me was that the following morning our doctor said that two of his colleagues would be prepared to see the man. I declined the offer in that I had taken action and would leave it to the shore authorities to handle it when the ship arrived at Cape Town.

Maiden Voyage *Everett F Wells* 1977

When I was appointed to the Very Large Crude Carriers (VLCC) I had a great deal to learn as had the other officers who joined with me. We were a good team I have to say. We had all attended the appropriate courses in operation at that time but had no real hands on experience. We carried out builders trials in the North Sea over 12 days when there were around 200 people on board and as the normal complement was around thirty-four, every bit of space was utilised. I shared what was to be my bedroom with four others, all men I at least knew. The company's superintendent engineer was in charge and the operations on board carried out by the shipyard personnel and navigation by three Tyne river pilots. We the ship's officers, tried to witness as many tests as possible and it was a somewhat stressful time. Finally, we took over the vessel at Cuxhaven. In my own accommodation at last, the handing over documents were signed and the ship's papers checked. At the end of this I suggested a toast but when I opened my cabinet there were two cans of beer left by the shipyard! I do believe the yard manager had the grace to look embarrassed and someone found an unopened bottle of coca cola! The day was 7.7.77. Not one I will ever forget!

We then had our own crew join and store up the ship for our ensuing voyage. On departing Cuxhaven, and having disembarked our German pilot, we took the large vessel buoyed channel to the Dover Straits. We passed Dover as the sun was setting when the chief engineer informed me that one of the main bearings of the propeller shaft was running hot and we would have to stop so that he could examine it. These things do happen but this was not the most convenient place, close to land, and ships all around. We informed Dover Coastguard that we were going to anchor and why and they would then inform other shipping. With the vessel empty and a fresh wind blowing our anchoring was an interesting and useful experience. Four hours later the chief announced he was happy with the adjustments he had made and again Coastguard Dover were advised we were getting under way again.

The following day as we were all settling down and getting familiar with the vessel, we reached Ushant and were turning into the Bay of Biscay. Fortunately it was a clear day because as we commenced our turn the steering engine jammed and as the vessel continued to swing we warned all adjacent shipping of our problem and sounded our siren. By the time the vessel had stopped the engineers had rectified the problem but have to say I have never seen French fishermen get out of the way so quickly.

Now settled down for our long haul around the Cape of Good Hope – we were too big for the Suez Canal – we commenced our own testing of the equipment on board. Before long we found a fracture in the cargo loading pipeline and head office were informed. As a result we put into Cape Town for three days while shore fitters worked round the clock to repair the pipework. On our departure from Cape Town we encountered the heavy swell common to that part of the world and the movement of the vessel caused our boilers to shut down as the automatic controls had been incorrectly set. The engineers had to return to manual control until we were far enough off the shore to risk stopping the vessel until adjustments made. As we proceeded towards our loading port of Kharg Island in Iran we discovered a fault in the hydraulic system which controlled the loading and discharge of our cargo and it would seem that grit had entered the system prior to it being assembled at the shipyard. Whether accidental or deliberate it should not have happened. This problem was beyond the ship's staff who had other duties to attend to. The ship was informed that a hydraulics engineer would join at Kharg Island.

One of the operating instructions the ship was given was that the cargo tanks had to be inerted with gas prior to and during loading and when the vessel was discharging. The machinery providing the gas failed prior to arrival at our loading port and so London was informed as we anchored and the engineers worked flat out endeavouring to make the plant operate. This was the month of August, the hottest time of year in the Gulf and these engineers were working in a very hot, restricted space. I had to order the chief engineer to his cabin for rest and point out that dead men were not what I wanted. All the time, pressure was being exerted by the US owners on our company. Meanwhile a specialist engineer was being flown out. I then informed our London office I was going to commence loading as the vessel, being new, had never carried an oil cargo. I saw no risk and no one in higher authority over-ruled me. The specialist engineer arrived and promptly fainted in the heat and it was twenty-four hours later before he started work. By this time we had been advised that we would load a half cargo and then proceed to Ras Tanura in Saudi Arabia to load the balance. In the meantime our cargo was loaded by having to operate the valves locally at the tanks instead of at the control room. By the time we departed from Klarg Island the inert system was still not in operation.

Our Ras Tanura call brought its own problems as we had no local charts of the area as the US owners had indicated we would not be loading in Saudi Arabia. We had to take a pilot for berthing and he was prepared to come out the extra mile to board us. Once alongside I asked the agent to supply us with the relevant charts to be told that none were available, but the harbour master would allow me to make my a copy from their own chart. I was then advised that when loading was completed we would be moved from the loading berth with pilot and tugs and anchored in the swinging area. Because we would have a draught of seventy-two feet when loaded, we would remain at anchor until there was sufficient water in the channel to give us a minimum clearance of six feet. On this information being given we were then to proceed out of the thirty mile channel to deeper water. We had on board 257,000 tons of crude oil giving a total displacement of 302,000 tons. By this time it was night as we carefully and slowly made our way out to open waters. During this passage I was aware of an extra man on the bridge who turned out to be the guarantee engineer sent out by the builder to join at Kharg Island and check on the problems. I suggested to him that he would be more useful with the chief engineer in the machinery space. He then told me that the last time he was here was as chief engineer in a Shell VLCC, when they had a black out due to sand being sucked into the vessel with the cooling water. He had informed our chief engineer of this hazard and decided he was better out of the way – hence his presence on the bridge. By this time we were half way along the channel and entered open waters without further incident but with considerable relief to the chief engineer and myself.

We now began our long haul round the Cape of Good Hope with our destination Bullen Bay at the Island of Curacao. As we departed the Gulf and entered the Arabian Sea it was the time of the South West monsoon which we were pushing into. One had to become used to seeing the deck forward of the bridge covered in white water and in the distance the forecastle head and foremast visible. The ship just pushed on with no pitching and tossing one would experience in a smaller vessel. Running down the South African coast, loaded tankers were obliged to be twenty-five miles off the nearest land, unless making port. We made a store call off Cape Town which would be either by helicopter or large launch depending on the weather. This was much looked forward to because of the mail sent and received and more reliable than at either end. However to the younger members of the ship's company it was very unsettling to see Cape Town five miles away, 'so near and yet so far'.

We then preceded to our discharge port, an oil terminal called Bullen Bay on the island of Curacao. The terminal gave us a target of thirty-six hours to discharge our quarter of a million tonnes of crude oil otherwise a penalty was imposed. Since it was our first discharge, I advised the terminal that we would discharge at what I considered a safe rate to make sure all equipment was operating correctly, our hydraulic fitter having completed his work. One of our engineer superintendents attended to learn of all our problems and our very hard worked chief engineer was relieved to have some well earned leave. We overstayed our terminal time by four hours which I thought very satisfactory and as the crew were on watches throughout initially there was no time to go ashore.

On departure, once everyone had had some decent rest, we commenced the big job of tank cleaning which involved carrying all the oily water in special slop tanks for discharge at our loading terminal. This period is the most dangerous time on a tanker as tanks are washed and gas freed. At this period I would take over the chief officer's bridge duties on the four–eight watches to allow him to devote his time to the cleaning operations. During this period we were heading into what is called the SE Trade winds and the ship, now empty, was pitching in the seas. Standing on the bridge one saw the bow rising and dipping 1,000 feet ahead of the bridge and see the ripple effect down the length of the ship and if you stood at the stern of the ship it was similar to standing at the end of a diving platform at a swimming pool, quite unsettling. When the first of these very large vessels came into service, some broke in half in heavy sea conditions when empty because they were too rigid. Now they are more flexible and much safer in coping with the ripple effect.

On our return to the Gulf, half of our crew left at the first loading port when their replacements joined and the chief officer and I stayed on till the ship was fully loaded and then handed over to our own reliefs. We two were out of luck however in flying home with Kuwait Airlines which did not serve alcohol and we had to make do with coca cola. Somewhat of a let down after a gruelling four and a half months.

After some time on leave I was contacted by our London office to say the ship had developed a major problem just prior to arriving to load another cargo. The vessel was now bound for Singapore during which time it was tank cleaning and gas freeing, prior to dry docking for repairs. A fracture of the steelwork in what was known as the collision bulkhead had developed which seriously affected the vessel's sea worthiness. Fortunately the vessel was still within the guarantee period of the ship's builders Swan Hunter on the Tyne. The American owners were not pleased and wanted everything made good including loss of earnings while the ship was out of service.

I was now instructed to proceed to Singapore and take over from the current master who was unwell. When I booked in at the hotel where I was to stay overnight I met up with the company engineering director who had been on the same flight but in first class. When we met up for breakfast the next morning, before going to the shipyard, we exchanged views of our previous night. I was at the back of the hotel and kept awake by the barking of dogs at a nearby dog pound. The poor man, in the best rooms to the front of the hotel, had been kept awake by telephone calls from ladies of pleasure offering him their services! This, I have to say, raised my spirits no end as he was a very sober Scots Presbyterian with no sense of humour!

On boarding the ship I took over from my colleague who was not in very good shape. He was taken to a hotel for the night where he collapsed and was taken to hospital. I was informed of this the next morning by our local agent and once I could find time I arranged to visit him. The hospital was one of the older ones and each ward was in a separate chalet in the grounds. With the assistance of a nurse I was shown the right ward and was told I could go in. To my surprise I found the patient strapped to his bed and asleep. I was somewhat concerned and withdrew to find the nurse. She told me that he had become some-what agitated earlier in the day and had bitten the doctor and so was sedated and secured for his own good. He was flown to the UK a couple of days later with a medical attendant and I departed with the vessel.

Pigeon Passenger 1978

I was Master of a VLCC from 1977 to end of 1979 trading between the Arabian Gulf and Curacao with crude oil for the USA. At that time the vessel was too big to use a US terminal.

When we passed Cape Town east or west bound, we took the opportunity to replenish our stores supplied either by helicopter or launch depending on the weather conditions, On one occasion, fully loaded westbound, we commenced storing just before sunset, completed after dark, and proceeded on to the West Indies. At dawn the following day the chief officer discovered he had a passenger. This was a pigeon which had landed when the vessel was undertaking storing in daylight and of course there was no land in sight. It did seem somewhat uneasy and we noted at the time that it was also ringed on one leg. It obviously and wisely decided to remain with the ship and became an additional lookout walking back and fore on the bridge wings. It was not encouraged into the wheelhouse except during rain storms where it messed up the place somewhat. It was supplied with food and water and all in all had a comfortable passage.

As the vessel approached Curacao about five miles away it took off without a backward glance. However, we speculated as to whether the first bird watcher, pigeon fancier who checked its ring markings would be claiming a world record for a pigeon flying from Cape Town to the West Indies with the SE Trade Winds. If so it would have become a local hero and only those on the *Everett F Wells* knew the truth – and our lips were sealed.

This thought occurs to me every time we see news coverage of thousands of twitchers converging on a spot where some enthusiast has seen a lesser spotted warbler known only in Russia. Did he fly or was he carried in comfort like our pigeon?

To Russia with Oranges
Winchester Universal 1980

In the summer of 1980 I was master of one of our refrigerated, usually referred to as reefer, ships called the *Winchester Universal*. We were instructed to proceed to Agadir and Casablanca to load a full cargo of oranges destined for the Moscow Olympic Games.

In Casablanca I had the agent arrange to visit the ship to see our electrical officer who was not well. I had expected the doctor to say he required hospital treatment but said he was alright to sail and prescribed some medication. We duly sailed bound for the Baltic and the following afternoon the purser/catering officer called me to the electrical officer's cabin where he was dead in his chair. The company was immediately informed and would contact the next of kin. I then said that unless otherwise informed by head office we would have a burial at sea as landing a dead body in most countries caused considerable problems. We held the burial with the ship stopped and position and details of the event recorded in the Official Logbook. We then continued on passage. British ships carried a very informative book called the *Shipmasters Medical Guide* and at the back of the book was the form of service for a burial at sea.

We were now instructed to unload our cargo at a port called Ventspil in Lithuania which meant traversing the Kiel Canal where we would take fuel and fresh water on board at the end of our transit. We were informed that we would be at anchor outside Ventspil until a discharging berth was available. In the meantime, I requested a British Consulate official to attend the ship at Kiel to record the death at sea and obtain all the necessary documents for endorsement.

We arrived at Kiel on a Saturday evening and the Consul from Hamburg came on board with his wife. I don't think he was best pleased at having his weekend spoiled. I said I would arrange for his wife to have tea or coffee in the officer's lounge which would be quiet as everyone was busy. However, he asked if she could remain in my cabin while we carried out our business and I provided her with refreshments. I was somewhat put out when she started to question the procedures I had followed without her husband making any comment. In the end, I had to ask him if this was correct. The ship departed from Kiel and when we anchored off the port of Ventspil we were ordered by the port authorities not to use our radar while at anchor without their permission. We now realised we were within the control of the Soviet Union. After dark each evening searchlights would sweep the beach off which we and other vessels were at anchor. All part of state security I was told. Not sure whether it was to prevent people leaving or trying to enter the country.

When we finally tied up in port there became a very interesting time for me. Our agents for a start was a department of the State and on arrival the agent's one man and one lady boarded along with the immigration, customs and police officials. The male agent, the manager of the office in the port, informed me that there would be someone on duty twenty-four hours a day in their office ashore and these turned out to be ladies on shift round the clock, all fluent in English. All the crew were checked individually and their seaman's discharge books checked. Each man was issued with a pass which had to be shown to the armed border police at the bottom of the gangway when going ashore. There was also another border policeman stationed on shore at the bow of the vessel. Everyone was told that no items were allowed ashore that the guard thought unsuitable which included books, magazines and newspapers and that everyone had to be back on board by midnight. The one exception was the captain which I found curious and had possibly ulterior motives. I did point out that at my age I was unlikely to take up the privilege!

When cargo work commenced it was interesting to discover that each gang unloading the boxes of oranges were given a target to meet each shift. If the target was not met, their wages were reduced accordingly and they had to work very hard to achieve these targets. Very different to the work practices in UK ports at that time. The workforce was very poor and we even found them scavenging for food and even taking the empty beer cans ashore.

The lady agents when they visited the ship I found most interesting. They would accept a cup of tea or coffee and would ask to look at my book shelves. I offered to let them take books and return them if they wished. Each one told me this was not allowed and every time they left the ship they were searched even to their handbags. They told me that some of the books could be bought ashore but that the Russian translations were quite different in places to the original. One of the ladies, all Russian by the way, no Lithuanians, told me that her husband had recently been transferred here as the manager of a large chemical plant. This lady, a graduate teacher of English, had applied for a teacher's position after they settled here. She was informed there were no vacancies at the schools; she could have a position at the agency but it would involve shift work. She said that would not suit her as she had two young teenage daughters and was told she had no choice and would start work the following day. It was indeed illuminating to talk to these ladies during the short occasions they called on duty.

There was a seaman's club within the docks which had a bar and a variety of local drinks including sparkling wine. There was also a games room and a juke box, pay as you play. There was a dance hall and a number of attractive young ladies to dance with. It turned out that the young girls were not allowed to board ships, which dashed any hopes of a party on board, nor were they allowed to meet up with any seafarer out-with the confines of the club which dampened the ardour of some of our younger crew. Two of our young seamen missed the midnight deadline one night by a couple of hours. Next morning they had to appear before me with the border police who withdrew their passes and informed if they returned to Russia on another ship they would not be allowed ashore. They objected but were dismissed. When the officials left, the two culprits came to see me and complained about the ban and I reminded them that it was out of my hands. They said that they were going to write with their complaint to the National Union of Seamen and I offered them pen and paper as at that time I knew that their General Secretary Jim Slater was holidaying in Russia with his Russian colleagues and being royally entertained I was sure. I did suggest that their letter would get little attention. They were not amused.

The purser/catering officer decided he would have to replenish some stores as when we left Ventspil we had no idea where we would be ordered to load. We then discovered that food in general was in short supply and especially meat. We were told the agents could buy a pig from the many small holdings around but we would have to pay for the whole animal as it were and they would slaughter and dress if for us. The work force, unloading our oranges, were searched at the end of each shift to make sure they were not taking an orange out of the dock area.

I would take a walk ashore in the afternoon for some exercise and that I found most interesting. Certainly all were equal there and a gang repairing the railway line were all women wielding pickaxes and heavy hammers. On the outskirts of the town every little house had a patch of garden and every space taken up by vegetables growing. What shops there were had little or nothing to display though a couple of churches I found open were quite beautiful inside. In general, the people I met appeared very poor and worn. On two occasions I was approached by locals, the first time by a young family with a motorbike and sidecar who were obviously lost and came to me for directions. Needless to say I was of no help nor could communicate and the young wife was helpless with laughter. On another day, I was approached by an angry old lady at a bus stop, very annoyed I could gather at the non appearance of a bus for which she seemed to blame me. When I related this during our evening meal the general consensus was that they had taken me for a plain clothed policeman by my appearance. They could have been right.

When we sailed we now knew that many people quite close to us were not as fortunate as we were. Our orders were to proceed to the English Channel and I was relieved by launch off Dover for leave and appointment to my first container ship.

MV *Barcelona* 1980

When I joined the MV *Barcelona* as Master, it was the company's only containership at the time. The ship had been chartered to Zim Line, an Israeli company trading from the Mediterranean to North America, Japan, Taiwan, Hong Kong and back. The ship's original name was *Table Bay* and had been initially employed in the South African Trade.

I joined *MV Barcelona* at Barcelona with my wife and once we had completed the discharge of cargo at other ports we proceeded to Malta for dry docking and some repairs. When we arrived off Valetta it was blowing a full gale. The decision was taken that we would not attempt to dock until the weather had moderated. The dry dock we were to use had been built and paid for by the Chinese government to service the largest vessels and we were to be its first customer. In time the weather improved and the harbour pilot boarded after a bumpy ride out to us. We discussed our docking plan and elected for the assistance of two tugs because the vessel was empty and riding high and the wind still fresh. We had a very tense time docking because of the weather conditions and being watched by what seemed like hundreds of tourists from the adjacent cliff. We finally berthed safely and I invited the pilot to my cabin for a restorative drink after a very competent performance. I commented on his name Thornton, and how it was common in Scotland. Apparently his father came from Glasgow originally and had been called up in the First War and joined the HLI. They were sent to Gallipoli where he had fought in that disastrous affair. At the end of the war they were returning home and the troopship called at Valetta to obtain fresh water. He and some others decided to jump ship rather than return to Glasgow. With the war over, the authorities were not bothered and there were fewer men to pay. His father found employment and married and his son had gone to sea, obtained all his qualifications, and was now a pilot. In turn, his son was captain of the Malta to

Sicily ferry. I was very pleased to learn that when we came to leave the dry dock he would take us out.

The day before our repairs were completed the agent asked if the Chinese management could be shown around the vessel. This was arranged and at the end came to my accommodation for afternoon tea. The group were the dock manager, engineering manager and the accountant all three men. The two ladies were the political commissar and the interpreter. My wife was in the party and even she could not raise a smile. Everything was passed through the commissar. Time to go and I took the party to the lift which would take us to the deck where the gangway was situated. This lift ran from the ship's navigation bridge to the engine room/control room with stops at each deck and doors at either end. One door led to the main stairway and the other to changing rooms, pantries, store rooms etc. When we arrived at the gangway deck I managed to press the wrong button and instead of the door into the stairway opening the other door opened into the engineers' changing room. It was filled with engineers who had just finished for the day, who were getting out of their boiler suits ready for the shower. Both the engineers and the Chinese party were taken aback but I had achieved a reaction from the Chinese. By the time I had closed the door even the lady commissar had lost her composure!

When on hire to the Zim Line, the owners paid for weather routing advice to the Master, saying their expertise saved money on fuel and weather damage. I received weather routeing on departing from Valencia in Spain to Halifax in Canada. Even with my own information I could see we were heading for a rough passage. We then received a change of route and again I informed them of the situation ahead and had another change. This time we were really being thrown about and this confirmed to me that containers were safe if properly secured. When I explained again and said what next they replied "choose your own course" which I did, having said I should have done that from the start. The result was we were thirty-six hours late at Halifax which certainly upset our schedule. In due course we were due to leave Long Beach in California bound for Kobe in Japan. I was then given two different routes by two different routeing experts. One American and one British. One sent us via Hawaii and one north of the Aleution Islands. I enquired of our agent as to which one to take and he said it was up to me. I elected to go up to the Aleution Islands but keep south of the islands as I had no charts of that area. We were fortunate as when in the area a full storm crossed ahead of us to the north of the islands where we might have been had we had the right charts. So much for the work of experts as consultants on weather.

On the return passage from the Far East we had departed Long Beach California for the Panama Canal. During the first night at sea a fire broke out in the engine room at about 4 a.m. The duty engineer was fortunately doing his rounds when a fuel pipe fractured and sprayed hot oil over even hotter machinery. The alarm was sounded and the ship's emergency party entered the engine room with equipment and masks to battle through smoke and fumes, and reached the duty engineer who was just holding his own. The fire was eventually extinguished but the damage was considerable. The ship had six diesel generators and normally two were required at any one time to provide power with others on standby or under overhaul. The damage to the control equipment was considerable and now the machines had to be manually controlled and only two of the generators were serviceable. We had a big problem as we were due at the Canal in two day's time and on the request for transit one had to declare that all plant on board was in good order. At the same time, we were aware if the vessel was refused entry we could be held up for weeks for repairs and spare parts with a big cargo from the east on board. With an excellent engineering department led by a very good friend and great engineer we decided we could manage the Canal transit, if luck was on our side, and not to admit our shortcomings. This was what we were paid for and carried out much of the time. As a large container ship we had to take on four American Canal Pilots and commenced our daylight transit. We were very mindful of our situation and I kept in constant touch with the team in the engine room. Just before the last locks the pilots indicated we would have to anchor for at least an hour to allow the other ship to clear the locks. This was fortuitous as when I informed the chief engineer he told me one of the remaining two generators was giving concern and with the delay he would now be able to deal with the problem. He managed and we cleared the locks and headed for the open sea. The Pilots bade their farewell and pleased with the smooth passage, I urged the Chief Officer to get them to their launch as soon as possible. As we headed into the Gulf of Mexico, and by this time in darkness, we heaved a sigh of relief. About an hour later we had a total blackout power failure and had to stop and carry out emergency repairs using our emergency generators. We were fortunate and after two hours of hard work we were underway again en route for Kingston, Jamaica with the engineers continuing their efforts. When we reached New York, the company had flown out additional electrical staff to restore the ship to reliable power.

We had a lighter moment on arriving off Kingston. Our scheduled time of arrival was 6 a.m, about an hour before sunrise. However, we could not raise the port control by VHF which the chief officer was dealing with. He was also an RNR officer and very much into correct naval procedures on the phone. At last he received an answer from the port control operator in a very relaxed West Indian drawl which sounded as if he had just wakened up and that was probably true. He then informed us that we could not expect a pilot before 8 a.m. The chief officer then repeated the message in a very snappy manner ending up with 'Roger and Out'. There was a long pause and then this operator came back with "Who is this man Roger"? It cheered us up immensely. When the pilot boarded he also looked as though he was just up and I felt I had to keep a watchful eye on him.

Our last port of call in North America was Halifax Nova Scotia in January, the middle of the Canadian winter and very cold. When we departed, bound for the Mediterranean, on leaving port we entered what is known as the Labrador Current which comes down from the Arctic past Labrador and Nova Scotia and the water is very cold This is the current which brings the icebergs down to the North Atlantic. There was a very cold North Easterly wind blowing and as the sea spray landed on board it froze. Even our bridge windows were frozen despite being nearly eighty feet above sea level. Then about eighty or so miles from the shore the sea water spray melted and our windows cleared. This showed we had now reached the influence of the Gulf Stream which flowed in the opposite direction coming from the warm water of the Gulf of Mexico; the main reason why we in the UK have a moderate climate. The change in the readings of sea water temperatures showed up very dramatically in our bridge read out. The thought of the huge movements of sea water flowing in opposite directions has always fascinated me.

MV Edinburgh Universal 1980

Prior to my being transferred to the container vessels I had five months as master on a refrigerated vessel usually employed carrying fruit. It was a very handy and fast vessel and had been bought from a German company and was nearly new. I joined in the UK and we proceeded to Porto Bolivar in Ecuador to load bananas for Jeddah. It was a new trade for me and we had to give an accurate time of arrival of forty-eight hours beforehand. The bananas we were to load were then harvested to be in the right green condition when the ship arrived. I did not know until we arrived there that the port had a very bad record for theft and the army was employed patrolling the port allegedly to prevent it. Our agent advised us to take all precautions and have only one entrance to our accommodation available and have it manned continuously by a crew member. The vessel loaded through the night and day and the first morning after we started loading our life raft was stolen. The officer of the watch had heard a splash just as the sun was rising, and on investigation, found that our life raft had been thrown off the boat deck and was being towed away by a launch. He appealed for help from the soldiers on the jetty but they just shrugged their shoulders. When I raised this with the agent he said this was not unusual as the army did not check the harbour waters. He then told me about the German ship which had loaded here prior to our arrival. Thieves had managed to get access to the chart room and had stolen the vessels chronometer which was essential for navigation prior to the days of sat nav. This was serious and no way could a new chronometer be obtained at short notice. The ship's master was taken by the agent to the general market where he had to buy back his own chronometer as the seller allegedly bought it in good faith whilst to go through the police would have delayed the vessel for days. One lighter aspect of our stay was the visit by three young Americans two men and a girl, Jehovah witnesses. They were based in Quito the capital for at least a year on the basic

162

living allowance while evangelising. A request came, if it was in order, for them to have lunch as they were very hungry, and then hot showers. They were back the next day for the same treatment with little evangelising, just anxious for company and English spoken. The downside was that the third mate fell in love with the girl, who was very attractive, and lived in a state of euphoria until we had reached the Panama Canal. I often wonder if he was able to follow this up as he was relieved not long afterwards.

We unloaded our bananas in Jeddah and any banana that was not still green was left on board to be disposed of. Though not much, it meant that the cook used bananas in many imaginative ways and considerably reduced the daily rate for some time until the ship's company had had enough of bananas! Our final part of the cargo was for discharge at Hodeida in North Yemen. We had arrived off the port on the day of the wedding of the Prince of Wales and Diana. Ahead of us was a Royal Navy frigate coming to show the flag and he picked up the only port pilot and so we just followed in. The navy ship anchored and so did we until we received orders to come alongside a floating pontoon to discharge our cargo. This was to the relief of the RN ship who insisted we were too close to it but assurances were given that we would do him no harm!

Our agent when he boarded told me the Navy ship was holding a reception on board that evening for VIP guests in honour of the Royal Wedding and that the guests would be taken by the naval launch from the pontoon to the ship and so our cargo work would cease before then. We watched with interest the guests arriving in their finery having to embark on the launch from a very dirty pontoon. Shortly after the ferrying of guests was started a very smart young midshipman arrived at my cabin to say his VHF communication with his ship had failed and could we help so we immediately gave him access to our equipment. He was very relieved but it did not get us an invitation to the party. A short time later our very agitated purser, chief steward arrived at the cabin door with a very drunk local policeman brandishing his firearm and demanding beer. As alcoholic drink was banned in Yemen and our liquor bond locked and sealed there was no way we were going to break the rules. It was quite unpleasant but we managed to lead him back to the shore and promptly raised our gangway without being shot at. I did think of calling up the frigate to request protection of a British ship but thought it might spoil a good party on board. Where this man had obtained his liquor goodness knows but I hope he was elsewhere when the guests came ashore.

Later, on the same ship, we were bound for Jeddah again with a cargo of fruit from Seattle and Long Beach. We encountered very bad weather as we approached the Philippines caused by a typhoon travelling in the South China Sea. One evening our radio officer picked up a message from the Japanese Coastguard giving the position of a ship in distress and taking water. This we acknowledged and indicated that we were about three hours distance and would proceed as it was not far off our present route. The radio officer then tried to contact the ship with little success. Before we had reached the distress area we passed no fewer than three vessels going the other way which must have passed the distressed vessel without offering assistance. We eventually picked up a target on our radar and managed to make contact to be told they were abandoning their vessel and suddenly the target disappeared from the radar screen. The sea at this time was still very rough but the wind had abated. Our crew was on standby with all the equipment necessary and it was a clear night. Two lifeboats were sighted and with us being loaded, and a very handy vessel, we were able to make an approach and come along side the two boats and picked up the men, eighteen in total. The master did not have much English allegedly, but the chief engineer was able to tell me they were Panamanian flag, South Korean crew and Japanese owned and gave me an address in Tokyo. I informed our London office with all details with the hope they could find the owners to accept responsibility for the crew. Meantime the Japanese coastguard requested we proceed and rendezvous with their cutter which would have taken another day and additional miles steamed and the rescued seamen did not wish another small boat adventure. I informed the coastguard that we would proceed as normal to Singapore and land them there. London was also able to find the owner responsible who would liaise with the Singapore Authorities to land the men . In the meantime, we had no spare cabins so these men were settled in our lounge, mess room and alleyways and were fed and watered.

A very amusing incident happened later on, about 07.00 hrs. The engine room ratings had not been needed and slept through the incident and came into the pantry to make tea. One was a chap called Charlie Chin, a Liverpool Chinese, who had a shocked look on his face when he encountered three Koreans in his pantry. For a moment he thought they were from outer space. Later in the day we thought we should make sure there were no medical emergencies to deal with and then the chief steward informed me all eighteen were indicating some symptoms. I told him to speak to the second officer's wife who was travelling, and I knew was a nursing sister, and ask for her help. When she arrived only two remained for treatment! Two days later we passed Singapore and landed the crew onto a launch with all matters dealt with without involving the ship. They were quite sorry to leave as they had never been so well fed before but it was good that we had the vessel to ourselves again. We were glad to have been of assistance and all details were written up in our official log book. All British flag vessels have a duty in law to render assistance where possible. By the time I retired, so many ships were sailing under flags of convenience with no government to enforce them, the rules have largely been overlooked for different reasons, but mainly because of the costs incurred.

Incidents that come to mind

We were on one ship loading fruit for Jeddah in Long Beach USA. The loading was taking place through the night and in the early morning I saw the duty officer and inquired as to whether it had been a quiet night. The only minor disturbance was caused by our young steward wheeling the ship's cook along the quayside in a supermarket trolley, the latter being out for the count as it were. Once the cook was returned to his cabin the young lad had his story to tell.

Four or five of the crew had headed for an evening ashore including the young steward who was a teetotaller. Whilst the others went looking for refreshments and entertainment this young lad went exploring round the town. When the steward was heading back to the ship he came across the cook, in the street, very much the worse for wear, his companions having gone their own ways. The cook had no money left and the young lad not enough for a taxi so he obtained a trolley and managed to get the cook into it, who then passed out. To get back to the ship, he had to push this trolley along one of these US highway interchanges for over a mile with no pedestrian footway, before reaching the safety of the docks. He was fortunate it was not too busy and he was not picked up by the police. I have to say the cook was on duty for breakfast if not very enthusiastic. I made sure to remind him how indebted he was to his shipmate as he could have missed the ship as we sailed at midday.

That same day, I went to see the chief engineer, a real character, and a very good engineer. I could not find him and in asking one of his men if they had seen him was told he had said he was going on the quayside to read the ship's draught. Not something that usually concerned an engineer. I decided to go and look for him on the quayside as we were due to sail in a couple of hours. One of the longshoremen told me that he thought he saw him go to the café at the end of the dock area. There I found him clutching a glass of beer in his hand, mesmerized by the girl behind the bar who was topless! The chief was short sighted at the best of times but the lady was getting a bit uneasy at his stare. I broke into his trance and we returned to the ship with him remarking it was never like that in Clydebank where he came from!

Our next port was Seattle and the chief asked me if I would like an evening ashore as he was going for what he called a 'a small sensation'. I declined the offer as a quiet night was what I was looking forward to. The chief would always engage with people and was very entertaining. Next morning when I saw him, bright and breezy as usual, I enquired if he had an enjoyable evening. He told me that he had met a very pleasant married couple of about his own age. At one stage, as it was getting late, the wife said it was about time they went home. The husband and wife then departed with the man saying he would be back. Quite soon afterwards the husband returned and the chief assumed his wife was safely home to which he had said "no I have just locked her in the car in the car park and told her to be quiet till I came back" Even our chief was a bit unsettled by this . To make amends he then invited his new friend to bring his wife aboard the ship the next evening. Despite misgivings on the chief engineer's part the couple appeared with another couple and a very social evening was had. All seemed to be serene but maybe this had happened before.

Another occasion comes to mind which took place in Curacao. Five of us were relieved after five months on the large tanker. We had to spend one night in the Hilton Hotel as the ship was departing and our flight to Miami was not until the following day. The group consisted of two young engineer officers, the radio officer, chief engineer and myself. I had suggested that once settled in their rooms they would join me for a drink before our meal. The chief was the first to arrive looking somewhat put out and said he had been propositioned by a Venezuelan lady in the lift who had invited him into her room. She was obviously wealthy but not attractive according to the chief. In the middle of this story the young radio officer arrived and when the chief finished he leapt to his feet and headed for the lifts 'to try his luck' as he left. The spirit of youth we decided. In due course he returned looking somewhat subdued and when questioned had to admit that his only contact was another man who had propositioned him. We were suitably sympathetic! At breakfast the next morning the chief and I were sitting at a table our backs to the wall and had exchanged views. I was then suddenly aware that the chief was no longer beside me and then I saw him under the table. He whispered that the lady of his meeting of the previous night had come in with two men and he did not want to be recognised. I sat back and ordered. I also identified the lady, not attractive and accompanied by two large men, they could have been minders or one of them could have been the lady's husband. Fortunately they only had coffee and departed. The chief then surfaced and had his breakfast! After a discreet enquiry we were told that rich Venezuelans were regular patrons of the hotel because of the casino where they laundered their money.

We then flew to Miami where again we had an overnight stay. Once settled in, I arranged to meet the others in the cocktail bar before dinner. Like many of these lounges in the US it was very dimly lit. One almost had to feel your way to a table. Once seated a young lady arrived to take our orders. Her total uniform appeared to be a bikini and at the sight of her I thought the young engineers would lose control. They had been locked up, as it were, on the tanker for five months. I settled them down with a cold beer. After our meal, they were away to enjoy the night life having been reminded to meet me at reception at 10.00 hrs the following morning to proceed to the airport. At that time, the two young engineers told me they were going to stay on for a few days as they had such a good time the previous night and were now on leave. I had to explain to them that we were all on a transit visa attached to the plane we were to board for the UK and if they did not board they would be picked up by the US Immigration and locked up. I understood their disappointment as with money and single I think they thought it the Promised Land. We all boarded but I have the idea they held it against me rather than Immigration.

Some time following, a group of us were flying home from Curacao. It was a weekend and the US Consul was closed so we could not get a visa but the agent assured us our tickets were sufficient. Not so, when we arrived at Miami we were placed in a secure enclosure in the main hall at the airport with a guard for four hours until our flight was called then escorted to the check-in desk. We were not amused but over the years I have learned to be very careful with Immigration Officers whatever the country. You do not exchange jokes with them!

Introduction to the Container Ships

Container Fleet Line was formed to operate the original vessels of Overseas Containers Limited to Australia and New Zealand. With the best of intentions the conditions for sea staff were very good when the operation started in 1968. The accommodation was excellent as was the catering and there were officers and ratings bars provided. There were changes of duty which included General Purpose (GP) ratings. All these changes were agreed with the respective trade unions. At the beginning of each voyage the crew would elect a member as their union spokesperson. This was something I was familiar with in my previous company. In the early days of operating, these ships' industrial disputes, principally in Australia, New Zealand and the UK, resulted in the vessels being frequently delayed in port with crews becoming used to too much leisure time in some very acceptable surroundings. As the fleet expanded and the newer vessels were diesel engined, the delays were fewer, and the port times reduced to what was expected of an efficient container ship operation. This was not acceptable or appreciated by some of the ratings in particular.

In 1981 the fleet management was reorganised to control all the vessels in the OCL group. I was then fortunate to join the company with *Table Bay* on the South African service. It was a big change for me at fifty-one and with a new management to work under. The chief engineer transferred with me, a very good friend and shipmate over the years, which was good for both of us.

Initially it was a swift learning curve but I soon came to the conclusion that there was a feeling that the crew and their wishes were more important than the efficient operation of the vessel. After eleven years as master in a variety of vessels, I felt confident in being able to run the vessel efficiently. Any individual who did not respond to warnings was entered in the ship's official logbook as required by the Merchant Shipping Act of 1972. However, I was hearing from some sources that the logging of individuals was not common practice. I was at the same time hearing some stories of crew behaviour in the past which I found difficult to believe. Names of individuals employed on the ships were mentioned, who were known as organisers of discontent or unacceptable behaviour as far as I was concerned. When discussing these matters with my superiors, they agreed with my views.

On my way to rejoining my ship at Tilbury I made my visit to head office. While there I took the chance of checking the crew who were joining. Among others was the name of a seaman who had been frequently mentioned as a nuisance on board. I raised this with our head of the crewing department and to my surprise he told me he was considering promoting him to petty officer deck at the end of the voyage. I said I would report on his suitability on completion of the trip. At the same time, I was informed that the chief officer joining had been in command for two voyages in an acting capacity and was expected to get his permanent command at the end of this voyage.

Once the vessel had sailed from the UK, I was informed that the seaman mentioned earlier, was now the union spokesman, having put himself forward for the position and no one objecting. It was not long before he was making himself known over trivial matters and in an irritating manner. I asked of the chief officer if this was his usual behaviour and he was non committal; I then inquired of the bosun a man of long experience, what he thought or felt. He told me he was a trouble maker whatever ship he was on and appeared to get away with it. According to what he had been told by other masters, they were not given backing to take action by head office and that this seaman had direct access to the NUS London office. I reminded the chief officer to warn the seaman when his behaviour was out of line and if necessary bring him before me. By this time I was beginning to think that the chief officer was nervous of this man. It all came to a head when the vessel docked at Auckland New Zealand. By company instructions and Board of Trade regulations, all ships personnel had to obtain a pass from either the master or chief officer to have friends or visitors on board. All visitors had to be ashore by 23.00 hrs. In the event of fire or accident the officer in charge would know exactly who was on board.

I immediately had a request for a meeting with the union delegate which was arranged with the chief officer present. At this meeting I was told these regulations were unacceptable and no way would his members comply. In the past, on other ships, friends were allowed to stay over-night and be fed if required. I said this is how it would be on this vessel and everyone who did not comply would be entered in the ship's official logbook. I also said I was taking notes of all of which he was telling me for the record of which he would have a copy. He then informed me that he was going to call all the union members on board out on strike. I told him to go ahead and arrange a ballot of his members as soon as possible and let me know the result. I would then advise London of the decision. He left my office and I told the chief officer to have the bosun muster the men as soon as possible and remind the men of the government and company regulations in force. In due course a ballot was held and the one to vote for a strike was the union delegate. This was all recorded in the official log book and the regulations observed by the ship's company.

But the following morning at sailing time, the shore police advised the ship that a known drug addict from ashore was on board. A search was made and a female person was found with a crew member, both under the influence of drink and drugs. The lady was handed over to the police and once the ship sailed the seaman was brought before me to have the offence recorded in the official log book. In the next couple of days, the chief engineer advised me that this man was a safety risk in the machinery spaces and he refused to work on deck. This was also recorded and arrangements made to have the man repatriated to the UK with copies of entries from the log book for the company to deal with in London.

Meantime, the New Zealand customs had issued instructions to all the ships in port that all ships' bars in recreation rooms on board had to be closed up one hour before sailing. Once again the union spokesman objected to this and his complaint was duly recorded in the official log book, but not withstanding, the regulation was carried out. On route for Melbourne the pilot boarded around midnight outside the entrance to Port Philip Bay. The entrance through the Heads is narrow and with strong tidal currents. The helmsman was changed and the relief was the union spokesman. On reaching a critical alteration of course he put the ship's wheel in the opposite direction to the pilot's orders. I was able to correct this immediately before any damage and was then aware the helmsman was smelling of drink and had him replaced. After the vessel was berthed, I had the helmsman appear before me with witnesses to have an entry made in the official log book of the incident and an official warning given to the seaman concerned.

In the course of the homeward passage other incidents arose concerning the behaviour of this man. He also informed me, in front of witnesses, that he was reporting me to the National Union of Seamen at their headquarters in London. I advised him that he was perfectly entitled to do so if he thought fit.

Our first port in Europe was Flushing and the company informed me that an official from the NUS would board the ship to investigate a complaint of discontent by the crew. At Flushing the union official boarded and made himself known to me before meeting the crew. He said at this time that he thought there was a clash of personalities between the crew spokesman and me and it could all be settled amicably. I told him that this was a disciplinary matter with a crew member and not a personality clash. I suggested that he should carry on and meet all his members of the crew and then to let me know of their complaints as individuals or collectively. By the time the ship was ready to sail I was told the union official had left without making any comment to me.

The ship was due in Tilbury on the Saturday morning but the crew change would not take place until the Monday around midday. Any wives who wished to join over the weekend were issued with passes. The chief officer, to my surprise said he would not have his wife down as he expected trouble with the crew. In fact, there was no problem with the ship's company and the change of personnel took place on the Monday.

I had left word that the seaman, union spokesman, was informed that his performance was to be reported to head office with relevant log entries. I was in my cabin dealing with the company superintendent and marine surveyors when I was advised that the seaman in question had said that he had never been warned about his conduct by the chief officer. When I asked the chief officer he admitted that this was true. I was not amused and proceeded to see the man in person informing him I was dismissing him from the ship and it was for the company to decide his future.

I had been informed before going on leave that I would not be returning to the ship and was to be appointed to the *Tokyo Bay* which was on the European Far East service. I must add that when I arrived to join the *Tokyo Bay* in Southampton, the bosun came down the gangway to fetch my bags. He was the man who had told me on the last ship of the trouble maker. He was in high spirits as he had just heard that the seaman in question had been dismissed by the company. I was pleased to get the news and it spread quite fast around the fleet and I was very pleased with the support I had from the Fleet Management. I found that provided you followed the correct procedures, which did involve considerable time and typing, satisfactory results could be achieved.

SS *Canberra* – A Near Miss

I was master of the TMV *Table Bay* a container ship trading between the UK/North Europe to South Africa at the time of the Falklands war.

North bound from South Africa, as the war was ended, the vessel was having mechanical problems, due to having taken on board contaminated fuel in South Africa. On arrival at the Solent I advised the pilot about our mechanical problems and that this might affect our manoeuvrability. As we approached Southampton port we were aware of the TSS *Canberra* berthed at the main quay with flags flying after her triumphal return from the Falklands war.

As we approached the container terminal we made fast two tug boats at our stern. Once abreast of the *Canberra* we had to turn *Table Bay* 180 degrees so that we could approach the container terminal stern first and so facilitate the cargo handling and allow an easier departure from the berth on completion of cargo. There was limited space for this manoeuvre but was normal procedure. As we started our swing the vessel was still making a little way through the water and as we were reaching half way into our swing and our bow was pointing directly at the midships section of the *Canberra*. Both our engines were ordered astern and refused to start while the vessel still with headway continued towards *Canberra*. The two tugs were doing their very best to stop our progress and the officer at our bow was regularly reporting our reducing distance from the other ship. He said later he was even considering putting his arms out to stop them colliding.

As this was unfolding I was already imagining the headlines in the next morning's papers. "British flagged ship manages to do what the Argentina forces were unable to do – seriously damage the *Canberra* with possibly a dramatic picture and of course the telling by-line "ship's master refuses to comment". However we managed to stop the vessel, aided by the tugs, with only feet to spare and then had them tow us stern first to our berth and made secure without engines. The chief engineer joined the pilot and me to discuss our near brush with fame and enjoyed a medical dram to sooth our nerves. To compound our problems it was a Bank Holiday weekend and we could not obtain spares so the ship's staff had to work round the clock to make temporary repairs to allow the vessel to sail on time. Just another day in the life of seafaring.

Tolaga Bay

In 1982 I rejoined my ship. It had been renamed *Tolaga Bay* as it was now to be employed on the New Zealand and Australian trade. Incidentally, this was to be the third consecutive Christmas I would be in this vessel under three different names *Barcelona* in Hong Kong, *Table Bay* in Durban and *Tolaga Bay* in Botany Bay, Sydney.

As the vessel was making its first call in New Zealand, and was the largest container vessel to do so at that time, the Company were to make an occasion of it. *Tolaga Bay* was one of the original landing points of Captain Cook's voyage and was now a small town, In fact, that year was the centenary year of the local school founded by the settlers

When we arrived at Auckland we took on board two passengers, both elders of the original Maori tribe from Tolaga Bay. The Chieftain had been invited but he decided he was too old anb sent these two other gentlemen, the younger of whom was also a member of parliament. I was informed that when the ship arrived at Wellington we would receive the traditional Maori welcome. In the meantime, I was given the traditional Maori reply with which I would be expected to respond. The two elders, who had joined us, drafted out a copy phonetically which I had to learn before arriving at Wellington! I was also informed that a small reception would be held on board after the welcoming ceremony. First question from me was how many to cater for and I was told around twenty-five. Having been involved in events like this before I told the chief steward to cater for fifty at least. The old Boy Scout motto 'Be Prepared' always holds good.

On route from Auckland to Wellington, we took the ship in as close as was safe to Tolega Bay where the Chief and many of his extended family were on the beach. We exchanged greetings with Gisborne Radio and sounded the traditional three long blasts on the ship's siren of farewell. Then back to learning my speech.

The vessel arrived at Wellington around 06.00 hrs and the welcoming ceremony took place on the quayside at 10.00 hrs. As you know from the All Blacks show before rugby internationals, the ceremony was impressive and of course in traditional garb and with traditional music and singing. The vessel was then blessed by an Anglican Maori priest. After that came the traditional Maori greeting of touching noses. This was the photo opportunity the press were waiting for and the attractive Maori lady and I had to repeat it to suit the photographers much to the enjoyment of the crew who were watching.

The welcoming party was then invited on board as the cargo operations resumed. In all, we entertained about seventy people and as I recall the officers lunch disappeared as well. It was a very pleasant social occasion but had to end. The Anglican priest thanked us and invited the guests to sing the traditional Maori farewell. It was wonderful and we were all very moved by it as everyone departed in good order and spirits. Our office staff thought they might stay a little longer but I reminded them we were departing at 18.00 hrs and I would be up all night and so the party was over as we went our separate ways.

On that same voyage we spent Christmas Day at Botany Bay container terminal in Australia. No cargo was worked on that day and so we had an unhurried excellent Christmas lunch. As the festivities continued I decided that a walk ashore would be the answer for me. Once outside the terminal gate I found myself next to the Botany Bay cemetery and in walking around it I realised it was the original resting place from the days of the first settlement. From the grave stones I could read it was a history of Australia as we now know it. I found it very moving. It was also very hot being midsummer there and there was no shade in the whole area. Life had been unbelievably bad in those days.

MV *Tokyo Bay*

I joined this ship in 1983, and in her time she was one of the largest container ships around. Nowadays they are more than twice as big. She was one of five built by Ocean Steamships or better known as the Blue Funnel Line and I was the first person appointed Master of one of these ships who was not a Blue Funnel man. This vessel was on the European Far East service with which I was not familiar. However, I had a senior chief officer with me who was excellent. Alister Leslie, and also a very good chief engineer called Alan Jones. I could not ask for more.

On my first voyage, we dry docked in Yokohama for routine repairs and inspection of our two large diesel engines which had been fitted one year before, replacing steam turbines which had become too expensive to operate. The time gave me an excellent chance to get to know the ship and familiarise myself with the Japanese way of working and learn something of their etiquette in dealing with them. They were efficient and our agents, Squires, were very good.

Prior to completion, the shipyard management entertained us at a Japanese restaurant where we sat cross legged at the table and enjoyed very good, if somewhat different food and drank saki. Towards the end of the evening we were introduced to karaoke which was very popular at the time. The chief engineer and I both refused the offer of singing but the chief officer and first engineer took front stage and could not be stopped. The London superintendent engineer and I were seated either side of the Mama San who was acting as hostess. A lady of mature years who revealed her gold teeth when she smiled. To my surprise I found her squeezing my thigh but saw she was doing the same to the engineer superintendent who assured me she was just assuring herself that the bill for the evening would be met!! We all left and returned to the ship in good order if the singers were somewhat hoarse.

For the following voyage, the chief officer's wife Anne and my wife Carol joined, departing from Southampton for Suez Canal, Jeddah,

Singapore, Busan, Kobe, Tokyo and back to Rotterdam, Hamburg, Bremhaven, Le Havre and Southampton. We also had a director of the company travelling to Singapore on a work experience exercise. En route from Jeddah to Singapore our first engineer was killed in a tragic accident. Early one evening he went to inspect the repair to a valve in one of the hold spaces. As he was entering the space on his own he had reported his intentions to the officer of the watch on the bridge and to report his whereabouts at fifteen minute intervals. When a call was missed and the crew could not raise a reply the general alarm was sounded and the ship's company proceeded to their designated positions. With a search under way the first engineer was found by the chief engineer and chief officer trapped by one of the ship's mechanical watertight steel doors in the working alleyway. He must have opened the door and then, before stepping through, had returned the control to the closed position and was trapped and killed. No fault was found in the door controls or any of the others and this was very difficult to accept. Our head office was informed and I said that a burial at sea was arranged subject to the company's approval. However a message was received to the effect that the widow wished the body to be returned to the UK. We were fortunate to have spare domestic refrigeration space which was utilised. With a few days to go before arriving in Singapore, reports and documentation were completed as landing a body in many countries can cause problems. It hardly needs saying but the ship's company were saddened by the death of a shipmate and it was somewhat unsettling for some having the body on board. At the time my concern was for the chief engineer, a man of few words normally, he became completely withdrawn and took the responsibility for the accident which was certainly not the case.

On arrival at Singapore, our cargo commitment had a stay of ten hours. Fortunately with Singapore, a very busy and efficient port, the paperwork was in order and the body was landed without problems. I had requested the presence of an official from the British Consulate to countersign the ship's official logbook as required by UK Shipping Regulations. We departed without the logbook being signed and I radioed ahead to our Kobe agent, our next port of call, requiring an official from the Consulate there. In the meantime, our passenger had left, experiencing more than he expected. A lawyer joined to take statements from various members of the ship's company relating to this unfortunate accident.

We arrived in Kobe on a public holiday and it was the next day before an official from the Consulate appeared. Our agents Squires, had arranged for a function on board for shippers and officials and for the first time wives were invited which was unusual in Japan at that time. The party went off well, helped by having two wives on board. I had been briefed that two of the Japanese wives who were to be there were teachers of English so I made a point of addressing them. In each case they replied through their husbands who passed on their comments to me in English. Another custom I had not been aware of.

I have to say that our agents were very good to the two wives on that voyage. Arranging to show them around in the time available when their husband's duties required them to be on board the ship. We called at Pusan in South Korea on the homeward passage and had enjoyed an amusing incident on our departure. It was the custom at Pusan for the National Anthem of each vessel arriving or sailing from the port to be played as they passed the breakwater entrance. We would respond by dipping our ensign. On this occasion, our harbour pilot informed me that a large US warship was due to enter as we departed but would wait outside until we had cleared the entrance. When we cleared and was passing the warship we of course dipped our ensign to it. Our navigating bridges were about the same height and there appeared to be as many personnel on its bridge as we had as a total complement. All the seamen forward of the bridge were smartly to attention. To our enjoyment the seamen at the stern of the vessel, out of sight from the bridge, were lounging about smiling and totally relaxed. I was sorely tempted to comment on our radio telephone but thought it rather unsporting if I did. Or it might even have caused a diplomatic incident!

On another voyage, we were to make the first call of a company ship to the port of Nagoya. I was advised by our agents that a reception was to be held on board to mark the occasion and around twenty VIPs were to be invited. It was to be held in my dayroom which was spacious and not unattractive. I warned our agent that, as we had limited staff and there would only be two stewards to serve drinks, it would take a little time. On the day after the formalities, introductions had taken place which involved me being presented with a bouquet of flowers by Miss Nagoya, the Beauty Queen of the Province, and another young lady who had just won an International piano competition; they were the only ladies present. To get things moving I, along with the purser catering officer, started to offer savouries, etc. to the guests until I was asked by the agent to desist as I was embarrassing our guests having the captain serve them and they did not mind waiting for the stewards. Another lesson learned but the occasion was considered a success

One of our following calls at Nagoya was of a very different nature. Japan, like most other countries by this time, was very strict about pollution and on board ship we too had strict procedures. On the *Tokyo Bay* the chief engineer had all discharge valves in the machinery spaces locked with padlocks to avoid accidental spillage and only the valves involved in discharging water ballast were exempted. As we were leaving the container terminal in Kobe, the harbour pilot and I noted traces of oil in the water as we left the berth but I assured him this would not be caused by us. En route to Tokyo our next port of call I discussed the matter with the chief engineer and chief officer and the only discharge that had taken place in Kobe was ballast water from the forepeak tank at the bow of the ship. As we could access this tank we decided to inspect the interior. On doing so we found traces of oil. The pipe used to ballast and de-ballast this tank ran through our oil fuel tanks to the pumps in the engine room and somewhere the ballast pipe must have developed a leak. We immediately informed our agents, London office and the port authorities in Kobe and Tokyo. Also requested that a comparison made of the sample of water from Kobe and our ballast tank. If this was positive we would accept responsibility. This turned out to be so and the Japanese Marine Authority accepted our responsibility. Our next and final port in Japan was Nagoya where we expected a forty-eight hour stay to lift our cargo before returning to Europe.

On berthing at Nagoya our agent informed me that a group of officials asked to see me led by the young head of Nagoya Marine Safety Agency. He was accompanied by an interpreter who introduced him as this gentleman did not speak or understand English. At the same time, a very concerned chief engineer arrived at my cabin to say that a squad of Japanese fitters had arrived in the engine room and were endeavouring to disconnect pipes which would cause a serious accident. This was repeated to the head of the Marine Safety Agency and they were informed that any if any damage or accident resulted, these people would be held responsible. I was informed by our agent that they were looking for evidence of oil pollution but would be guided by the chief engineer. I explained that the company had admitted responsibility and the cause appeared to be a leaking ballast pipe running through a fuel oil tank at present full of fuel. I was now told that the Marine Safety Agency would require the person responsible for the leak to appear in court at Csaka in the province where the offence took place. Unless this was agreed the vessel would not be allowed to proceed. The situation was now serious and both offices in London and Tokyo were informed. I suggested that I agree to go to court as the person ultimately responsible and the chief officer take over until I could rejoin at Singapore. This was put to the MSA official which caused some disquiet and was refused. He wanted the chief officer who had given the instruction to discharge the ballast and the bosun who had opened the valve to appear in court. The meeting was adjourned until the following morning when a negotiator from Osaka would attend. This is a common practice in Japan. I discussed with the chief officer and bosun their possible appearance in court which they, understandably were not happy about. News had got round that in Japan a person appearing in court was handcuffed irrespective of the charge.

The following morning the negotiator appeared, a mature very prosperous looking gentleman along with the deputation from the MSA. I explained the situation to him from the ship's point of view and of the reluctance of the chief officer and bosun to appear in court as my presence in court was not acceptable. He withdrew to consult with the official from the MSA. By this time we had completed cargo operations as scheduled but had not be given clearance to sail. The agent meantime informed me that the official I was dealing with was a very ambitious gentleman and a court case would enhance his reputation even if the owners had accepted responsibility. During the afternoon the negotiator boarded with a written agreement that if the two men voluntarily agreed to appear in court they would at all times be in the care of the agent and with no restrictions. At the end of the hearing they would be flown to Singapore to rejoin the vessel. The two men reluctantly agreed to this. At 16.00 hrs the head of the MSA and his assistants boarded and informed me that we had clearance to sail. He stated this himself in perfect English, wishing me a safe voyage! At least we had only lost four hours time in a very competitive operation.

I kept the chief officer's watch keeping until we arrived off Singapore where the two men boarded from a launch so we proceeded on passage. Their experience had not been unpleasant and they had been well looked after by the agent. The actual court appearance had taken about three hours. When I reported to the Head Office at the end of the voyage the cost of the operation was eye watering. For a minor leak it appeared as though the Japanese Sea had been polluted. The company though was able to take action with our four sister ships to prevent a recurrence of this incident.

Towards the end of my time on *Tokyo Bay* our three year dry dock was due. All repairs and essential maintenance would hopefully be carried out. Until now the dry dockings had taken place in Japan and had been very satisfactory. However, when the work was put out to tender, for the first time, a South Korean shipyard at Ulsan submitted a tender. The price was considerably less than any other but the yard had no knowledge of the vessel. Despite protests from the technical department in London, and our chief engineer, the Korean option was taken up. Prior to our arrival at the shipyard the area had been buffeted by a cyclone which had also affected work at the shipyard.

The vessel dry-docked at Ulsan, South Korea on arrival. We were to share the very large dry dock with three smaller vessels which in due course caused us problems. The ship was transferred to shore power as soon as we docked which caused us endless problems and averaged two blackouts each day. It was very inconvenient to say the least, as well as giving the crew cause for complaint. The work force from shore was working round the clock and it was not uncommon to find them asleep at their tasks. They were totally unfamiliar with our type of vessel causing the chief engineer, in particular, some anxiety. He and I did not leave the shipyard during our stay to try and avoid mistakes being made or corners cut. The shipyard had an agreed date for completion of repairs and the ship was scheduled to commence loading at Busan the following day. The chief engineer and I were soon aware that we would not be ready to depart on the agreed date and I informed London accordingly. At the same time, our Head Office was being advised by the yard that they would meet the completion date. The day before our due date the yard admitted our departure would be delayed forty-eight hours. This stretched to sixty hours and the yard had made no allowance for the testing our engines and other items and I would not sail until the chief engineer was happy. This caused a heated exchange between the yard manager and myself. Later the chief engineer told me that when checking the list of repairs with the ship manager, the manager fell fast asleep over the desk and when aroused admitted not have had a proper break for forty-eight hours. We finally sailed with some work not carried out and the ship in a disorderly and filthy state. The figures would look good in the final bill but there would be a price to pay before the next docking in three years time.

One immediate result of our departure was our bosun refusing to turn out the crew on overtime to start cleaning up the ship. The chief officer reported this to me and had the bosun brought to me. When I repeated the instructions he still refused on the grounds that the shipyard should have done it. As a result I had to officially charge him with disobeying a lawful command. The crew were then offered the work at overtime rates and they all came forward to work and we made a considerable overtime payment in getting the ship back in reasonable shape. Unknown to me at the time the bosun was on a warning for a similar earlier offence and left the company's employ at the end of the voyage.

Towards the end of my time on the vessel we were bound for Hamburg in midwinter and when we picked up the Elbe sea pilot in late afternoon Iit was bitterly cold and freezing fog was forecast. At Brunsbuttal we changed pilots and two river pilots boarded. They informed me that there was dense freezing fog in the river and most traffic at a standstill. We could anchor or proceed up river using the very efficient radar control system and two pilots who would give us a nearly clear passage. I decided to proceed with the freezing fog thickening and the temperature dropping to minus 15C. I warned the chief engineer and asked him to make sure the heating in the accommodation was adequate. We had a safe passage up to Hamburg with competent advice from pilots and river control. We berthed at the terminal in the early hours and it was still bitterly cold. The ship itself was like a Christmas card. Everywhere was totally white and spotless even the funnel, all caused by the freezing fog. Having dealt with the agent and terminal staff and due to depart in twenty-four hours I looked forward to turning in. I then discovered that my bunk was soaking wet due to a leak from a pipe in the heating system and this could not be dealt with unless the system was shut down. Not possible in the circumstances. I retired to my armchair.

After four years as Master of the *Tokyo Bay* I returned to the *Tolaga Bay* for my last two years before retiring. At that time I was appointed Commodore of the P&O Container Fleet, the first to hold that position. This entitled me to fly the commodore's flag on the vessel I happened to be on. It was wholly unexpected at the time but to add to my pleasure, my good friend and old shipmate on different occasions Robert Gemmell was appointed Commodore Chief Engineer of the fleet. Both of us had started our seafaring career with the Clan Line Steamers of Glasgow sometimes known as the Scots Navy.

On my return to the *Tolaga Bay* the ship was doing one last voyage on the New Zealand Australia service and so my wife Carol joined me.

We went outbound through the Panama Canal and homeward bound round Cape Horne at the bottom of South America. Carol left the ship at Melbourne and flew up to stay with old friends in Brisbane. She then flew to Auckland where she rejoined the ship having had a very pleasant time. When we completed loading at Port Chalmers, the port for Dunedin New Zealand, we headed for Cape Horn. The next time we saw anything, other than Cape Horn light flashing, was when an RAF plane buzzed us as we passed the Falkland Islands. We were carrying a big cargo of refrigerated lamb and beef from Australia and New Zealand as well as other produce.

En route to the UK, the ship was having its weekly emergency and fire drill. Unfortunately our cook, who had been teetotal for the voyage up until then, had broken his fast. He presented himself at his lifeboat and was making a nuisance of himself. He was hustled away to his cabin in case his language was overheard by my wife who was also attending the drill. In the meantime, I was on watch duty on the bridge with a deck boy allowing everyone else to be in attendance at the exercise. Meanwhile, the cook escaped from his cabin and apparently had decided to see me on the bridge to tell me what was on the menu for the evening meal! The ship was sailing gently to a low sea swell. To my surprise the cook burst through the door into the wheelhouse and managed to steady himself using the chart table. By this time, I was aware of the cook's state but he set off again unsupported and, with the rolling of the ship, ended up flat out on the deck repeating the evening menu over and over again. The young deck boy was transfixed by the scene. Eventually, others arrived having found an empty cabin and the cook was hustled away.

The next morning he appeared before me, very repentant but anxious to see my wife to apologise for the bad language he had been using and also to have her support in his difficulties! I said I would pass on his message thus stopping the chance of getting her sympathy. The incident livened up our passage home and he did not repeat his moment of glory.

For the following voyage, the vessel was transferred to the Far East service and for this penultimate voyage Carol came away with me. She joined the ship in Southampton and prior to sailing we had a weather forecast of very bad weather in the Bay of Biscay which was heading for the English Channel. I had our Southampton pilot leave us in the sheltered weather off Cowes in the Isle of Wight otherwise he would be with us until the Suez Canal

By the time we had reached the Channel Islands it was blowing a full gale and the radio officer had picked up a number of distress messages but none where we could help. Later in the evening we received one from a vessel ahead of us and enquired if we could be of assistance. They replied that conditions were bad but at present they did not require help. Later in the evening we received another call to say they were in real difficulty, giving a position. We replied that it would take us another hour to reach their position, subject to the current weather conditions, and a very wild sea. In the meantime we made appropriate arrangements but were fully aware of the problem of being a high sided vessel and presenting a big area of windage with containers stacked four high on deck.

At the time we were in contact, the vessel advised us they were German owned, registered in Singapore, with a crew of eighteen – four German officers and fourteen Singaporean ratings, plus two wives. Shortly after that we lost radio contact with the vessel, which was not a good sign.

On arrival at our last reported position of the vessel, seamen were posted in suitable spots to keep look out and stay in exposed places wearing safety harnesses. The ship was stopped when floating debris was spotted which included an upturned lifeboat. Also around were the lights on floating lifejackets which ignite when in the water. In the meantime with engines stopped the vessel was at the mercy of the sea and lying broadside to the wind and weather. On the side of the ship, away from the wind our gangway door was opened and a net and pilot ladder lowered down to aide the rescue of anyone in the water. The force of the wind had the vessel listing over between 10–15 degrees. The seawater had also affected our internal communication system and so our two young cadets were employed as messengers. Meanwhile a

French coastguard plane had arrived at the scene which dropped a life raft and lit up the area with parachute flares which initially spoiled our night vision. At that time a cadet arrived on the bridge to tell me that two of the seamen had been swept overboard from the gangway door by a big sea and where the chief officer was stationed. It was a bad moment and engines could not be used in case these men were caught in the propellers. The young cadet rushed back to the bridge to tell me that one man had been washed back through the door by the next wave and that the chief officer had managed to pull the other seaman on board with the rope attached to his safety harness. What a feeling of relief and I did feel someone was looking after us. The two men meantime were immersed in hot baths and checked over for injuries.

It appeared as though there were no survivors and we reported this to the French Coastguard who instructed us to remain in the area and continue to search. However, the wind and high sea was pushing the vessel downwind and out of position. The engine room was advised that we would get underway and this would be when the vessel was most vulnerable. We would require to reach a speed of about twelve knots before the vessel could be steered up into the wind and sea and thus be able to maintain our position. Before we had steerage the ship was knocked around like a toy. The crests of waves came over our boat deck and we found in due course that we had badly damaged ten of the containers up in the bow of the ship and some damage in the engine room from heavy equipment breaking adrift.

Once we were hove to in the sea and able to keep the ship in the most comfortable position we were told by the French Coastguard to remain in the vicinity and continue our search. I then had the opportunity to go to my cabin and check up on Carol. I found her in bed wearing her life jack and not too happy. She was certainly in the best place as the furniture in my quarters was all in a heap and all the files in my office on the deck. I was able to give her a mug of tea and assure her that things would now be quieter as I returned to the bridge. The engineers had done a great job having to deal with spare equipment coming loose and causing a dangerous situation. Lookouts were posted again and I sent the watch keepers and others to bed while I remained on the bridge until daylight without any sight of survivors.

It was a bleak sight at daylight with the huge seas still running and we estimated the wave height to between thirty-five – forty feet. Again one feels very small and insignificant in the open sea. At 08.00 hrs I informed the Coastguard and our London office that I intended resuming our passage as we could not maintain our position without more damage to the ship. I received clearance and proceeded on our passage as best as the conditions would allow.

I understand that about 120 lives were lost during that storm in the Bay of Biscay. Mostly from small vessels and fishing boats which do not hit the headlines of newspapers. I took the opportunity of also reminding our younger members of the ship's company that because a ship is big the power of the sea is bigger. Also to remember that when ordered to make items of equipment secure, to be sure they did so as they had just experienced what happened when heavy items became loose in heavy weather and become a real danger to ship's crew members. The opportunity was taken to explain exactly what had happened and to thank everyone for their help.

Later that day I pointed out to my wife the seaman who had been washed overboard and rescued using the line attached to his safety harness. Carol immediately went to have a few words with him and his reply was that he would now have something interesting to write in his letter to his wife. The other seaman, a younger man, really could not remember what had happened to him but he found himself lying on the deck on being washed back on board.

When the ship arrived in Singapore, I visited the Marine office to report the sinking, as the ship was registered at Singapore. I handed in my report and entries in the Official Log Book and was taken aback with the seeming indifference of the vessel's sinking and loss of life.

The Seafarer's Wife

The Lord was creating a model of a seafarer's wife and was into his sixth day of overtime when an angel appeared and said "Lord, you seem to be having a lot trouble with this one, what's wrong with the standard model!?

The Lord replied "Have you seen the specifications of this order? This isn't a regular wife I have been asked to make. This order is for a seafarer's wife. She is going to be some kind of phenomenal creation. She has to be completely independent, possess qualities of both father and mother, and be a perfect hostess to four or forty guests at a moments notice. Handle every emergency without a manual, be able to carry on cheerfully whether pregnant or down with flu and she must have six pairs of hands."

The angel shook her head and exclaimed, "Six pairs of hands? Impossible".

The Lord continued by saying. "Don't worry, I will make some other seafarer's wives to help her out and encourage her, and I will give her an unusually large heart that she can swell with pride, brought through her husband's achievements, capable of saying, "I understand" when she really doesn't and I love you in the bleakest of circumstances. She has to have a strong heart to sustain the pain of separation and to beat soundly when she is overworked and tired".

"Lord", said the angel, touching his arms gently. "Go to bed and get some rest, you can finish this project another day".

"I can't stop now", said the Lord. "I am close to the finished product. Already this model heals herself when sick, can play gracious hostess to as many as six unexpected guests, wave good-bye to her husband from the pier or airport without totally understanding why he must go".

The angel circled the model of a seafarer's wife looked at her closely and signed "It looks fine but it is too soft".

"She might look soft" replied the Lord. "But she has the strength of a lion. You would not believe what she can endure.

Finally the angel bent over and saw something down the cheek of the Lord's creation. "There's a leak, something is wrong with this model. You are trying to put too much in this model".

The Lord appeared offended at the angel's lack of confidence. "What you see is a tear, not a leak".

"A tear? What is that for?" asked the angel.

The Lord replied "It is for joy, sadness, pain, disappointment, loneliness, pride and dedication to all the values she and her husband hold dear".

"You are a genius!" exclaimed the angel.

The Lord looked puzzled and replied "I didn't put that tear there".

The Watch Ashore

The ship sailed on Sunday afternoon bound for Corner brook and the snow. On our way we were instructed to keep a lookout for survivors from an American tanker which had sunk two days previously off Cape Hatteras. We did not see anyone and learned afterwards that thirty-one men had been lost. On reaching the Gulf of St Lawrence we discovered that most of the ice had disappeared and arrived in Cornerbrook on 3rd April.

On filling up with newsprint again we sailed on 5th April bound for Buffalo on Lake Erie. This meant going up the St Lawrence River to Montreal, then into the St Lawrence Seaway, across Lake Ontario, through the Wellend Canal into Lake Erie and then just round the corner to Buffalo. Unfortunately it was not quite as easy as all that and it turned out an eventful trip one way and another. We picked up our first pilot on the Wednesday at a little place on the north shore at the mouth of the St. Lawrence River called Les Escoumains. Because we started to encounter ice in the river we anchored when darkness fell and got under way at 4 o'clock the next morning just before dawn. Arrived at Quebec City an hour later, changed pilots, and continued on our way. We reached a town called Three Rivers by ll o'clock and changed pilots again. This proved a little difficult as the pilot boat could not reach us because of ice. We arrived at Montreal at 5 o'clock in the afternoon and took oil fuel and passed inspection by the various officials. However, because of the severe weather in Canada this winter the opening of the St Lawrence Seaway was delayed and so we went twenty miles down river from Montreal and anchored to await the opening of the Seaway. We were there for eight days which included Easter weekend but it was not possible to go ashore mainly because of the ice floating past. As you can imagine everyone was very bored though there was plenty of work to do.

On Saturday 17th April we headed up to Montreal again and by this time there were fifty ships waiting patiently to get into the Seaway. We entered the first lock on the Saturday afternoon and were the twelfth ship to do so that season. At this point, I should explain what a lock is. It is really a lift for a ship, and is like a long box with no top and gates at each end. What happens going up the Seaway is that the *Nina* arrives at one end of the lock, the gates at this end open up and in we sail. We are so low down in the dock that only the masts and funnel can be seen and the men who take our ropes are looking down at me on the bridge. The gate behind us is then closed and water allowed into the lock from the higher level and within five minutes we have risen over forty feet and are looking down on the men on the lock. Then the gates at the other end are opened and we sail out at the new level of the water. Coming down the Seaway as you will understand in each lock we are lowered down. In the Seaway itself there are seven locks to go through to raise the ship about 220 feet from the level of the St Lawrence River at Montreal to the level of Lake Ontario. Between these locks there are three lakes partly formed by the damming of the River St Lawrence and they are called Lake St Clair, Lake St Francis and Lake St Lawrence. At three of the locks there are huge power dams used to make electricity both for Canada and the USA.

As you can imagine, it is all very interesting and you get a wonderful view of the countryside. It is also very wearying for the ship's company as it takes us nearly twenty-four hours from Montreal to Lake Ontario if there are no delays which there are with a lot of ships on the move. After the last lock until the ship reaches the open waters of Lake Ontario we pass through a stretch called the Thousand Islands. It is a narrow stretch of water full of very attractive islands and on virtually every one there are summer houses. The deep water channel for the ships wends its way through between these islands and it is very interesting; one island has a Scottish castle which was taken out stone by stone from Scotland and rebuilt here by some very wealthy person.

Appendix A – Letters

During my time as master of the *Nina Bowater* I was asked to write to (a class at a School) to give them an insight into a life at sea which inevitably included a geography lesson on many of the places we visited in the course of transporting cargo across the world. Here are a selection of letters written in 1970 although I wrote many more and built up quite a relationship with the pupils.

MV Nina Bowater
At Sea
Monday 27th April 1970

Dear Girls and Boys,

I am the new Captain of your ship the *Nina Bowater* and am looking forward to getting to know you all. I joined the ship in March at a little place in the Thames Estuary called Ridham Dock. The ship was in there unloading wooden logs to be used for paper making at a big paper mill in the town of Sittingbourne in Kent.

A little information about myself may help to know each other better. I went to a training ship called HMS *Conway* in 1944 when I was a boy of 14, and spent two years there training for the sea. This old ship had a long history and when it was first built fought in battles under Lord Nelson and was called HMS *Nile*. I left the training ship in 1946 and joined the Clan Line as a cadet and have been with the same company ever since. Passing the different examinations, I became 3rd Officer, 2nd officer, Chief Officer, Staff Commander on a passenger ship, and now Captain on your ship. I live with my wife and son in a village called Dunblane in Perthshire. My son is five years old and like you goes to school. I hope, too, that like you he is working hard at his lessons and enjoying *school.*

I think you know quite a bit about the ship itself and the crew she carries. There are a lot of different men here now since you last heard from the ship. However I think I will just tell you of our voyaging so far and anything of interest that I think of. I am sure you have a good atlas to be able to see some of the places we go to. I hope to be able in time to get interesting information about the different places we go to and it will certainly help my own history and geography.

When the ship left Ridham we proceeded to the River Tyne up through the sand banks of the North Sea. On reaching the River Tyne we went to a place called North Shields, near the mouth of the river, which is well known for its ship building and ship repairing. Here we remained for a fortnight doing our spring cleaning, just like at home, and repairing which is carried out once a year. We went into a dry dock which is just like a very big bath set into the river bank with one end open to the river. Once we were in the dry dock, the river end was closed by a big gate, the ship was put right in the middle, and big wooden poles wedged between the ship's side and the side of the dry dock. Then the water was pumped out of the dry dock till the ship sat on big blocks on the bottom of the dock and the poles kept her from falling over. The water was completely pumped out and there was the *Nina Bowater* high and dry.

In dry dock, the bottom and sides of the ship are inspected and any damage is repaired. Our propeller was taken off and another one fitted. All the pipes that come out from the ship checked which is very important in case the sea gets back inside the ship. When all this is done the underwater part of the ship is given a good scrub, just like when you get dirty, and then given a coat of special paint. I used to go down into the dry dock to inspect the work and it was a funny feeling to be walking under a ship just sitting on these blocks on the floor of the dry dock. Once all this work was completed, the water was slowly allowed into the dock until the ship was afloat again. The poles were taken away, the gate was open, and we moved out into the river again, Here we completed the repairs inside the ship, and took all our stores for the voyage. It is a big shopping day for a ship going away for four or five months. We have to take everything we need to eat with us as it is cheaper in Britain than in America. Then there is the oil for the engines, water to drink, and sheets to put on the beds. You just think of everything you need at home that we had to take before sailing.

At last we were ready. The Chief Officer, Chief Engineer and the Purser/Chief Steward said they had everything they wanted and the repairs were finished. We said cheerio to the shore people and sailed from North Shields on Thursday 26th March in a snow storm.

The shortest way to Canada from the River Tyne is round the North of Scotland through the Pentland Firth. This is known as a wild bit of sea and as the weather was very bad up there at this time I decided to go the other way, so on Good Friday as you were eating your hot cross buns the *Nina Bowater* was proceeding down the English Channel. We now headed across the North Atlantic Ocean for Nova Scotia. At first we had good weather and hoped to reach our destination by Sunday 5th April but when only 700 miles from our destination we ran into a gale. This delayed us two days and we did not arrive until Tuesday 7th April. At this time of the year, as well as bad weather, ships have to be very careful not to run into icebergs. From March to July these icebergs drift down the coast of Newfoundland into the North Atlantic where they finally melt away when they meet the Gulf Stream.

The town we arrived at in Nova Scotia is called Liverpool and it is on the bank of the Mersey river. As you can guess by the names, many years ago some people from Liverpool in England must have settled there. At Liverpool NS there is a big paper mill called the Bowater Mersey Mill which is very important to the town, it being the place where most of the people are employed. The mill had its 40th Birthday last year. It makes newsprint from trees. These trees are cut down in the forests in Nova Scotia, cut into logs and brought to the mill. Here they are crushed down and come out as great big rolls of newsprint.

Our job on the *Nina Bowater* for the next few months is to carry these big rolls of newsprint to the newspapers that need it in the United States of America. Most of the paper we carry is for a newspaper called *The Washington Post* and also for the US Government. We take it to a town called Alexandria which is six miles from Washington the capital city of the USA.

Enough for now however. The next time I write I will tell you of our trip from Liverpool to Alexandria and the interesting things we saw. Meanwhile I hope you are enjoying school and getting warm weather now. I expect you are already thinking about your summer holidays.

Yours sincerely
R P Royan

MV *Nina Bowater*
At Sea
21st June 1970

Dear Girls and Boys,

Here I am once again with a letter before you finish school and go on your summer holidays. You will all be looking forward to that time I am sure. So also will your teachers. With these lovely long summer evenings I don't suppose you want to go to bed at all. The only trouble is getting up and going to school in the mornings.

Since I last wrote to you the *Nina* has been back to Alexandria a couple of times but has been other places too. To Cornerbrook in Newfoundland, Richmond in Virginia, Charleston in South Carolina and Port Canaveral in Florida. I am sure you will be able to find all these places in your atlas. It is getting quite warm out where we are now and most of the time we now wear our summer uniform of white shirts and shorts. It is so much cooler to wear.

Now let me tell you of a ship we were lucky enough to see a short time ago. This was a ship built by a very rich American at a little town just above Liverpool. She is called the *Rose* and is built exactly like a warship of the same name which fought out here over 200 years ago. Isn't that a long time. It has no engines only sails. This new ship is going to a seaport in the United States where it will become a museum. At this very town a long time ago the first *Rose* blockaded the port, not allowing other ships to enter or leave. One afternoon as we left Liverpool I saw this ship away in the distance on its way to its new home. Decided it would be nice to see it closer and so that is what we did. It looked beautiful with its sails and all the flags that were in use a long time ago. It had a beautiful carved figurehead as ships had long ago. We lowered our ensign on the *Nina* in salute to her and then sounded three long blasts on our siren which at sea means 'farewell'. Some of our crew were able to get good photographs as well.

To get to the city of Richmond we had to pick up our pilot at Cape Henry as for Alexandria but turn left as we enter Chesapeake Bay and go to Hampton Roads which is an area of water at the mouth of the James River up which we have to go to reach Richmond. On one side of Hampton Roads is the port and naval base of Norfolk and on the other side the port and shipbuilding yard at Newport News. These are both very busy places and ships come from all over the world to load thousands of tons of coal every week.

At Hampton Roads we changed pilots getting one to take us up the James River. As we passed close to the Newport News shipyard on our way into the James river we had a good view of two huge ships. One was the famous American liner the *United States* which has been taken out of service and was lying there looking very sad. The other was the American Navy aircraft carrier the *Enterprise* which is the biggest ship in the world. It looked enormous.

The distance up the actual James river is about the same as it was on the Potomac. However the James is more interesting and very much narrower, especially for the last twenty-five miles. In this last part the banks are as high as the ship and are so close you think you can almost touch the leaves on the trees. There are some very sharp corners in the river here and we blew our siren each time to let any small boats know we were coming. Each time we blew all the birds used to fly out of the trees. We had two road bridges to go through and all the traffic had to be stopped as the bridges opened to let us through.

On the way up the river we passed an island called Jamestown and this was the very first place that English people settled in America. You will see it on the map I am sending with this letter. At this place they made friends with a famous Indian Chief called Pocahontas. Nearby is a town called Williamsburg part of which is like it was in the early days. If you visit it you will find people wearing the clothes of long ago as well. People from all over America come to visit these places. Through the trees on the banks of the river we caught glimpses of some of the lovely old plantation houses. Where the ship tied up at Richmond was about six miles down river from the city and it was very quiet here. All you could see were the trees on top of the high river banks. I did not see very much of Richmond but did visit the house of the Governor of Virginia. I also did a little shopping. It was really too hot to do much walking around. We do not stay long enough in our different ports of call to have a good look round.

This last voyage we went up to Cornerbrook in Newfoundland to load the paper. At Cornerbrook is one of the biggest paper mills in the world and the town grew up around the mill. When you come in from the sea on a ship you enter what is called the Bay of Islands, which is full of islands, which we have to go round. Then, at the end of the bay is a narrow stretch of water called Hember Arm and Cornerbrook is at the very end of this arm of water. It is a very pretty run up the bay to Cornerbrook but the shore is very stern looking. Mountains, rocks and some trees. There was still snow to be seen on the high ground. The houses dotted along the shore just look like a picture postcard as they are nearly all painted bright colours and built of wood. Our stay in Cornerbrook was 1½ days.

From Cornerbrook we sailed to Charleston and arrived there in the middle of the night. It had been quite cold in Cornerbrook but now it really was very warm. We sailed the same afternoon right in the middle of a big yacht race. There seemed to be hundreds of them around with their different coloured sails. It made a very pretty sight. Unfortunately, because of our short stay, I can't really tell you anything about Charleston, except that it was important in American history.

Our next call was at Port Canaveral in Florida. This is a small place and has only developed since the Americans started firing rockets in this area. The first thing to be seen as we approached the port were the big rocket towers sticking up in the sky. Poor old Cape Kennedy lighthouse which I was looking for was like a dwarf alongside these towers. We stayed at Port Canaveral for two days and enjoyed our visit. The beach was close to the ship and the sea warm and quite a few of the crew went for a bathe when off duty. On the Monday afternoon the Chief Engineer and I went to visit Cape Kennedy and the space centre. We took a bus at Space Centre tourist building and were taken on a two hour trip round Cape Kennedy. As you can imagine it was very interesting. We saw the old control centre where the earlier rockets were controlled from, the launch pad where the Apollo space craft had been launched from and the enormous building where the Apollo rockets are fitted together. You will see some good photographs of these different places in the book I am sending with this letter. There were quite a few boys and girls on the bus with us and they were very excited at seeing all these different things. At the end of the tour we were able to see the clothes the men wore on the Moon and the food they eat when they are flying through space It was very interesting and all the crew who wished to see Cape Kennedy were able to take the tour.

We had for company in Port Canaveral a British submarine called HMS *Revenge*. She was down in Florida doing exercises with rockets. It was nice to see the British flag on another ship.

Coming down to Port Canaveral and after leaving it we were right in the centre of the Gulf Stream which is a current of warm water which travels a long way over the Atlantic Ocean. Down off Florida the Gulf Stream is full of different kinds of fish. People come out for the day to try and catch the big ones with very heavy fishing rods. However we were lucky as on different occasions we saw big turtles swimming lazily along, sharks swimming by looking for something to eat, and porpoise and dolphin diving around and chasing the ship. They are very graceful. Every now and again flying fish would skim over the tops of the waves trying to get away from the big fish that were chasing them. As we came further north we saw quite a few big whales and often the first thing you notice is a spout of water going straight up in the air out of the sea. Then when you look closely there is a whale swimming there.

Now we are on our way back to Liverpool NS and our usual run. It is possible that we may return to Britain at the end of August with a cargo of logs from Newfoundland. This would be lovely as I could get home for a couple of days Anyway we are all hoping this happens.

Well boys and girls that is all my news from the *Nina Bowater* once again and do hope you all enjoy your holidays. I know how I used to look forward to the summer holidays when I was at school.

Yours sincerely,
RJ Royan

MV *Nina Bowater*
At Sea
Sunday 9th August 1970

Dear Girls and Boys,

I was very pleased to get your very interesting letters last Wednesday when we arrived at Hare Bay in Newfoundland. I quickly passed over the ones addressed to Mr Coleman. It was good to learn of all your activities. I must say you have been busy. Making a doll's house, swimming, playing rounders, I hope you win next time and learning French. It is terrible to have to admit that I have forgotten most of my French. Some of you have had a very interesting day with Miss Whittaker at the 'Discovery'. I am sure I would not have been able to answer anything like forty-two questions.

I was interested to hear about Honey the Hamster. It was lucky your caretaker had such a clever idea for catching it after it ran away. Our ship's cat had four kittens about 4/5 weeks ago exactly the same colour as the mother. They were born on the bed of the steward who looks after me. He has given me some photos of our cats to send to you. The grey one is the mother. However we left them behind at the last port because cats are not allowed to come into Britain just now. Everyone on board were sad to leave them but we did find them a good home with a family.

I do hope you all enjoyed your summer holidays as by the time you get this letter the *Nina* will have been home and away again. We expect to get to Ridham next Sunday 16th August and be there for five days. Then the ship leaves again for Newfoundland. Everyone is looking forward to getting home and most people will get a holiday. I have not heard yet if I will get away but I am hoping. You see since I left home my wife has had a little baby girl so I am anxious to see her. With this letter I am enclosing one or two things. One is a cutting out of a Richmond newspaper all about the ship. We carried a newspaper writer down the James River one voyage and he wrote this article. The sailor with the long hair and the beard when he saw his photograph quickly had a shave and a haircut as he said if his mother saw the photograph she would not know him. There is also a little book from the 2nd officer about two very big people who once lived in Nova Scotia and I have a postcard of one. The 2nd officer has also written a little bit about the history of Liverpool. There is also a postcard of the Coat of Arms of Nova Scotia, as well a badge which I forgot before commemorating Apollo 13.

Since I last wrote to you in June we have been sailing back and fore between Liverpool in Nova Scotia and Alexandria in Virginia. We left Alexandria for the last time on Friday 31st July and headed for Newfoundland. This took us past Liverpool this time, not stopping across the Cabot Strait and up the west side of Newfoundland, going past Cornerbrook where we had called before. Then through the Belle Isle Strait which lies between Newfoundland and Labrador. This stretch of water is closed for six months every year as it freezes over completely. Once through the Strait we turned sharply right or to starboard as we say on board and entered a place called Hare Bay. Tucked away in the far bottom corner of the bay was a little village called Mainbrook and it was near here where we stopped. There was a very narrow entrance and once inside it was very difficult to see where we had come in from the sea.

Here at this little village we loaded logs for the Bowater paper mill at Sittingbourne. These pulpwood logs are all cut in lengths of 42" at the sawmill ashore and then pushed into the sea. There they float inside a log boom until we arrived. Then this boom full of logs was brought alongside the ship and a crane lifted them into our holds all dripping water. Once the holds were full up we carried on loading them on the top deck till the pile was seven feet high. Now you can hardly see the ship for logs!! This all took us two and a half days. As soon as the crew had tied down the logs on the top deck we set sail for Ridham and home.

On leaving Hare Bay the good ship *Nina Bowater* headed just about due East for the isles of Scilly. If the weather is clear they should be the first of England that we see. The first two days out was quite worrying as that was when we passed through the area of water where the icebergs float down from Greenland in. We saw about ten and passed another five in the fog. They are huge ice islands and if a ship hit one it would sink. We were all keeping a very keen lookout for these icebergs and one night we stopped the ship for three hours and waited for daylight before carrying on again, as there were a few icebergs around and it was very thick fog. Now I am glad to say we are clear and are left with just the rain and the fog.

We must be getting near to Britain don't you agree?

Now I must get all my end of voyage reports ready for our London office. A lot has happened in four months and some things have to be explained! It is the only thing I don't like about going home. However I am sure your teachers know what it is like similar to the end of term. The 3rd Officer and I are the only two officers not leaving the ship, but I hope to get home for two days. Anyhow I should be able to write you a letter next time out in Newfoundland.

Meantime, I hope you are all fit and well after your holidays and pleased to be back at school. You will have a lot to tell your teachers of that I am sure. I must say 'Hello' to the new pupils and hope you enjoy being at All Hallows School, the Ninaos school.

Yours sincerely,
J S Ryan
Master

MV Nina Bowater
At Cornerbrook

Dear Girls and Boys,

Thank you very much indeed for the two packets of letters I received when the ship arrived at Cornerbrook on Monday 25th October. I enjoyed reading them all very much, some of you I have had letters from before. I recognised the names of five girls and some of you for the first time. The letters are now being read by the rest of the ship's company with much enjoyment.

I last wrote to you at the end of May before the summer holidays, it seems a long time ago. However I knew you were going to join up with another school so thought I would wait and hear from you first. Now that you are St Pauls and All Hallows Junior School I wish you all success in the future and say 'Hello' to all the children of St Pauls from the *Nina Bowater*. It is very disappointing that the new school is not yet complete and I hope you will be able to move in to it fairly soon. I am sure it will be very nice.

It was very interesting to read of all your activities especially about the football team. I expect the girls will have a netball team by now too. Once the football team has a bit more practice I expect to hear about the games they win as well as the ones they lose. What with the swimming as well you should all be very fit this winter. I do not get enough exercise on the ship, walking back and fore on the deck is very monotonous, so when in port I enjoy going for long walks when the weather is kind.

You have been doing some interesting projects too. One was on Tottenham which I am sure you could tell me a lot about. I really know every little about the London area and am anxious to learn. Another project was the weather which as a seaman interests me very much. I will include two barograph papers, one will show you where we passed through the middle of a tropical storm called 'Kristy' and the other shows you what happens when the ship rises in the locks in the St Lawrence Seaway. This autumn freize you have been doing must be most attractive now that it is completed. I am sure your efforts at the Harvest Thanksgiving would be very much appreciated by the old people of the district to whom you gave the gifts.

Now I must answer some of your questions which I may not have done before. The *Nina* was launched at Dundee on the 29th June 1961 by the Marchioness of Linlithgow from the yard of the Caledone Shipbuilding Company. The ship's speed is about 12½ knots which has us doing 300 nautical miles a day which is about 345 statute or land miles. The voyage we are now is No.189 and we are carrying 3,975 rolls of newsprint weighing 3,000 tons to Cleveland in the State of Ohio. Most of this paper will be used to produce a paper called the Cleveland Plain Dealer. Last voyage we carried 22,080 bales of woodpulp weighing 5,037 tons. Our longest passage so far in the life of this ship was last voyage from Charleston, South Carolina to Durban, South Africa. This was a distance of 7,702 nautical miles which took us 28 days eight hours six minutes. Of this 26 days were out of sight of land. I will enclose what we call a Crew List which is required at each foreign port we call at. This list shows every member of the crew and where they were born. AB means able bodied Seaman, DHU means Deckhand Uncertified, SOS means Senior Ordinary Seaman, ERS means Engine Room Storekeeper, DKY/GRS means Donkeyman Greaser. All the other ones you will understand.

In my last letter I told you about our calls at Buffalo and Montreal. After that we did one voyage to Rochester, two to Detroit, one to Port Huron and Muskegon and one to Cleveland and Muskegon calling at Port Alfred, on the Saguenay River in the Gulf of St Lawrence on our way back to Cornerbrook. This took us to early August when you were all enjoying your summer holidays I hope. Then we loaded paper for Port Newark and Baltimore and proceeded to Charleston to load for South Africa.

Rochester lies on the south shore of Lake Ontario in New York State. It is known as the Garden City which is understandable when you see the number of beautiful parks there are in the vicinity. It is best known as the headquarters of the world famous Kodak Company and they are by far the biggest employer of people in the area. The port itself is very small and lies at the mouth of the river about ten miles from the city centre. I have marked with a cross where the *Nina* lay on the postcard of the river I am sending to you.

There was an attractive beach just beside the ship but unfortunately the lake water is polluted and it is dangerous to swim. Nearly all the waters of the Great Lakes system are affected this way and it is very serious.

Detroit in the state of Michigan, lies at the extreme west end of Lake Erie on the bank of the Detroit River. It is one of the biggest cities in the United States and is the centre of the car manufacturing industry. Coming up the river to Detroit you pass big steel mills and as you can imagine there is a lot of smoke and dirt in the air. There is an island in the middle of the river on the way to Detroit which has been turned into an amusement park. It is very colourful when you pass it at night with all the coloured lights switched on. The river itself forms the boundary between the USA and Canada. At Detroit the Ambassador Bridge joins the two countries. Windsor is the city on the Canadian side. I was fortunate in being able to visit the Henry Ford Museum on one-call at Detroit. The museum is situated just outside the city where the Ford factories are sited, in a suburb called Dearborn, The museum is part of Greenwich Village which is a replica of a village and life in early America. I only wish I had more time to spend there as the museum was very interesting with all sorts of different things including the early motor cars. The city of Detroit I did not see much of but I was not very impressed. Like many places in America it was not really very safe to be out after dark and so I remained on board the *Nina*.

Port Huron lies at the south end of Lake Huron and to get there we had to sail up the Detroit River past Detroit, under the bridge and into Lake St Clair which is only 15 miles wide. Then up the St Clair River to Port Huron. It was very interesting going up these rivers during the hours of daylight and having a good view of the shore. The rivers were full of small pleasure boats which were a bit of a nuisance at times. The banks of the rivers here are very low and there are houses right to the water's edge in places. Because of this there is a speed limit for ships and if you are caught exceeding the speed limit the ship is fined. Otherwise the wake of the ship sometimes washes into the gardens and sometimes even the houses. Our stay at Port Huron was very short and I did not get ashore but it appeared to be a pleasant little town. On the Canadian side of the river is the city of Sarnia which has a very big refinery and chemical plant. A few miles inland from Sarnia is the town of London!! At the entrance to the St Clair River is another bridge joining the USA and Canada. This one is called the Bluewater Bridge which does describe the colour of the water there on a sunny day as I was able to see for myself.

From Port Huron we went to Muskegon which is on the east side of Lake Michigan. This meant we had to sail up Lake Huron, through the Mackinaw Strait into and down Lake Michigan. The Strait is spanned by the beautiful Mackinaw Bridge which has been opened quite recently. This area is a popular holiday spot and is pretty wild country. The people come up to the forests to hunt deer and bear. There is one holiday island in the Strait on which no cars are allowed. They use horse drawn carriages instead. I think Muskegon was the most attractive port we called at on the Great Lakes, possibly it was fairly small and not crowded out with cars. It lies on a little bay called Muskegon Lake which has a very narrow entrance into Lake Michigan which makes it a very sheltered harbour. During one of our calls the town was holding the Muskegon Seaway Festival which comprised of many activities including a boys' and girls' fancy dress parade through the town which was very good. Another event was an exhibition and sale of all types of hand work, paintings, glass blowing and many other things. This was held in the open air in the town square under the trees and I found quite fascinating. We were lucky too in being able to store up the ship with lovely vegetables and fruit as this is a big market garden area and the best time for fruit. The strawberries were delicious!!

We called at Port Alfred on one occasion on our way back to Cornerbrook to pick up 500 tons of alum. This is one of the chemicals used by the Cornerbrook mill to make newspaper. Port Alfred is the port for a very large aluminium mill and lies at the head of the Saguenay River which enters the Gulf of St Lawrence at the mouth of the St Lawrence River. You will be able to see it on an atlas. This Saguenay River is very deep right close to the banks which are, in fact, cliffs. It is very wild country and not many people around. It was a lovely day when we called at Port Alfred, going up the river in the morning and down in the afternoon. I enjoyed the scenery very much and imagine it was like some of the Norwegian fjords. Some of the navigation beacons on the cliffs were statues of religious people holding the navigation light in their hands. At the mouth of the river there was a religious cross on the hillside which was lit up after dark and really stood out.

On another voyage we took newsprint to Port Newark in the State of New Jersey. This city is only about two miles from New York City itself but lies on the opposite side of the Hudson River on Newark Bay. However we had a wonderful view of the famous New York skyline with all its famous skyscrapers but turned off to Port Newark before reaching the famous Statue of Liberty. The last time I had been up this river was 25 years ago on my first voyage to sea as a cadet. It was my first foreign port and was very exciting. I did not go ashore this time as the area the ship was berthed was not very nice. However, as we were in port on a Sunday, I was able to pass the day trying to read the whole of the Sunday paper which had over 200 pages!!

From Port Newark we proceeded to Baltimore to discharge the remainder of our cargo. To get there, we sailed down the coast till we reached Cape Henlopen at the entrance to Delaware Bay where we picked up our pilot.

We proceeded half way up the bay and then turned into the C. and D. Canal which is short for Chesapeake and Delaware which are the two bays it joins up. This canal is twelve miles long and is on one level but saves ships many extra miles steaming especially between Baltimore and Philadelphia which are two big ports in the US. The canal is through open country but it was a hazy morning when we passed through and did not see very much. A very sad sight when we reached Baltimore were the many American cargo and passenger ships lying tied up with no employment. The wharf where we tied up was at the oldest part of the Baltimore waterfront which goes back to the early days of America and the sailing ships and is being preserved for historical reasons. Beside the ship was the river police station and in the evening saw the policemen all jump into a police launch and dash away with sirens sounding. Further down the harbour the Chinese crew on a ship had mutinied and a man was killed. Anyway the police took some crew back in the launch and away to jail. It was all very exciting but I am glad it does not happen on the *Nina*. Leaving Baltimore we passed one of the biggest steel works in the world at a place called Sparrows Point. We then proceeded all the way down Chesapeake Bay to Cape Henry, a distance of 140 miles, where we dropped our pilot. Going down the bay we passed through both the States of Maryland and Virginia.

At Charleston in the State of South Carolina we loaded wood pulp from a Bowater mill further inland to take to South Africa. It was very hot and humid when we were there and every evening at about sunset there was a tremendous thunderstorm with every heavy rain. However, I have some friends there and it was very pleasant being able to visit them. Charleston is one of the very early towns of America named after Charles II. It has very strong links with the American Civil War too. There is a very big naval base at Charleston with many warships including nuclear submarines. When we passed the naval base the cadet was quite exhausted dipping our red ensign to each warship as we passed. This is a courtesy that most merchant ships observe when passing a warship of any country. The ship lowers its ensign half way and then the warship acknowledges the salute by lowering its ensign and then hoisting it again whereupon the merchant ship hoists its ensign up again. We also dip our flag when we meet another ship of our own company

We left Charleston on Thursday 26th August and next morning we were rather unfortunate to run right through the centre of a tropical revolving storm or cyclone. The American meteorological people give these storms girls names. A name starting with A at the beginning of the season and going through the alphabet. This storm was called 'Dora'. The *Nina* was so heavily laden that we had to close all the big steel doors to the accommodation as the decks were awash. We were more like a submarine for two days when involved with Miss Dora. However after that the weather was kind to us and the sun shone.

Our long voyage to Durban took us down past the West Indies, past the NE corner of South America and across the Equator into the South Atlantic. It was the first occasion the ship had crossed the Line and we used it as a reason for having a celebration dinner. Father Neptune did not call, he must have been busy elsewhere, but only two of the crew had not crossed before. This long passage gave the crew the opportunity of overhauling all the ship's equipment and getting her looking lovely and clean. Once we were well south we were joined by the albatross. Some days there were two and other days many more. These birds look like seagulls but are very much bigger, their wing span sometimes reach as much as 12 feet! They are really fascinating to watch as they swoop and glide past the ship. I think they must have competitions to see who gets the closest. They stayed with us till the day before Durban, The first land we saw since leaving Charleston were the mountains behind the Cape of Good Hope. It was quite exciting to see land again after 27 days. We rounded Cape Agulhas which is the southernmost point of Africa and headed up the coast towards Durban. There are always big waves or swells in this part of the world even when there is no wind. These swells are known by seamen as the Cape Rollers and we did our share of rolling as we sailed along. We kept close to the land going up the coast to try and avoid the very strong Agulhas current which come down from the Mozambique Channel between Africa and Madagascar. This meant we passed quite close to the city of Port Elizabeth and very close to the city of East London. As we passed along the coastline, there was a fine mist hanging over the shore and this was spray caused by the big rollers breaking on the shore which is pretty rocky.

We arrived at Durban on the 24th September and spent seven days there. Our cargo was going to a new paper mill nearby which had commenced operations a week before. When this mill is in full production South Africa will not require to import any newsprint. Durban is the biggest port and second largest city in the Republic of South Africa. It is both an industrial and holiday centre and is growing rapidly. There is a very attractive beach front lined with large hotels and apartment buildings. This area is lit up by a variety of lights and looks very attractive at night especially from the sea.

The esplanade runs round part of Durban Bay, in which the port is situated, and is very attractively laid out with trees and gardens. When we were there it was early spring in South Africa and the blossoms and flowers were just beginning to come out. In a few weeks time the flowering jacaranda tree would be out in all its glory in Durban and is quite a sight. It never gets as cold in winter time as we know it at home but it is cooler than their summer. It was two years since I had last been there and during our stay my last ship came in for two days on her regular six weekly call from Southampton. I was able to go aboard and pay a call on her captain and say 'hello' to some of the people I knew on board.

The *Nina* sailed from Durban on the morning of the 1st October not really knowing where we were to go. We were originally supposed to return to Charleston and load a cargo for home but on the day we sailed the American dockers had come out on strike. Anyway when we rounded the Cape of Good Hope we headed up the middle of the South Atlantic and awaited orders. A week later just as we were passing the island of St Helena, I received instructions to proceed back to Cornerbrook calling at the Cape Verde Islands for oil fuel. We passed close to St Helena and everyone had a good view. As you can see by the atlas it is in the middle of the ocean and is mountainous with cliffs down to the sea. I have called there in the past and there is no proper harbour, People and cargo have to ferry out to the ship in small boats. One of our seamen was born and brought up there but now lives in England. He wished we could have stopped long enough for him to visit his relations but this was impossible. St Helena belongs to Britain, about all that is left of the Empire and is the place where Napoleon the famous French Emperor, was imprisoned and died.

The Cape Verde Islands are situated about 300 miles off the coast of West Africa and belong to Portugal. This was my first time there and we went to a tiny port called Porto Grande on the island of St Vincent. The islands are volcanic and practically nothing grows there. What people there are are even poorer than those on St Helena. We arrived in a very heavy rain storm to find everyone very happy. The reason for this was this was the first proper rain on the island for three years. Can you imagine that? We took our fuel aboard quickly and two hours after we arrived we were on our way to Cornerbrook again across the North Atlantic.

Our journey from Porto Grande to Cornerbrook was uneventful except that we ran into another tropical storm, just to the east of the island of Bermuda, catching us by surprise. In fact our weather message probably indicated to the people ashore how severe it was as it was given the name of Kristy. Just see how many storms there had been since we met Dora six weeks before? One of the disconcerting things about these storms is if you go through the centre, or eye as it is called, as we did is that one minute the wind is blowing at gale force from one direction and then, with a crack like thunder, it starts blowing just as strongly from the opposite direction. It is quite awesome and the sea gets all mixed up. The crests of the waves being blown in the opposite direction to the waves, and creating a very uncomfortable motion on board.

On our arrival at Cornerbrook, I discovered to my disappointment that, instead of loading for home, we were to make two further voyages up the Great Lakes to Cleveland before going home. Right now we are on our way down the Seaway after our first trip to Cleveland. We are held up right now because it is too windy to transit the Welland Canal and we have another 15 ships with us for company. The temperature is below freezing and every now and then we have a snow shower which certainly means winter has reached Canada. Many ships have been diverted up here because of the continuing dock strike on the US East Coast which is causing a lot of congestion in the ports and St Lawrence Seaway. The important thing is that everyone has to be clear of the Seaway by about the middle of December as that is when it usually closes because of ice.

We have just spent two and a half days in Cleveland which is the largest city in the State of Ohio. It is an industrial city with big steel works among other things. The ship lies very near to the centre of town and so I took the opportunity of doing some shopping. There are some big department stores in the city one which had ten floors! Luckily it has lifts. There is rather an attractive square in the centre of town but of course all the leaves have fallen from the trees now. Ten days ago when we came up the Seaway the leaves were beautiful though the pilot told me as they had been even prettier the week before when the maple trees changed colours. The maple leaf being of course the emblem of Canada and is in the centre of their flag.

Well girls and boys, I think I have brought you up to date with the movements of the *Nina Bowater*. She has covered quite a few miles since leaving the UK. I hope to enclose some postcards with this letter and others when we eventually return home. Everyone on board has their fingers crossed that we get home in time for Christmas as we have been away for a long time. My son Bruce has his seventh birthday on 10th December but unfortunately I will not be able to make it. I am sure you are all starting to look forward to Christmas yourselves. Are you doing anything special at school this year I wonder? I hope the weather is not yet too cold and I hope to hear again from you soon.

Yours sincerely
Signed RP Royan
Master

MV *Nina Bowater*
Purfleet, Essex
Tuesday 16th February 1971

Dear Boys and Girls,

It is well over a month since I posted my last letter to you from Cornerbrook. However with this unfortunate postal strike there has been no point in sending another letter to you before arriving in the UK. I wonder how you are all getting on? Working hard at school I expect and learning all about the new pennies which start now. You will have to help your parents give the right money when out shopping. By now I am sure you are looking forward to the warmer weather coming along. Somewhere your letters are held up and I do hope they reach the ship alright once the mail starts moving again.

We sailed from Cornerbrook at 4.30 pm on New Year's Eve just as everyone from Bowaters mill were going home for their two day holiday. In Newfoundland it is the custom at Christmas time to decorate the windows, outsides of houses and trees in the gardens with coloured lights Some houses are completely outlined in lights and it is very attractive. As we sailed down the Bay of Islands to the sea it was a beautiful cold, clear night and the coloured lights on the houses with the background of pure white snow made a very pretty picture.

The weather was reasonably kind to us on New Year's Day 1971. It was cold but quite calm as we left the land behind us. Once again our catering staff put on a very good meal though not quite so elaborate as the meal at Christmas time. I certainly enjoyed it but there were no sixpences in the plum pudding!

Our first port of call was Barcelona where we arrived on the evening of the 11 January after a good crossing of the Atlantic. We just missed a big storm by a day and were pleased about that. It was late at night again when we passed through the Straits of Gibraltar into the Mediterranean Sea. Was just like speaking to old friends again when Lloyds signal station on the Rock called us up by Morse lamp to ask our name and where we were bound for. The Mediterranean was calm and we had a good passage along the coast of Spain, just seeing the lights of Alicante at one stage.

We were in Barcelona from the Monday evening to Thursday at midday. Most of Tuesday was spent entertaining Spanish newspaper people. Two newspaper proprietors came to lunch on the ship and in Spain this is rather a long affair. Then in the evening, there were 20 guests to a cocktail party. It is always interesting meeting new people but unfortunately many of the guests did not speak English and I did not speak Spanish. However I think they all enjoyed themselves.

I was ashore on the Wednesday afternoon and enjoyed myself walking around the city. The main street in Barcelona is fascinating. It is very wide and quite long with high buildings along each side. In the middle of the street there is a wide pavement which runs the full length which is lined with trees and is popular with people out for a stroll. There are stalls all the way along this pavement selling books, magazines, postcards, lovely flowers and even birds of many different colours and kinds. The noise from these birds was quite something especially the parrots. However, it was a bit sad to see them in the small cages and the wild birds outside flitting about the trees. As you can imagine there are many churches in Barcelona and the cathedral is very old with a very beautiful main entrance. There is also a very strange looking building called the Church of the Holy Family. It is a memorial to those who died in the Spanish Civil War and so building only started at the end of that war. It is not yet completed because the builders have used all the money and so more money has to be collected to finish it. Just behind the city there is a monastery built on top of a hill. It can be seen from the ship arriving at the port. It is called Montserrat after the hill and is quite famous. It has been in the news lately because of some protest meetings held there.

At the bottom of the harbour end of the main street there is a tall monument to Christopher Columbus not unlike the one in Trafalgar Square. It was from Barcelona that Columbus set off to discover America. You can climb to the top of this monument and, I imagine, get a wonderful view. I did not go up. Just a short distance from this monument in the harbour itself there is an exact replica of the *Santa Maria* which was the ship Columbus sailed in. It looks tiny even compared with the *Nina* and she is not very big.

Barcelona has quite a big and busy harbour which is understandable as it is the largest city in Spain now I believe, with a population of one and a half million people. Both harbour and city have grown since I was last there nine years ago. There are regular shipping services to all parts of the Mediterranean with ferries running to Majorca, France and Italy. From the cliff at the shore side of the harbour entrance to the far side of the harbour a cable car runs. The wires are suspended from large steel towers which look like smaller editions of the Blackpool Tower. The ships pass under these wires when they enter the harbour. The cable car is used by people going to work on the ships and by sightseers. It certainly offers a bird's eye view of the whole harbour.

On leaving Barcelona we called at Gibraltar again for oil fuel but this time it was in daylight. However, we were only there for three and a half hours on Saturday morning and so no time to go ashore. There were one or two Royal Navy ships in port on this occasion.

Our next port of call was Las Palmas in the Island of Gran Canaria in the Canary Islands group. These islands belong to Spain and are governed just like a province on the mainland. It took us just over two days to get there arriving 5 o'clock on the afternoon of Monday 18th January just in time to see the flagship of our company leave port. She is called the *Windsor Castle* and was on her way to South Africa. She made an impressive sight.

We did not dock in Las Palmas until 5 am on the Tuesday morning as there was another ship in our berth. We started discharging the remainder of our cargo of newsprint and sailed again on Wednesday at midday. Las Palmas is a very busy harbour nowadays, especially since the Suez Canal was closed. Many of the big fishing fleets operating in the area use this harbour as a base for their vessels. They come into Las Palmas and transfer their catch to cargo ships to take to the various destinations. The Japanese, for example, send their fish all the way to Japan. The Russians too send the fish they catch to Russia. When we were in Las Palmas there were three other ships of the size of the *Nina* loading tomatoes and fruit for Britain. The mild climate of the Canary Islands enables the people to grow fruit and vegetables which they supply to us in winter when we cannot grow it ourselves.

I had been to Las Palmas many times before but only for a short time and with no chance of going ashore. However, I was able to have a look at part of the town this time. I was amazed at all the new buildings which are going up and they are mainly hotels and apartment houses. The growth of the town is due to its popularity with the holidaymaker. The pleasant climate with plenty of sunshine attracts people from Britain and Northern Europe. I did not see anything of the old town but look forward to going back one day and seeing some more.

On leaving Las Palmas we headed back across the Atlantic to Canada again. This time our destination was St John in the province of New Brunswick, and situated in the Bay of Fundy. We arrived there on Saturday 30th January and loaded huge rolls of corrugated paper for packaging and bales of wood pulp for paper making. The paper is going to Purfleet on the Thames and the pulp to Bremen in Germany and from there it goes to Hungary. The loading took us until Thursday afternoon, the 4th when we set sail again.

St John is one of the oldest ports in Canada and was at its busiest some years ago. It lies at the mouth of the St John River which has its source in the United States of America. The Bay of Fundy is well known to seamen for having about the biggest tides in the world. This meant when the *Nina* was tied up at St John she rose and fell 28 feet with the tide. This made life quite difficult as sometimes you had to climb up the gangway to the ship and at other times climb down to get on board. These very high tides and fast running water is the reason St John manages to remain ice free in wintertime which is important. One of the things the city is well known for is the Reversing Falls at the mouth of the St John River. These rapids are caused by a peculiar rock formation and at low tide the river runs down to the sea. Just before high water, the sea runs over these same rocks into the river in the opposite direction and hence the name.

During our stay there the area experienced a very severe spell of cold weather. Certainly the coldest I have ever experienced or want to again. At night the temperature was dropping to 50F below freezing and during the day was still 30F below freezing. Even well wrapped up you could not remain outside very long especially in the wind or your nose and ears felt like dropping off. The ship was warm inside but even so the pipes were freezing up. I walked up to town a couple of mornings but it was too cold to stay out for long and so I saw very little of St John. Everyone was glad to get away and when we first sailed any salt water spray that splashed on deck froze straight away. However, we are now in the warmer waters of the Gulf Stream and things are back to normal for which everyone is glad.

I was unlucky in not being able to obtain any leaflets or books in Barcelona. I had arranged to go to the city Tourist Bureau before sailing but was unable to go. However, I did manage to obtain one or two more leaflets at Gibraltar, a few of the Canary Islands and some quite good ones of St John New Brunswick, as it is in the summer and not when we were there. The officer's social club on board bought a Spanish doll for the school, at Barcelona. I hope you like her and find some corner for her where she can watch you all working hard at your lessons. I must be careful how I pack her so as not to spoil her rather pretty dress.

At the same time I am sending you a chart of the North Atlantic Ocean. It is a bit worn and grubby looking but this is because it has been in frequent use in the chartroom up until recently when we obtained a more up to date one. On this chart I have traced out some of the passages made by the *Nina* since I joined. Have marked in each Noon position and by using coloured pens hope you find it easy to follow. You will notice that at times the Noon positions are very close together, this will have been due to bad weather slowing the ship down. Other places we suddenly seem to leave our course and this has usually been when we have been trying to avoid the worst of bad weather. I have made a note of the nautical miles of steamed ports in each case.

On the same chart I have shown the position and names given to the Ocean Weather Stations. At these positions a ship is stationed all the year round. These ships usually do a month on station and then are relieved by other ships. On board are meteorological experts as part of the crew and various scientific instruments. Weather information is being recorded all the time and the results transmitted to weather centres ashore in the US and Britain. Merchant ships can use these vessels for position finding if they pass close enough and transatlantic airliners are in contact all the time for safety reasons. The ships are maintained by the principal maritime countries using the North Atlantic. The Meteorological Office looks after the British ships and the US Coastguards the American ones. I will also enclose a small map of the sea forecast areas round the British Isles. The next time you are listening to Junior Choice on the radio and the announcer interrupts with a gale warning to shipping you will know where they mean and how important it is to us at sea, whether merchant ships, fishermen or pleasure craft. Bravo, Charlie, Delta, Echo are looked after by the US. Juliet and Kilo by France, Holland and UK. India by Holland and UK. Alpha by France, Holland, Norway and UK between them.

Well that is all my news I think. Unfortunately I only expect to be one day in Purfleet and am not going on leave. We do not know where the ship is going after Bremen as yet, though I expect back to Canada. However, I will be writing to you again sometime. I just hope the post office is working again as we all miss getting our mail. Meantime,

Yours sincerely
Signed RP Royan
Master

PS Please excuse the mistakes in typing but the ship is rolling quite a bit and the typewriter sticks.

MV Nina Bowater
At Cornerbrook, Newfoundland
27th December 1970

Dear Girls and Boys,

By the time you receive this letter you will be back at school after the Christmas holidays. I do hope you had a happy time with your families and I wish you good health and happiness in the year 1971.

I am sure you had lots of good things to eat over Christmas and did many interesting things. Do you have a school choir and go carol singing I wonder? I do enjoy listening to the Christmas carols and hymns that are sung at this time of year. It was a relief to hear on the BBC news that the electricity supply was back to normal. It would have been a cold and dark Christmas otherwise.

As I write, some of the crew are putting up our decorations in the officer's smoke room and in the crew recreation room. We have also two trees and lights to attach to them. What we are hoping for is a fairly calm sea on Christmas Day to be able to enjoy the good food the ship's cook will provide. If it is not too windy we will also hoist a Christmas tree to the very top of our mast. We are just going to miss being in port as we expect to arrive in Cornerbrook on the afternoon of Boxing Day unless we run into some very bad weather.

We left Cornerbrook on Sunday 29th November after six days

there. Our long stay was due to three days of very heavy rain. This stopped the loading of the cargo. By this time of year it is usually snow that falls not rain. One day there was quite serious flooding in parts of the town. One was sure of getting at least wet feet walking from the ship into town.

When we first arrived the *Nicolas Bowater* was in port. She is the largest ship of the Bowater family. Then before we sailed the *Elizabeth Bowater* arrived in. She is our sister ship along with three others but she is the eldest and we the *Nina* are the baby of the family. Isn't it strange that ships are always thought of as feminine by seamen, it does not matter what they may be named. There are many reasons given for this but I wonder why you think it might be so. I would be interested to hear. However, we had a little chat with the people we knew on the other ships and of course we had the latest news from home as both these ships have been away from the UK since last April.

The cargo of newsprint that we loaded was for Alicante in Spain and for the time of year we had a very good passage across. This took us past the north of the islands of the Azores, and then on the afternoon of Tuesday 8th December we sighted land again, our first since Newfoundland. It was the north west point of Africa at the entrance to the Straits of Gibraltar and is called Capo Espartel. We passed through the Straits on Tuesday evening keeping to the African side as is the general practice when going into the Mediterranean Sea. We had a good view of the towns of Tangier and Ceuta on the African shore as we passed but the lights of Gibraltar itself were blocked from our view by a severe hailstorm. This was accompanied by thunder and very vivid lightening. The hailstones were large enough to make us take shelter in the wheelhouse on the bridge. By 10 o'clock that evening we were through the Straits and in the Mediterranean Sea, heading for the south east corner of Spain. We reached this point, called Cape de Gata, and there turned up the east coast of Spain towards our destination.

The lights on shore, as we approached Alicante, looked very pretty on Thursday morning when we arrived. The moon was full and hanging very low in the sky by this time. All around us the lights of small fishing boats bobbed around us in choppy seas. The pilot boat came out to us at 06.30 hrs the Spanish pilot climbed the ladder, and we were alongside ready to unload our cargo by 07.30 hrs just as the dawn was breaking.

When I was on the training ship I did one year of trying to learn the Spanish language. It would have come in very useful in Alicante as the ships agent spoke very little English. However because I did not bother to keep practising my Spanish, we had to try and speak with a little of both and the never failing sign language.

The ship stayed at Alicante for four and a half days unloading the newsprint. The weather during that time was beautiful and I can understand why there are a number of people from Britain and Northern Europe retired to this part of Spain. Because of the lovely climate, supposed to be the best in Spain, this is a very popular holiday area, and in summer over half a million tourists come. This is more than twice the population of Alicante so I imagine it must become very crowded. The coastline is called the Costa Blanca or White Coast because of the sun and the sand I gather. All around big new hotels and flats are being built for the holiday maker.

Alicante is the capital city of the province of the same name. The main industries are fruit growing, tourism and fishing. The oranges, lemons, figs, grapes and melons are of the best quality but limited in quantity by the lack of water, the rainfall being so small. However water is now being brought in by pipeline from other parts of Spain to irrigate the land and to greatly increase the crops. We had some melons delivered to the ship before sailing and they are delicious.

I did quite a bit of walking during our stay and saw quite a bit of the town and of course the harbour. Parts are very old with narrow streets and sometimes strong smells, other parts quite new but all very interesting. There is a big rock overlooking the town on top of which is perched an old castle called St Danta Barbara. From there you get a very good view of the surrounding area. The esplanade is very attractive and there is a nice beach. It was warm enough in the early evening to sit outside the cafes at tables on the pavement and have coffee or a drink.

The harbour itself is not very big but there is a special basin for yachts and other pleasure craft and one for fishing boats. The fishing boats come mainly from little villages along the coast and come to Alicante to sell their fish at the fish market and be repaired and overhauled at the little shipyard. I enjoyed watching the fishing boats and most of them were painted very bright, gay colours. One of the many fish caught in this area is a huge one called the Tunny. I will include a postcard of one.

I was taken by the ship's agent for a drive in the country outside the town. It was very interesting and we passed many orange and lemon trees. He took me to have lunch in a very pleasant restaurant where I had Spanish food. One dish was called paella which is rice with meat and fish. The other course we had was a whole fish baked in an oven inside a crust of salt. It was really extremely good. I did not require any more food that day!

The *Nina* sailed from Alicante on Monday 14th December at 18.30 hrs. It was a beautiful evening and again the lights looked very pretty as we sailed away. However I think everyone was quite glad to be at sea again and most people had spent all their money It would be nice to visit Alicante again.

Tuesday evening at 20.00 hrs we called in at Gibraltar for oil fuel. This did not take us very long and we were on our way again at half past midnight. There was no time to go ashore but the lights of the town did look very inviting.

The Rock of Gibraltar is very impressive both at a distance when coming out of the Mediterranean and close up when lying in the harbour and the top towers above the ship. It is 1,392 feet at its highest point. The Rock itself is full of caves which made it such a strong fortress in the past. Some of the caves you can visit and others belong to the Army. It is just like an underground city. It is still a big base for the Royal Navy and important to Britain. It has a very interesting airport in that the runway sticks out over the sea at each end, this is because it is situated on the very narrow neck of land which separates Gibraltar from Spain. The pilots cannot afford to make a mistake otherwise the plane will end up in the sea. Fresh water is in short supply on the Rock and they have to collect as much rain-water as possible. To help with this a huge concrete watershed has been built on the steep side of the Rock to guide the rainwater to the reservoirs.

It was a beautiful clear night when we sailed and with the moon it was almost like daylight. We turned , as we were bound west, we kept close to the Spanish shore staying about one and half miles off the coast. Once we passed a lighthouse called Tarifa, built on top of an old castle, we were clear of the Straits and set course to pass south of the Azores, leaving the land behind us again.

The southernmost point on Gibraltar is called Europa Point on which there is a lighthouse. Behind this lighthouse there is a signal station operated by Lloyds of London the famous shipping insurance company. The men on duty 24 hours a day in the signal station call up every ship which pass through the Straits either by Morse lamp or radio telephone. They ask the ship for her name and where she is bound. If you wish, they will report your passing in the Lloyds Shipping List which is published in London every day.

I am enclosing some leaflets I obtained of Newfoundland, Alicante and Gibraltar which I hope you will find of interest. On the road map of Newfoundland I have drawn in the route the *Nina* took to get to our various destinations. There are also some postcards of Alicante which give you an idea of what it is like. Also enclosed are letters from the Radio Officer and the Cadet which I hope you will enjoy.

We have arrived at Cornerbrook now, docking on Boxing Day morning having to slice our way through the ice in the Bay to reach our berth. We had a very wild day on the 25th and the ship was bouncing around. However, everyone enjoyed the lovely meal and I must get a menu to send to you. There was two feet of snow here at Cornerbrook on Christmas Day. However, from what I hear on the news they have had a white Christmas at home as well and it is now very cold.

The *Nina* is expected to sail from here on New Year's Eve and we are going first to Las Palmas in the Canary Islands and then to Barcelona in Spain. Then I believe back once again to Newfoundland but I am not too sure about that.

Yours sincerely,
Signed RP Royan
Master

MV *Nina Bowater*
At Cornerbrook, Newfoundland
Monday 23rd November 1970

Dear Girls and Boys,

Here I am back on your ship the Nina Bowater. I have just had a most enjoyable spell at home though the weather up north was not very kind. My wife had me organised very quickly into various household jobs such as fetching the coal, sweeping the floors, drying dishes and feeding the baby. This made me realise that everyone had been working very hard when I was away at sea. In fact I had to come back to the ship for a rest!

I left the *Nina* in mid September just as you returned from your summer holidays which I hope you enjoyed. That must seem a long time ago to you now. Everyone will be looking forward to Christmas now with the festivities and we hope goodwill to all. You will have all been working hard at school and joining in the various activities. These of course will be different to the ones you enjoyed during the summer term. Do you have a Christmas play I wonder! You are pretty certain to have a party and I expect you put up decorations. I wonder if you still have Honey the hamster or did she manage to escape again, successfully this time.

The ship has just completed four voyages from Newfoundland to Ridham with cargoes of logs for the Kemsley Bowater mill at Sittingbourne. These logs are crushed up to make pulp and from that the newsprint is made. Three of the cargoes came from Hare Bay in the north of Newfoundland near the Belle Isle Strait and one from a place called Tommy's Arm a little further south. These places are not near any town but inlets from the sea near to the forests where the logs are cut. In fact the first time I called at Tommy's Arm I used a road map of Newfoundland to help me find the place,

This voyage we are bound for Cornerbrook and the paper mill there. We are going to make two voyages to Spain with newsprint and the first one will to a place called Alicante. It is now eight years since I was last in Spain and so I am looking forward to it. After our Spanish voyages we expect to go to Charleston and load a cargo of paper pulp for Ellesmere Port which is on the Manchester Ship Canal. This should bring us back home about the middle of February.

Of the 35 people who make up the ship's company there are only seven left, not including myself, who were on the ship during our last spell away. Some have gone to other ships going to other parts of the world. Four are rather like you, back at school preparing to sit examinations for higher qualifications. A couple I believe have left the sea altogether to work on dry land.

The North Atlantic Ocean is not really the best place to be during the winter months. It does get very rough at times and life is very uncomfortable for all on board. This is especially so when the ship is on its way out to Canada as it has no cargo on board. Then we tend to toss around rather like an empty bottle.

Just before sailing from Ridham this time I telephoned the Meteorological Office and told them where the ship was going. I was then told what sort of weather to expect and as it was much worse up north we came down south quite near to the islands known as the Azores. By doing this we missed the worst of the bad weather. Every day the 3rd Officer draws me a weather map from the information we receive over the radio and from this get an idea of the type of weather we can expect. Every six hours while at sea the ship sends a message with her position and the type of weather she is experiencing to the Meteorological Office which assists them in drawing the map and forecasting the weather you see at 6 o'clock every evening, on television.

Another organisation we deal with on the Atlantic is the United States Coastguards. They operate something called the Atlantic Merchant Vessel Report System and all ships are invited to join in. When the *Nina* leaves the UK I get the 2nd Officer to send a message to the US Coastguard in New York of where we are, where we are going, which way we are going and when we hope to get there. Then every 2–3 days a message with our present position. In the Coastguards headquarters a record is kept of all the ships that have sent in messages while they are at sea and if a ship or aircraft is in trouble and requires assistance the Coastguard, by this record, can help to organise something very quickly. As you can imagine it is a very good system and is frequently required.

Well girls and boys that is about all my news at present. Once we have been to Spain I hope to have something interesting to tell you. I must remember to write you before the Christmas holidays if I can manage. I expect school will finish about the 23rd December. I hope all goes well with you and look forward to hearing from you sometime.

Yours sincerely,
Signed RP Royan
Master

MV *Nina Bowater*
At Belfast
Friday 26th November 1971

Dear Girls and Boys,

This is just a short letter to let you know that the *Nina* is now on her way to the United Kingdom. To our surprise our last voyage up the St Lawrence Seaway to Cleveland was cancelled because the Seaway authorities could not guarantee to get the ship out of the Lakes before the big freeze up takes place. I certainly was quite pleased as the idea of being stuck fast in ice for the whole winter did not appeal to me. However when we arrived at Cornerbrook on the 14th and found the ship was to load newsprint for Belfast and Newport, Monmouthshire, I was very pleased indeed.

We arrived in Cornerbrook on Sunday just as the snow was starting and we were lucky as this was the start of a very bad storm. It affected the whole island and the surrounding sea areas for four days with very high winds, snow and very low temperatures. Two boys and two men out hunting were caught and died of the cold, very sad. Four ships all due to arrive shortly after us at Cornerbrook were still not there when we sailed due to the bad weather.

The *Nina* sailed at midnight on Thursday 18th and when we cleared the Bay of Islands turned right and up to the Strait of Belle

Isle which separates Newfoundland from Labrador on the mainland. We passed through the strait in daylight and without fog. It really is a very bleak part of the world. Once clear of Belle Isle itself, which is just a great big rock with two lighthouses on it, we were in the North Atlantic Ocean and pitching to the big seas. In another month's time the Belle Isle strait will be closed to shipping because of ice and by January you can drive a car across the ice from Newfoundland to the mainland if you don't mind a rough ride!

We are hoping to arrive at Belfast by Friday 26th if the weather is not too bad. It should take us about 2/3 days to discharge but with the trouble there I don't think I will be going ashore. It is very sad people fighting with each other and giving the poor soldiers a very difficult job. From Belfast we go to Newport in South Wales to complete unloading from where the ship will return to Cornerbrook. However, practically everyone is leaving Newport to go on leave which is rather exciting for us. With any luck I should be home by about 1 December in good time for Christmas.

I am including with this letter one from the cadets and some more postcards. There will also be a chart of the Great Lakes on which one of the cadets has drawn in our voyages. There is also a photograph of the *Nina* taken from a helicopter by the ship's electrician.

Well boys and girls I will take this opportunity of wishing you all a Happy Christmas and a Good New Year. I do hope Father Christmas is good to you and you have a good party. I don't know whether I will be returning to the Nina after my holiday I will just have to wait and see.

Yours sincerely,
Signed RP Royan
Master

MV *Nina Bowater*
At Cornerbrook, Newfoundland
Sunday 30th May 1971

Dear Girls and Boys

I was very pleased indeed to receive your letters just before we sailed from Cornerbrook on Saturday 15th May. Your letters were full of news and made most interesting reading. You certainly have been busy. Thank you too for the photograph of the girls who were confirmed. A very important day in your lives. The photograph, along with your letters, has been seen by the rest of the crew. The photo been shown as some of 'our girls'.

I do hope your Easter concert was a success and I am sure your parents would enjoy it. Did you all have a good time in the holidays I wonder? There must be more good swimmers at All Hallows than on this ship with all the medals that have been awarded. I think it is a very good thing to be able to swim well – both for pleasure and safety. Those of you who were sitting music exams I hope you were successful too. I must say you do have some interesting projects to follow and only wish I could see you at them. I am glad to learn that the new money does not bother you even if you do not like the new halfpenny. It is very small. I have not had enough practice yet to be fully confident.

Well now where have we been since I last wrote to you? I sent the last letter from Purfleet on the 15th February but the Post Office strike was still on. The ship only stayed there one day and we changed quite a few of the crew. Then up the River Weser to Bremen where we remained one and a half days discharged wood pulp for Hungary. I did not get ashore at all as the weather was unkind and I had a lot of sleep to make up. From there we sailed to North Shields on the River Tyne for our once a year spring clean and repair, staying in the drydock for six days. We arrived there on the 21st February and I dashed home for one week. It was very short but it was so nice to see my family again and as we say better than nothing.

We sailed from the Tyne on the 2nd March bound for Cornerbrook with the not so good news of probably staying away for nine months. There is now only one person left on the ship who has been here since I joined 14 months ago. We were lucky in having a good crossing of the Atlantic for that time of year, not too uncomfortable. Once we reached the Cabot Strait, however, we had to force our way through ice the rest of the way to Cornerbrook. As you can imagine it slowed the ship down quite a bit but fortunately was not quite thick enough to stop us altogether. The noise of the ice bumping and grinding along the side of the ship was considerable, making some people wonder if we were going to sink. However, we arrived safely in Cornerbrook on the 12th March without any damage I am pleased to say.

After loading a full cargo of newsprint we sailed and had to push our way out through the ice again until through the Cabot Strait and clear of the Gulf of St Lawrence. Our first port of call was Richmond up the James River of which I wrote last year. This time, being earlier in the year and no leaves on the trees, we had a very good view of some of the old plantation houses. The ship spent a little less than a day at Richmond and then set off for Miami with the rest of our cargo. We encountered some bad weather on our way but it cleared up on the day we arrived. For the last 60 miles into Miami we sailed very close to the shore to avoid the full strength of the Gulf Stream. This gave us a very good view and it just seemed like mile after mile of hotels and new houses and a continuous beach. The land is very flat and so there is nothing to see behind the buildings. We had to keep a very sharp lookout for small pleasure boats of which there seemed to be hundreds. Too many of them liked to see how close to the ship they could get which I found a little nerve wracking. Despite this we arrived in Miami on the afternoon of Saturday 27th March. It was very pleasant to be back in a warm sun.

Unfortunately I did not see very much of the area as once again we were only there for a day and work came first. However I had a couple of walks in town in and through the park. It is nearly tropical in this part of Florida and some of the streets were lined with palm trees. This area had been without rain for three months, can you imagine that, and everyone was very concerned. All the fruit and flowers were just withering up and water was rationed. I gather that even now there has been little rain. I was surprised to find there were two cities of the same name just six miles apart. The best known one is called Miami Beach and the one we were at called Miami City. Both are very popular holiday centres and many people come there to retire because of the warm weather. There were aeroplanes flying around pulling advertisements behind them and a barrage balloon just like the one which floated over London during the last war. You could go on a trip under this balloon which must have given the passengers a wonderful view.

MV *Nina Bowater*
At Cleveland, Ohio, USA
5th November 1971

Dear Girls and Boys

Having read your letters, we saw that you wanted to know about the crew, so we decided to tell you about ourselves. Our names are Mark Williams and Nigel Hughes, and we are both cadets on the *Nina*. Each of us is eighteen years old. As cadets we are training to be officers, although we have exams to pass before we are recognised as such.

During long sea passages, one of us goes on the bridge from four o'clock to eight o'clock (morning and evening) to keep watch with the Chief Officer, and to learn all about navigation. The other one only works throughout the day, (just like you do), and is not woken up at four o'clock in the morning like the Watch keeper. The Dayworker gets up at seven o'clock. It is easy to see why we both prefer day work! Each week we alternate. Before breakfast at eight-thirty, the dayworker has to take the soundings. For this he has a four-foot metal rod, joined to a long piece of rope. As you know, all ships carry fresh water in large tanks beneath the decks, plus ballast sea-water to keep the ship stable. This can amount to over one thousand tons of water! The level of the water has to be checked each day. So every morning, the Dayworker puts his rod into a pipe on deck that goes right down into the water tank. When he pulls it back out again, he can see from the wet rope just how much water is in there. He has to do this for nine separate tasks, after which he enters up the readings in a special book. Then he rushes in for a good hot breakfast, as it is usually quite cold outside on deck. For the rest of the day, the Dayworker does any odd jobs that need doing around the ship, such as chipping, painting and varnishing.

Nigel and myself were originally on the *Nina* when she sailed in March. We both joined her on the 25th September at Durban, South Africa. Durban is a large and very interesting city, with a long sea front. It is safe to swim here, unlike most of South Africa, as wire mesh nets have been positioned some distance out from the beach so that sharks do not swim into the enclosure! The water is very warm in Durban and it is not unusual to see many people sun-bathing and swimming under the hot sun.

Not very far away, one can find Zulu warriors in full ceremonial war costume complete with spears, shields and 'witch' doctor' horned head-dresses. Each warrior has a hand-cart, (similar to a Japanese rickshaw) gaily decorated with animal skins, long feathers and bright paint. For a small price, they will take tourists for a ride along the sea-front, running along the road, and pulling their cart behind them.

We travelled down to Durban in another ship called the *Clan Sutherland*. She is much bigger than the *Nina*, but very well built in 1950. After we left her, she sailed on to Shanghai where she was sold to the Chinese.

It was 1st October, when we eventually left Durban in the '*Nina*', and it took almost one month to reach Cornerbrook mainly because we were slowed down by hurricane Kristy. The sea became quite rough, and we experienced winds of over 60 mph at one time. This storm almost stopped the ship completely, although we were going at full speed! We berthed in Cornerbrook on 25th October, and I found it very cold compared with the tropical regions we had just come from. Cornerbrook is surrounded by picturesque pine forests, and most of the houses are made completely of wood. The inhabitants are very friendly, but I found it difficult to understand the Newfoundland accent, although English is their native tongue everyone seems to speak an extremely broad Cornish/American dialect virtually impossible to comprehend.

Three days later, we left for Cleveland, Ohio, USA carrying a full cargo of newsprint. Cleveland, as you will see from the chart, is in the second lake, Lake Erie. As we sailed up the St Lawrence River, the weather became much milder. The sea lost its unpleasant greyness of the past few days, and turned a dark green as we entered fresh water. Neither Nigel nor myself had ever been on a voyage to the Lakes before, and so we were fascinated with the land being so close for a change, and seeing in detail the tiny rustic villages situated right on the river banks. All the way up the river, we experienced beautiful dawns and sunsets with the sun lingering above the horizon for what seemed like hours, setting the sky ablaze with red, yellow and purple streaks of light. One evening we even saw an aurora in the northern skies, hanging down from no where like a gigantic sheet, shimmering with its luminescent glow.

Our next stop was Montreal, where we berthed to take on fuel. Shortly after that, we entered St Lambert lock – the first of many that we were to pass through before we reached Cleveland. It is a cadet's job to steer through the locks, (taking orders from the pilot) and so one of us was always occupied whenever we went through one. Captain Royan has already told you about the locks, so I will not attempt to enlarge on that. However, I will give you my first impressions; the lock seemed extraordinarily narrow, but we entered it with no difficulty whatsoever, and were soon secure inside. Then the gate closed behind us, and we began to rise with astonishing rapidity as water flooded into the lock. Within minutes we were out, and steaming up the calm and silent waters of the St Lawrence Seaway. Six locks and seventeen hours later, we entered Lake Ontario. Towards the far end of the lake, we passed through an area called The Thousand Islands. The sun was shining and the water a calm and vivid blue as we came upon a fairy-tale land of hundreds of pine-covered islands, some with dark rambling mansions looming above a carpet of trees, and on others just a colourful cottage peeping between the vast array of foliage, glistening in the morning dew.

Then the magic seemed to dwindle as the skies took on their

morbid grey appearance once more, to stay with us for the rest of the trip. At the end of Lake Ontario we had to anchor as the Welland Canal, (a series of eight locks, the entrance to Lake Erie) was moderately congested. We waited three days before we were allowed admission, and subsequently passed through all the locks in the equitable time of ten hours. Leaving the Welland Canal, it was only a matter of hours before we reached Cleveland, where Captain Royan berthed the ship himself, without the aid of a pilot. Cleveland struck me as being a very dull depressing city, not how I had visualised it at all. Tall, grimy buildings and grey smoking factories seemed to envelop the whole area, and I was not sorry when we left three days later.

Well, that was our trip up the lakes, and I hope you have enjoyed reading it. I think I'll stop now, as I have ground my forefinger into a stub from typing!

Yours sincerely,
Signed; Mark Williams and Nigel Hughes
Cadets

Appendix B
Ships Sailed on Foreign Going

TSS *Clan Cumming*
Jnr Cadet. Two voyages 12.8.46–13.6.47. Maiden voyage of ship.
First new clan ship after the war. Cayzer family took cruise round
Ilsa Craig and back to Greenock after trials. Master A. R. Cossar
who had been p.o.w. after torpedoed in Pedestal Convoy.

SS *Clan MacFadyen*
Snr Cadet. One voyage 23.6.47–23.11.47. US Liberty ship. First
voyage in company as clan vessel. Master A. V. Gordon. In Calcutta
at buoys for Indian Independence Day.

SS *Clan Macnair*
Snr Cadet. One voyage 11.12.47–24.4.48. Oldest ship I sailed on built 1921. Master C. W. Jenkins. G. W. Potter other cadet Old Conway. In Bombay when Ghandi killed.

MV *Clan Macleod*
Snr Cadet. Three voyages 8.7.48–15.10.49. Maiden voyage. Master E. Gough Chief Officer. C W Mitchell later superintendent. In Durban during African Indian riots. February 1950 passed 2nd mates Foreign Going certificate. Glasgow at 20 years. Promoted 3rd Officer.

SS *Clan MacIlwraith*

3rd Officer. One voyage 10.3.50–24.7.50. Built 1924. Sold to Germany at end of voyage. Master T. O. Marr. His sister friend of my Aunt Isobel gym teachers. Named *Magdalen Vinnen.*

TSS *Clan MacRae*

3rd Officer. Two voyages 14.8.50–2.10.51. Refrigeration vessel. Master E. Courthart previous Liverpool superintendent. 1951 towed disabled *Clan Maciver* Bay of Biscay. December 1951 passed for 1st Mates certificate Glasgow exam held between Christmas and New Year. Promoted 2nd Officer.

SS *Clan MacQueen*
2nd Officer. Two voyages 25.1.52–1.5.53. Ex ocean vessel. Masters
T. O. Marr, A. S. Palethorpe-May.
1952 – 56 days anchored Mombasa Port congestion.

SS *Clan Sinclair*
2nd Officer. Three voyages. Twelve passenger vessel. Sister ship went
to Spithead for Royal Review. Master J. H. Crellin. Chief Officer
G. Emnett ex *Clan MaQuarrie*. Later married Marie from Borve,
Isle of Lewis. February 1955 passed for Master Foreign Going.

TSS *Clan MacTageart*
2nd Officer. One voyage 7.3.55–24.7.55. Master F. B. Parker.
Promoted Chief Officer August 1955.

SS *Clan MacBean*
Chief Officer. Three voyages 6.8.55–3.11.56. Master L. S. Jones
(Bangor). Last Clan vessel to call *Mormagoa*. Ex ocean vessel.

SS *Clan MacKinlay*
One voyage. 28.12.56–13.8.57. Ex empire boat. Suez Canal closed to/from India via Cape. Master J. P. Dunphy.

SS *Clan MacLennan*
Chief Officer. Two voyages 28.9.57–20.8.58. Sudan… doctor. Tonsils out on leave. Master J. J. Millar. Sunk Pedestal Convoy Malta p.o.w. Tuticorin search for fishermen.

MV *Clan MacInnes*
Chief Officer. Twelve passengers. Ten voyages 29.12.58–30.7.62.
Masters J. West. F. D. Bonney. 1959 Collision on Thames with
Mormac Pine. Dar Es Salaam for Tanzania Independence Day. On
leaving vessel ceased carrying passengers. Married Carol Squires
5.1.63. End of an era. On 27.11.68 was flown for first time from
UK to Bombay to replace Chief Officer. Landed at Aden to hospital.
Lucky me.

TSS *Clan MacTavish*
Chief Officer. Three voyages 7.2.63–26.2.64. Masters G. Rodger,
R. Shattock, C. A. Thomas. First voyage four month honeymoon.

RMHV *Stirling Castle*
First Officer/Chief Officer. Four voyages 15.4.64–13.11.64. Transferred to passenger ships, British crewed. Masters D. W. Sowden (Honey), A Hort. 2nd voyage north bound moth charter.

RHSS *Transvaal Castle*
Chief Officer. Two voyages. 16.12.64–26.4.65. Bruce born 10.12.64. (Capetown Castle bullion) Master N. M. Lloyd.

RHSS *Kenya Castle*
Chief Officer. 7.7.65–10.12.65. F. Pye, R. H. Wright. First call after resolution and riots.

TSS *Rhodesia Castle*
Chief Officer. One voyage. 30.3.66–7.7.66. Out of UK until last two days of NUS strike. Master R. H. Pape.

TSMV *Capetown Castle*
Chief Officer. Four voyages. 26.7.66–23.11.66. Second voyage
Mediterranean cruise. My parents travelled. Master D. W. Sowden
(Treasure), R. W. Wright. Vessel scrapped Italy 1967.

TSS *Rhodesia Castle*
Chief Officer. One voyage 9.2.67–19.4.67. Final voyage East Africa
Service. Master R H Pape. Ship scrapped Taiwan.

TSS *SA Oranje*
Staff Commander. Seventeen voyages 26.5.67–13.10.69. Promoted to Staff Commander 30.4.67. Masters J. P. Smythe, Freer, Mavitty, R. shattock. 1968 changed to South African flag.

MV *Nina Bowater*
Master. Two voyages 5.3.70–29.11.71. Promoted Master 1.1.70. 1971 Great Lakes season. Pilots licence. Daughter Nicola Rose born 11.7.1970. One passenge to South Africa. Two passenges to Spain. Stitching job mid Atlantic. Successful despite bad weather.

MVT *Hector Heron*
Master. Three voyages. 1.8.72 – 41.7.74. Union trouble in Calcutta.
West African calls! Independence Mozambique when in L. Marquies.

TSS *SA Oranje*
Master. Five voyages. 24.2.75–5.11.75. Family travelled out and home
from South Africa, voyage 2–3. Final voyage passengers to Durban.
Crew flew to UK via Jumbo Jet while 40 crew sailed to Taiwan for
scrap. Big send off from Durban.

TSS *SA Vaal*
Master. One voyage. 3.12.75–12.1.76. Christmas/New Year full ship. Planned Richards Bay opening call.

RMSS *Windsor Castle*
One voyage. 26.5.76–5.7.76. In whites all voyage. On leave in caravan at Findhorn. Nice contrast.

TSVLCC *Everest F Wells*
Master. Four voyages. 7.7.77–8.12.79. Panamanian licence. Cape-town for repairs. Maiden voyage. Singapore for repairs. Collision bulkhead. No problem. B. Trowsdale. Relieved by helicopter. Capetown in fog. Interesting.

TMV *Barcelona* (*Table Bay/Tolaga Bay*)
Master. One Voyage. 7.10.80–11.2.81. Carol sailed Med. Drydocked new dock Malta (Chinese) E. R. Fire Long Beach to Panama. Transited Canal then black out. NUS overtime ban which overcome. Cost crew money with adjusted schedule.

MV *Winchester Castle*
Master. One Voyage. 9.3.80–13.7.80. Drydock Capetown. Electrician died at sea. Oranges for Moscow Olympics at Ventsp.L.

MV *Edinburgh Universal*
Master. One voyage. 4.6.81–11.11.81. Puerto Bolivar banana experience. Distress rescue approaching South China Sea. 18 men.

TMV *Table Bay* (*Tolaga Bay/Barcelona*)
Four voyages. 3.12.81–8.8.83 Transferred to OCL. Great relief. Adjusted to new experience and management. Bob Gemmell transferred too. Carol and Nicola travelled to South Africa. Returned by air. Stowaway to Liverpool.

TMV *Tokyo Bay*
Master. Thirteen voyages. 23.9.83–2.7.87. Drydock Yokonama. Carol and Ann Leslie did second voyage. First Engineer killed. Kobe pollution. Korean drydock and many others.

TMV *Tolaga Bay* (*Table Bay/Barcelona*)
Master. Six voyages. 19.11.87–1.9.89. Final voyage. Carol did second last voyage with SOS in Bay. Officially retired 2.1.90. Appointed Commodore 1988 along with Bob Gemmell.

As matter of interest to me I sailed on the same ship on three consecutive Christmas Days with three different names. *Barcelona, Table Bay and Tolaga Bay*. Could at times be confusing.

Ships sailed on as coastal relief round UK and N. Europe

As Chief Officer

Clan Ranal, Clan Farquharson, Rustenburg Castle, King George, Clan MacIlwraith, Clan Brodie, Clan MacTavish, Clan MacTaggart, Clan MacIntyre.

As Master

Clan MacIndor, Clan Menzies, Clan MacIlwraith, Clan Ranald, Clan Malcolm. Was relieved at Hull to attend Clan Line 100th anniversary at Savoy Hotel.
British Respect in Gulf to see loading of VLCE. Very large crude carrier.
British Success in Europort and en route to Las Palmas to see discharge and tank cleaning of VLCE.
Now considered an expert.

Personal

Married 5.1.63; retired 2.1.90; 27 years married;
9 Christmas days at home; 16 Christmas days away.
Son Bruce born 10.12.64.
Sailed from Southampton 16.12.64 *Transvaal Castle* Chief Officer.
Daughter Nicola born 11.7.70.
Was at sea *Nina Bowater* as master.
Saw my daughter 15.9.70. Given seven weeks leave.
6.11.70 rejoined *Nina Bowater*.
21.2.71 Seven days leave. Ship in drydock.
1.3.71 rejoined.
29.11.71 returned home having left ship.